W9-AOG-279

EDUCATING ARCHITECTS

EDUCATING ARCHITECTS

EDITED BY MARTIN PEARCE & MAGGIE TOY

A.D. ACADEMY EDITIONS

Acknowledgements
We should like to express our gratitude to the many contributors to the Symposium, at
the University of Portsmouth, School of Architecture on 9-11 February 1994 (organised
with the cooperation of Wendy Potts, Head of the School) who contributed to this book
as well as the many architects, worldwide, who supplied us with informative material
on their own education and architectural education in general. We should also like to
thank Mark Lane for his editorial assistance and Sandra Haskett for the transcriptions.

All illustrative material is courtesy of the architects unless otherwise stated.
pp44-53: reprinted with permission from Dalibor Vesely, 'Architecture and the Question
of Technology' in *Architecture, Ethics and Technology*, edited by Perez-Gomez/
Pelletier, McGill-Queen's University Press, Quebec, 1994; *pp90-95*: © Ekkehard
Rehfeld; *pp111-115*: extract printed with permission from the original French edition
De la cave au toit © 1991, Presses polytechniques et universitaires romandes, 1015
Lausanne, Switzerland, all rights reserved; *p124*: Angela Carter, 'Universality' in *The
Sadeian Women*, Pantheon, New York, 1978 and *p125*: Gillian Naylor, 'Assessing the
Bauhaus' in *The Bauhaus Reassessed: Sources and Design Theory*, Herbert, London,
1985, reprinted in Paul Greenhalgh, *Quotations and Sources: On Design and the
Decorative Arts*, Manchester University Press, Manchester, 1993. A Carter and G
Naylor reprinted in this book with permission from Manchester University Press,
Manchester.

Cover: Metropoint, Lausanne, View of Interchange and Bridge from Valley Floor,
Bernard Tschumi Architects, 1993
Page 2: Oranienburg Competition for Sachsenhausen, Model Detail of 'Hope Incision',
Daniel Libeskind,1993

First published in Great Britain in 1995 by
ACADEMY EDITIONS
An imprint of Academy Group Ltd

ACADEMY GROUP LTD
42 Leinster Gardens London W2 3AN
Member of the VCH Publishing Group

ISBN 1 85490 391 8

Distributed to the trade in the United States of America by
ST MARTIN'S PRESS
175 Fifth Avenue, New York, NY 10010

Printed and bound in UK

CONTENTS

INTRODUCTION
MARTIN PEARCE AND MAGGIE TOY

EDUCATION IN THE EXPANDED/ING FIELD

If the heterogeneous and eclectic manifestation of current architecture is a product of the sheer enormity of diverse approaches practised by designers, the range of approaches in architectural education mirrors this condition, and the collection of essays which follow provide some fragments, at a moment in time, of that same diversity. The compilation of these fragments was generated initially from an international symposium of architectural educators in February 1994 held at the University of Portsmouth, School of Architecture, United Kingdom. From the proceedings of that symposium and the concerns and ideas gathered from other eminent educators, both before and after the event, many provocative and profound questions were raised, not least an attempt to identify some structural base of contemporary architectural education. In producing this publication the dilemma in identifying such a structural base quickly became apparent for the editors in their task of developing a cogent and coherent system for the reader. However, what came to emerge was far more than the articulation, stratification and territorialities which might have been expected and in some way provided an insight to the nature of the condition which had generated the material.

EDUCATION: HETEROGENEITY AND MULTIPLICITY

Gilles Deleuze and Felix Guattari[1] proposed a condition where the tap root of ideology has been aborted in favour of the shifting layers and boundless interconnectivities of the rhizome. While their biological dialectical model was forwarded as a challenge to the then current semiotic thought it is worth some investigation, as the model provides a useful analogue to architectural education today. There are four main constituents of the model:

The principles of connection and heterogeneity: that the rhizome inherently differs from the tree root's fixed position in its necessary possibility of connection from any one point to another;

The principle of multiplicity: that the rhizome cannot be unified, it must be treated as substantial in itself, as it cannot be treated as a subject or object but rather only as a multiplicity devoid of identifiable points and in a constant state of flux;

The principle of a-signifying rupture: synonymous with the rhizome's a-singularity it resists being characterised as a 'single' signified/signifying entity. Thus, it can be broken at any point with the result that it will adopt one or other (unpredictable) trajectories of division never ceasing to reconstruct itself;

The principle of cartography and decalcomania: The tree constitutes a logic of 'tracing' (*calque*) establishing a hierarchy of tracing analogous to its leaves. However, the rhizome is analogous to the map, recording the experiments and connecting all of its dimensions. In effect, the map reconstructs rather than reproduces.

These four principles: connection and heterogeneity; multiplicity; a-signifying rupture; cartography and decalcomania, provide a useful model for architecture and architectural education today. Education resists any single identity being inherently diverse and disparate in its components, which are in a constant state of flux with certain growth, mutation and transformation in a boundless and mapping field of possibility.

This model loses the definition of what *is* and what *is not* architecture[2] and in this inherently creates both the diversity and accompanying anxiety/paranoia of architectural education today.

We all experience this possibility and paranoia, particularly students in schools of architecture, as in one case the latest popular magazine presents the contemporary *avant-garde* which is quickly appropriated and reproduced (with various levels of success), while in another case students seek to be the creators of the *avant-garde* itself in a constant striving to change perceptions and recreate the world often at the margins of what might traditionally have been considered the edges of the architectural project. Of course, both dipoles bring with them their own peculiar forms of paranoia: in the former the ideological tap root provides an impression of a convenient and available world of firm ground, or at least offers reassurance and comfort, but it also brings with it the possibilities of sterility, retrogression and dogma. The latter brings the perhaps desirable marginalisation of peripheral activity. However, both are the necessary products of ranging the expanded and expanding field of the rhizome and perhaps against the very nature of that field trying to ground oneself.

The dilemma of ranging and grounding have, probably, always been present, manifest by the ways in which architectural ideas have cross-fertilised through the centuries; the history of which is well presented by Geoffrey Broadbent in the first essay of this book. But historically, this opportunity was limited to the privileged *cognoscenti.* Today, however, proximity to a vast range of architectural positioning is available to the many rather than the few. While creating multiple possibilities this situation has at its core a certain problem for students and educators alike.

EDUCATION: THE ECSTASY OF COMMUNICATION
While some may now feel Jean Baudrillard's observations are rather *passé*, his words demonstrate the dilemma faced by students in trying to orient themselves in a world of exponential growth of ideas, and symbiotically of the technologies which communicate those ideas.

The schizo [he who possesses] . . . too great a proximity of everything, the unclean promiscuity of everything which touches, invests and penetrates without resistance, with no halo of private protection, not even his own body, to protect him anymore.

The schizo is bereft of every scene, open to everything in spite of himself, living in the greatest confusion. He is himself obscene, the obscene prey of the world's obscenity. What characterises him is less the loss of the real, the light years of estrangement from the real, the pathos of distance and radical separation, as is commonly said, but, very much to the contrary, the absolute proximity, the total instantaneity of things, the feeling of no defence, no retreat. It is the end of interiority and intimacy, the overexposure and transparency of the world which traverses him without obstacle. He can no longer produce the limits of his own being, can no longer play nor stage himself, can no longer produce himself as mirror. He is now only a pure screen, a switching centre for all the networks of influence.[3]
This presents a bleak picture for beginning architecture

students. A world of operation in which the possibility seems only one of consuming overexposure blinding their individuality while at the same time requiring of them a positioning/grounding. This is the reality of what others might choose to call pluralism.

The reality (or lack of reality) of Jean Baudrillard's condition is most clearly demonstrated by the latest technologies of communication where access to a global network of computers through what is now termed *The Internet* enables students and teachers to have instantaneous proximity to information.

Rather than magazine or journal culture, or indeed televisual medium which has in-built editing deceits and production delays, anyone can access the world of information first hand. For example, Columbia University, as do many other institutions, provides instant access to its current work, At Columbia one can readily obtain entry to Greg Lynn's first-year fall studio almost as it happens. The possibilities are manifest for a worldwide School of Architecture as the work of Dean Bill Mitchell of MIT demonstrates. Here, Mitchell established a core project undertaken by students at various schools around the globe using computer-based experimentation as a vehicle, with the development of the project at each of its respective nodes informing the trajectory of the whole field of exploration, and this finds a direct analogue in the rhizome model.

So this is a kind of globalism with immediate proximity, and many of the following articles concern themselves with the global/regional distinction. This can be seen as worrying for both educators and students at once adopting the academy's responsibility to question the present and from this to construct a future, while the homogenising effects generated by these technologies of consumption create an antithetical paradox.

Importantly, the closed system engendered by these technologies presents, perhaps, the strongest feature for the architectural student, where concepts are the greatest achievement supplanting the traditional domain of objects which the architectural project has held at its core. Several architects are now projecting the possibilities of this condition, not least the internationally based group of architects and urban designers, Studio 333, who with Burton Hamfelt draw directly from these possibilities in their proposition entitled 'Opening the Envelope'.

WORLDWIDE WEB
One of the **strongest features** of our age is the fact that **concepts** are becoming our greatest achievements as opposed to objects. Who can deny that the transition from the modern, mass industrialised and protected state to the **mobile**, late capitalist and competitive state

is having a manifold effect on the **contemporary city**. These forces are projecting **new and wonderful maps** onto our current globe. These maps are without the physical edifices that have marked the traditional territorial dimensions of our cities. What is being mapped among other things are the **morphological structures** of trans-migrational business, interconnected technologies, fading political borders and **inevitable ruptures** of civilian populations in transition. In this **global solid state mix**, should one not ask what will be the effects of these behavioural geometries on the way our **cities are formed**?[4]

This raises the important issue of the relation between practice and theory, an issue which several of the following contributors broach. In the context of such pervading technologies the consequence and nature of practice (ironically *Techné* now disembodied from the concept of making), as that of the production of physical artefacts, becomes blurred as it enters a field where theory dominates the territory and usurps the product of the architectural project.

While Jean Baudrillard's death of the object highlights the growing paradox for the academies of architecture, the prediction of the dilemma can be traced back through Martin Heidegger as an illustration of a fundamental behind the current condition.

All distances in time and space are shrinking. Man now reaches overnight, by plane, places which formerly took weeks and months of travel. He now receives instant information, by radio, of events which he formerly learned about only years later, if at all. The germination and growth of plants, which remained hidden throughout the seasons, is now exhibited publicly in a minute on film. Distant sites of the most ancient cultures are shown on film as if they stood this very moment amidst today's street traffic. Moreover, the film attests to what it shows by presenting also the camera and its operators at work. The peak of this abolition of every possibility of remoteness is reached by television, which will pervade and dominate the machinery of communication.

Man puts the longest distances behind him in the shortest time. He puts the greatest distances behind himself and thus puts everything before himself at the shortest range.

Yet the frantic abolition of all distances brings no nearness; for nearness does not consist in shortness of distance. What is least remote from us in point of distance, by virtue of its picture on film or its sound on the radio, can remain far from us. What is incalculably far from us in point of distance can be near to us. Short distance is not in itself nearness. Nor is great distance remoteness.

Of course Heidegger could not foresee the Internet or the virtual worlds beyond which are creating these paradoxical conditions for students and educators. However, he does predict the central underlying paradox which is that of the one among the many and the paranoid schizophrenia of contemporary architectural education.

This is an important point for education. If the possibilities of information are both boundless and immediate while location and certainty are key, how can the educator enable the students to achieve the nearness of which Heidegger speaks. In this respect we should first question what nature or purpose such a nearness might have. The following essays provide some insight into the nature of such a nearness and, in particular, this is a nearness to what might be termed the creative act and its place in this new and uncertain territory.

Personal ranging through the expanded/ing field of educaton, the ecstasy of communication and the possibilities of remoteness and nearness, may seem distant from some of the texts which follow. However, by means of introduction the scene may in some way foreground the earnest importance of the positions expressed by the respective authors in teaching architecture in a world, as Pierre von Meiss describes it, *of growing permissiveness and speed.*

Notes
1 Gilles Deleuze and Felix Guattari, *On the Line-Semiotexte*, 1983.
2 Rosalind Krauss, *Sculpture in the Expanded Field*, October, no 8, 1979. Krauss' use of the Klein group to develop her argument of the landscape/architecture and not-landscape/not-architecture, along, respectively, complex and neuter axes.
3 Jean Baudrillard, 'The Ecstasy of Communication' in *Post Modern Culture*, edited by Hal Foster.
4 The words shown in bold resemble the pages of hypermedium format of the Worldwide Web computer network which allows information to be arranged in multiple ways simultaneously.

ARCHITECTURAL EDUCATION
GEOFFREY BROADBENT

Architectural education has always been in tension with architectural practice. That is how it should be; practice sometimes gets complacent and education is there as a kind of conscience, trying to correct what seems to be going wrong. So from time immemorial the architect has been subject to learning in two quite different ways; *theory* in a classroom of some kind and *practice*, on the job or in the office.

Vitruvius describes the syllabus that architects learned in ancient Rome at the beginning of his *Ten Books*: 'Theory . . . is the ability to *demonstrate and explain* [my italics] . . . [skill in] the principles of proportion'; while, 'Practice is the continuous and regular exercise of employment where manual work is done . . . according to the design of a drawing.'

There is a lesson in semiotics: the study of meaning in architecture. For as Vitruvius says: 'In all matters, but particularly in [the study of] architecture, there are these two points: the thing signified, and that which gives it significance.' Ferdinand de Saussure could not have put it better! As to the student of architecture: 'Let him be educated, skilful with the pencil, instructed in geometry, know much history, have followed the philosophers with attention, instructed in geometry, understand music, have some knowledge of medicine, know the opinions of the jurists, and be acquainted with astronomy and [with] the theory of the heavens.'

Nothing much has changed since the time of Jesus Christ; our syllabuses these days are much like those that Vitruvius describes. Our students are 'skilful with the pencil' – or these days the computer; they do indeed 'know much history' and, in the most productive schools, 'have followed the philosophers with attention', even though the philosophers may have changed from Plato to Heidegger. Certainly they are 'instructed in geometry', although that may be computer-aided. Few schools seem to teach music as they should; despite Von Schelling's insistence that 'Architecture in general is frozen music' and Roger Scruton's that the way in which 'form follows function' is much like that in which the melody of a song 'follows' the poem on which it is based. We may not know the language in which the poem is written but, nevertheless, 'the melody lingers on'.

'Some knowledge of medicine' has rightly become the province of environmental psychology. Our psychologists tell us what humans need of their environments in terms of thermal, lighting and other conditions. As for 'the opinions of the jurists', no architect these days can survive without knowing very clearly the Law of Contract; his rights and responsibilities in relation to the client and the contractor. As for the 'theory of the heavens', clearly that has changed dramatically since Vitruvius. But if we place it in the rather narrower context of the earth and its sustainable resources then that also has very much to tell us.

So what is new? Nothing much. Our problems are as they were in Roman times.

We know a surprising amount about both Classical design and Classical educational procedures. The original academy of course was Plato's school of philosophy, of which traces are still visible in the suburbs of Athens. Greek education was based on the principle of *arete*, struggle, and it was common for the young to practise physical combat in a courtyard while philosophers disputed in the shady colonnades. And when they had finished their boxing, their wrestling, or whatever, the young went to hear the philosophers. Thus, in a very literal way, Greek education was a combination of physical and mental exertion.

I suggested elsewhere in quite a different context – my little book on *Deconstruction* – that Plato, in various ways, provides five ways of thinking, all of which are needed for a balanced education. They are:

THE INTELLIGIBLE WORLD: the world of the intellect in which ideas can be developed – as in geometry – by the sheer exercise of reasoned thinking. He saw this as superior to

THE SENSIBLE WORLD: the world of the senses in which we gain from experience of the world around us. But the senses may be deceived by optical illusions, hallucinations, conjuring tricks and so on, therefore we cannot trust them.

Plato possessed but could not explain a sense of

DIVINE REVELATION: the belief in some kind of God, possessed of all knowledge and maker of all that exists in the world.

Then, since it subverted his pure thinking, Plato dismissed, as 'perverting all that is good in geometry,'

PRAGMATICS: the use of models or other mechanical devices.

He also excluded from his Republic

CREATIVE IMAGINATION: on the grounds that artists and poets think in ways which again may subvert his 'pure intellect'.

There is no way an architect can work at the level of pure thinking entirely in Plato's 'Intelligible World', nor can he ignore the World of the Senses; indeed everything he does is going to affect the senses of those who use his buildings. One hopes that he will display a few things more pragmatic than the actual processes of building as well as creative imagination. And in the most sublime of cases, no doubt Divine Revelation.

Plato had his views on architecture and they were fairly pragmatic. As he puts it: 'the most pleasurable and beautiful of houses is that in which the owner can find pleasant retreat in all seasons [of the year] and can [also] protect his possessions'. A matter, clearly, of design *with* climate. So architecture was clearly discussed at Plato's Academy, but there are no suggestions of formal courses taking place there. No doubt the Greeks, like centuries of successors, learned architecture on the job. Coulton suggests (1977) that they would not have needed drawings. Once the orders had been established they would know exactly what to do. Each temple, in a sense, was a refinement of the last; if it seemed a little squat then make the columns taller; if it seemed a little top heavy then lighten the architrave and frieze.

Coulton suggests that, like the Egyptians, the Greeks based their designs on grids, and indeed Haselberger found grids, not to mention other quite remarkable drawings, in his thorough study published in 1985 of the Temple of Apollo at Didyma in western Turkey. This dates from the time of Alexander, *c*300 BC, and while there was no scale drawing of a plan there were sec-

tions drawn on the actual walls. So why not floor plans on the floors? He searched intensively and found 'an entire array of thin lines engraved on the surfaces of the individual layers: alignments, axes and other construction lines'. So it seems that each layer was built onto a full-size plan incised into the layer immediately below. The topmost layer was to carry the columns and the walls: there, Haselberger found 'a precise rectangular grid' with 'markers . . . in the only suitable place: along the base of the wall surrounding the nucleus of the temple' – accurate to within one millimetre.

Even more remarkable, however, were the column details which Haselberger found incised into a wall. There was a full-size section lying on its side and 18 metres long with a subtle entasis. One end of this will be overlapped by half a circle; the column's lower diameter divided into segments where the fluting will be. Along side there was a section 'concertinaed'; its vertical central axis crossed by some sixty horizontal lines. These ran towards a diagonal and a curve, representing the entasis, greatly exaggerated. This drawing, of course, would be essential for determining the different diameters of the drums from which the column was constructed. More remarkable still is a detailed section through the base in which the profiles of the mouldings were first drawn with compasses and then 'corrected' freehand.

There is no reason to suppose that Roman practice was any different except that, having drawn their curves with compasses, they left them geometrically 'correct' but unrefined. Certainly we know from surviving drawings, such as the *Forma Urbis* – part of a great map of Rome – that they used rulers, compasses and set-squares. So, as Vitruvius says, an architect's education in Greece and Rome had two aspects: theoretical, which for Vitruvius included such things as proportion and practical, and training 'on the job' in the actual technicalities of building. And there have been these two aspects ever since, inevitably, although the subjects called 'theory' have changed over the years and been greatly expanded. At most times and in most places, too theoretical an education and practical training have taken place simultaneously, although as we shall see the first split between them took place surprisingly early.

MEDIEVAL DESIGN

One might even suggest that it started in the Middle Ages when the Masons had Lodges, where they taught their 'secrets'; inaccessible to the general public and even to ordinary builders. We know quite a lot about those secrets from several sources: first of all from books by several Master Masons such as Villard de

Honnecourt (*c*1235), the 'Magister II' whose drawings are bound in with Villard's (*c*1250), Mathes Röriczer (1486) on the design of pinnacles and a very early printed book by Hans Schmuttermayer, *c*1488. Between them these contain many drawings, and the Abbot Suger himself thinks it worthy of comment that the very birth of the Gothic depended on 'mathematical instruments' which were used to align his new east end at St Denis with the existing nave.

Some 2,000 Gothic drawings survive in various parts of Europe and it is clear that rulers, compasses, dividers, pen and ink were used in their preparation. For example, in the tombs of Gothic Masons, such as that of Hugues Libergier (died 1263) who is shown with the model of a church he designed and three quite specific instruments: a splendid staff about six feet long, a large pair of dividers and a 'square' (that is an L-shape of iron about 18 inches long). Mirgan shows such a 'square' which was actually found in Liverpool. It sets up, more or less, a 30°, 60°, 90° triangle (a proportion called *ad triangularum*), while the staff might be used for measuring lengths along the ground.

So setting out a cathedral may have been rather easy: draw a line along the ground, divide it into bays with the staff, set up lines with the 'square' at right angles to that first line then, from each intersection, set up an *ad triangularum* diagonally to intersect the next cross line. That would define the width of the nave. You might then use a 45° 'square' (*ad quadratum*) to set up the width of the aisle. That is exactly what seems to have happened at Salisbury. We also know that once Milan had been set out there was a dispute as to whether the section should be set out *ad quadratum* (too low and therefore rather dark) or *ad triangularum* (too high and therefore expensive). The result was a compromise.

This is not the place to trace a history of those proportions; they come directly from Plato's description in the *Timaeus* of how the Universe is constructed. Another description from Plato's *Meno*, of how to draw a square exactly half the area of a given square, forms the basis of Röriczer's procedure for building up a pinnacle in diminishing stages. And so one could go on in increasing detail, as John James does (1981) in the case of Chartres, to show how the minutest details of mouldings were derived from geometries of this kind.

RENAISSANCE

The Renaissance of course began with a revival of Classical literature and philosophy initiated by Dante (1265-1321) and Petrarch (1304-74). This naturally led to an interest in buildings surviving from Roman times – Greece was rather inaccessible – and the young Brun-

elleschi studied examples at first hand in Rome. He developed a fairly limited vocabulary of columns, arches and domes: the latter of a 'merging pendentive' kind which, built over a square, has a diameter equal to the diagonal of the square. So with arches on all four sides, the dome sweeps down into the triangular corners between them. So it was that Brunelleschi designed various permutations on these elements for the Foundling Hospital (started in 1419), S Lorenzo (1421), the Pazzi Chapel (1429), S Spirito (1436) etc.

There was, however, no theory behind any of these, just practical geometry. Morolli sees them (1993) as 'aggressive and aurorean'. Brunelleschi's perspective was 'practical' too; indeed his first small painting of the Baptistry to Florence Cathedral was painted on a wooden panel with a hole through the vanishing point, so one viewed it out-of-doors, backwards in a mirror with burnished silver leaf to reflect the real clouds.

Leon Battista Alberti was a prolific writer on matters to do with human relations, and in 1435 he turned his hand to a study of perspective and proportion, *Della pittura*, which may have had a supplement of practical exercises in geometry, namely *Elementa picturae*. He designed the Palazzo Rucellai in 1446, the facade of S Maria Novella in 1448 and the Tempio Malatestiano in 1450. In each case he designed and someone else carried out the building. Also in 1450 Alberti wrote his guide to the ruins of ancient Rome, with careful measured drawings and a map. And then in 1452 his *De re aedificatoria*, written in Latin, began circulating in manuscript form, after he had presented a copy to Pope Nicholas V.

In the treatise Alberti reasoned that of all the arts architecture was the most susceptible to theory. Unlike painting, sculpture, literature and poetry, architecture could be developed philosophically. That was because it was rooted in 'ideal' forms – the primary solids: the cube, the sphere, the pyramid and so on.

Alberti indeed saw himself as a philosopher, very much in the manner of Plato, and Landini reports a famous 'Disputation' of 1460 between Alberti and Lorenzo de Medici of the great Florentine family. Lorenzo thought of himself as a practical man; his constant aim was to get things done, whereas Alberti in his view was a theorist, a dreamer, who simply thought out how things *ought* to be. He preferred a contemplative life. Yet by 1485 Lorenzo had grown 'so fond' of Alberti – as his secretary puts it – that he volunteered the services of Angelo Poliziano, his 'man of letters' and a poet, to edit *De re aedifactoria* for publication, which he actually funded.

Increasingly, his discussions with Alberti had led Lorenzo to understand the importance of theory. There were academies already based on Classical models for the teaching of literature and other arts. So during the mid-1470s he had set up his own private school, the *Academia Platonica*, in a Garden which he owned on the Piazza San Marco in Florence, appointing Bertoldo di Giovanni, a sculptor who had studied with Donatello, as his Director. The purpose of the school was to counter what Lorenzo – and no doubt Alberti – saw as the baleful influence of the Craft Guilds which still survived from the Middle Ages. Lorenzo himself selected the students who studied, ate and slept in buildings within the garden, including a loggia where they used unwanted sculptures from the Medici collection as raw materials. There may also have been a collection of drawings and models by contemporary masters for them to study at first hand in the workshop. We therefore gain some idea of the quality, both of Lorenzo's selection and Bertoldo's teaching, when we realise that graduates from the Academia included Leonardo da Vinci, who entered in 1475, Michelangelo, there from 1480, and Antonio Dangallo the younger, not to mention sculptors such as Pietro Torrigiano and Andrea Sansovino. No doubt, Alberti's treatises were used there but the crucial point is that an Academy, in Plato's sense, proved a more than viable alternative to simply working on the job with a master by which architects, painters and sculptors had been taught until then.

ACADÉMIE ROYALE

As the Medici dynasty crumbled so the Academia was abandoned. But Chafer suggests (1980) that the tradition did not die, that Italian Renaissance and post-Renaissance models inspired the French, so that in 1635 Richelieu set up the Académie Française to regulate the language, Mazarin in 1648 founded a Royal Academy of Painting and Sculpture, while during the 1660s Colbert established a number of other institutions for Dance, *Belles Lettres*, History and Archaeology, Science, Music and in 1671 the Académie Royale d'Architecture for Louis XIV. Initially, it was a discussion group of eminent architects who in addition to advising the King on matters architectural also aimed to 'bring forth a more exact knowledge and a more correct theory'. They also set up a School, with François Blondel as Director who gave public lectures twice a week. There were lectures also on arithmetic, geometry, mechanics, military architecture, fortifications, perspective and stone cutting. By 1717 these had become a two- or three-year course.

Colbert's point, like Lorenzo's before him, had been to attack the trade guilds which were not under Royal control. The point was to raise architects from the status of craftsman to that of philosopher. The Acad-

FROM ABOVE: Ospedale degli Innocenti, Florence, facade; San Lorenzo, dome of old sacristry, Florence; S Maria Novella, facade proportions, Florence. Alberti was presented with the difficult task of building onto the existing Gothic base, merging the Gothic details into his Renaissance design

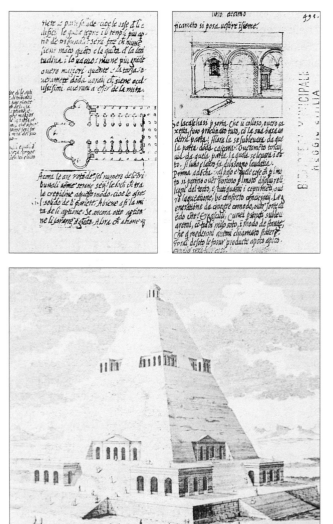

emy offered only lectures; there were no design studies in the school. Students learned drawing and design in the studios of their masters.

By 1720 the Academy had established annual competitions for student designs and by 1780 the Grand Prize had become available after three years of study at the French Academy in Rome.

The presumption behind all of this was that students would design with the Classical Orders, but in 1721 a strange thing happened. JB Fischer von Ehrlach, the great Baroque architect of Vienna, published his illustrated *History of Architecture* in German and French, which was meant to be a survey of all architecture 'from the earliest times to the present day'. Some drawings are accurate indeed, such as Stonehenge, but many others are Baroque versions of how Fischer's perspective-historical architecture ought to have been. That was true of the Temple of Solomon; it could have been drawn a hundred years after Fischer by Durand. And of the Seven Wonders of the World, from Babylon, Giza, Olympia, Halicarnassus, Ephesus, Rhodes and Alexandria, all are more or less Baroque in one way or another. Apart from the Pyramids at Giza, which are too steep, there are strange 'Egyptian' pyramids; clearly hollow and inhabited with doors and windows in several storeys. Fischer's 'Greek' temples have walls between their columns and the Palace of Nero looks like a grandiose version of Fischer's own Schönbrun outside Vienna. His Roman arches are by no means bad, nor Trajan's column, nor the ruins of Palmyra. He has twelve Islamic examples – if you count Hagia Sophia, the plan of which is commendably accurate. His oriental examples too, from Bangkok, Nanking, Beijing and other parts of China, are a little ill-proportioned but fairly convincing in their details.

There is a splendid section on Fischer's own designs – some built – in and around Vienna, including a triumphal arch, ie Schönbrun as he conceived it (not quite as grand as Nero's Palace) and as it was built. There are various smaller palaces: the Church of Nôtre Dame for Salzburg and the Karlskirche in Vienna. And finally there is a volume of basins, fountains and vases. Some periods are clearly missing altogether; not a single example of Early Christian, Romanesque or Gothic, apart from St Stephen's in the centre of Vienna. But that is not quite the point; nor are the inaccuracies. The point is that, for the first time, studies of comparative styles were brought together. Here was the material for a loss of nerve: 'Is the best I can do as good as the best of this?' And in many cases it was not, and still is not.

In any closed culture, of course, one knows the 'going manner' of doing things; if you were a Greek you designed Greek temples, and so on, which applies

FROM ABOVE: Illustrations of Alberti's De re aedifactoria, taken from the 1538 Reggio Emilia manuscript by Pieti; JB Fischer von Ehrlach, History of Architecture, *1721. A Theban pyramid synthesising disparate cultures united by common archetypes*

through all ranges of architectural grandeur. There are few cultures more closed than those who construct vernacular buildings. For them there is a 'one best way' in each case from which there is no reason to depart. But once the floodgates of history are opened then we have to look, consider and make choices. So it has been since Fischer; and there have been many reactions: the plagiarism of a chosen style; eclecticism in which any style is as good as any other; a search for rules; a *rappel à l'orde* which will tell us, after all, which style to use.

These processes have continued unabated in books, journals, television programmes, colour supplements. These days architects and clients know all there is to know about architecture, so, since Fischer, we have a number of choices: eclecticism based on what happened in the past and which Fischer showed; regionalism based on our local vernaculars; and Internationalism based on a 'one best way' that ought to be built everywhere.

All of this was not a problem at the Academy. The style had been chosen: Classical Roman. Apart from the annual competitions, Marigny set up monthly ones in 1763 which survived through the Revolution of 1789, after which, of course, there was no longer a place for a Royal Academy. The academies as a whole were under threat; the artists indeed had been demanding that they be allowed to draw from casts of the Antique. Their protests were suppressed by Jacques Louis David, painter of great neo-classical scenes; but he seems to have shared with David Le Roy, whose hasty drawings of the finest monuments in Greece had appeared before the more accurate, but much slower Stuart and Revett's. So David had great respect for Le Roy and his co-professor Vaudoyer. The Académie continued under their direction with Napoleon's favourite architects Percier and Fontaine as visiting critics. By 1793 there was a rival school, which was to become the École Polytechnique with J-N-L Durand as Professor. Durand's geometric approach to design, using grids no doubt, was appropriate in an institution devoted to the design of bridges, fortifications and other public works. Ever hungry for power, David became Chairman of the National Convention in 1794 and in 1795, at his behest, new schools were set up in astronomy, medicine, political science and music, including a Special School of Architecture to be linked with equally Special Schools in Painting and Sculpture. And thus finally were brought together the components of what was to become École Royale des Beaux Arts, formally named as such by Louis XVIII in 1819.

The architects' syllabus included lectures in the theory of architecture, the history of architecture, construction, perspective and mathematics, to which Chafee reports had been added, by 1900, physics and chemistry, descriptive geometry, building law, general history and the history of French architecture. Of those, only scientific-based subjects were examined. And, of course, independent from the lectures there were still the monthly competitions, most of them in architectural composition. These were of two kinds: *esquisses* (sketch designs) and *projets rendus* (fully finished drawings rendered in ink). An *esquisse* might consist of part of a facade, a small house, a public fountain or whatever, whereas *projets rendus*, at the second level, might consist of a small school, an assembly hall or a small railway station. A third kind of *projet* was added in 1876; this was *éléments analytiques*. In these, drawings were required of the Classical Orders. There were annual competitions also in construction: construction in stone, in iron or in wood and general construction. Indeed, these competitions in construction were elaborated greatly towards the end of the century when drawings would be required for the construction of a building with all the necessary details and calculations.

In all this there were several anomalies. Since the École presented only lectures, issued the programmes for the competitions, judged the students' entries – in secret – and announced the results, the students were therefore, in terms of design tuition, 'thrown to the wolves'. They had to fend for themselves; and of course they did. They might work for a *patron* in his office but that was rare. The most popular teachers had their own *ateliers* or, at least, *ateliers* organised by students who would find the premises and rent them. One of them, the *massier*, would administer the place, buying coal for the stoves, oil for the lamps, the few books the *atelier* could afford, and, most important, pay the patron. He would usually select the students *maintaining* a balance between *anciens* – senior students – and *nouveaux*. The latter would learn a great deal by helping out their elders on final drawings, casting shadows, repeating ornamental details and inking-in plans on a process known as *négrifier*.

For one of the larger competitions, such as the *Prix de Rome*, a senior student would register in March. The first stage of the competition would be an *esquisse*, prepared under en-loge conditions; that is locked in a room with cubicles for twelve hours – the result might be a facade design. Within a week of that the second stage would be held, a twenty-four-hour *esquisse* for thirty students again prepared under en-loge conditions; probably a complex planning problem such as placing a university within a city. Out of the thirty, eight were admitted to the final stage. That too would start with an *esquisse* produced *en loge* for a large and complex building: a museum of some kind, a hospice, a university or other centre of higher education, an embassy, a palace, a cathedral or whatever.

On completion, the student had to trace his sketch design and if the final building departed from this in any significant way he was disqualified, which, of course, is quite alien to that more recent theory developed from Karl Popper's philosophy of science as described in *Conjectures and Refutations: The Growth of Scientific Knowledge*. One puts forward an idea, tests it, and if it does not work, abandons it. Such an approach to process was probably a much greater source of weakness at the École than anything to do with an emphasis on Classical formalism.

The École is important in our scheme of things because its mode of education dominated architecture and the way architects were taught until the 1920s when the Bauhaus presented a different scheme. The point about all this is that there were two kinds of teaching at the École des Beaux Arts: theory in the classroom and design in the *ateliers*. Quite separate things, taught by very different people.

LE CORBUSIER

Le Corbusier, despite later denials, actually attended classes at the École, especially in history and construction. He blamed the engineer, as many students do, for making the latter more complicated than it need be, learning concrete construction directly from a Master in the subject, Auguste Perret.

Clearly, he gained a great deal from the history courses and did what every student should: he travelled, extensively, first to Italy in 1908, then passed rapidly through Bern, Lucerne, the Gothard, Lugano, Milan, Pavia – where he saw his first Carthusian monastery, the immensely ornate Certposa – Genoa, Carrara, Pisa – where he stayed for a day or two – and Florence – where he stayed for almost a month – fanning out to Galluzzo, Siena, Lucca, Pistoia, Prato and Fiesole. Then he hit the road again, via Faenza, Ravenna, Ferrara, Bologna, Mantua, Peschiera, Verona, Padua, Venice, Fiume, Budapest and Vienna. It was in Galluzzo that he saw his second Carthusian monastery, which he insisted on calling 'Ema'. The divided life of the monks, between the absolute privacy of the individual houses with gardens, and their meeting, as required for communal worship, eating and so on, struck him as some kind of model for the choices that all human beings ought to have.

The extraordinary things about Le Corbusier's Tuscan sketches are their delicacy, their sensitivity. They could have been made by Ruskin; and indeed used by Ruskin to reinforce his views on the nature of the Gothic. But somehow, in his later travels, Le Corbusier became a harder man. His trip to Germany in 1910 included Berlin, Weimar, Bamberg, Nürnburg and Stuttgart, and he became more interested in what industry had to offer. After which, in 1911, he made a more extensive German tour, to Karlsruhe, Heidelberg, Darmstadt, Frankfurt, Wiesbaden, Hagen, Mainz, Coblenz, Cologne, Düsseldorf, Hamburg and Berlin. There he worked for Peter Behrens for five months, alongside the young Gropius and the young Mies van der Rohe. Later he visited Dresden, Prague and Vienna.

Shortly after, starting in May 1911, he began his big adventure: the journey down the Danube by way of Prague, Vienna, Budapest, Belgrade, Bucharest, Tirnovo, Adrianopolis and many smaller places in between. He ended up in Constantinople. (Kemel Attaturk had yet to call it Istanbul.) After Constantinople he came back to La Chaux-de-Fonds via quite a circuitous route, by way of Mount Athos, Thessaloniki, Athens, Delphi, Brindisi, Naples, Pompeii, Rome, Tivoli, Florence and his favourite monastery at Galluzzo, Pisa and Lucerne. Again he produced hundreds of sketches, but this time in hard black line, not to mention many photographs which, bearing in mind the sheer weight of photographic equipment at that time, must have been quite a physical feat. All the time he noted three different kinds of activity: 'folklore', which we should call vernacular, culture – fine architecture – and industry.

On the second trip of 1910 to Vienna he could not have avoided the furore that was going on over Adolf Loos' Goldman and Salatsch Store on the Michaelerplatz. Loos designed a four-storey store on a corner of the Platz; the first two floors of which were given over to a gentleman's outfitters. These were chaste, Classical, with green Tuscan columns. The further four storeys had squarish windows between which Loos designed linear patterns in some unspecified material. But after much debate, he decided to leave off the patterns and paint plane white walls between the windows. Such was the furore in Vienna that the Emperor was involved. It could not have escaped Le Corbusier's attention, but he claims in the journal of his travels that he first noticed white-walled architecture a few weeks later in vernacular houses around Tirnovo on the Danube.

In Constantinople he seems to have learned two things in particular: the danger of fire in timber houses – hence one reason for his interest in concrete construction – and the use of the ramp for moving from level to level. Clearly, this travelling and observing was a splendid education. Observing also in different ways: by looking, making notes, making Ruskin-like watercolours, annotated or not, hard-like pencil or charcoal drawings, and in his later travels taking photographs. One obviously learns very different things from each of these media; looking, sitting down to sketch for minutes or hours at a time, moving around the building as one takes photographs and thus experiences it from different viewpoints in rapid succession, learning differences between the sunny and the shaded side.

BAUHAUS

While Gaudi, Wright and others of their generation had formal university education (Gaudi failed structures several times and Wright did not complete the engineering course), future architects, such as Gropius and Mies van der Rohe did not, though they still became educators, initially, at the Bauhaus. Gropius formed this in 1919 by combining two different kinds of teaching when the Weimar School of Arts and Crafts was absorbed into the Academy of Art. The point, for Gropius, was that there should be no distinction, that all the arts and crafts be brought together in the production of architecture, which he outlined in his Manifesto and Programme for the Bauhaus of 1919. His aim was that the crafts should be well established before the architecture course was started.

Gropius brought in some of the finest German artists of his time, including Lionel Feininger, Johannes Itten, Wassily Kandinsky, Paul Klee and Oskar Schlemmer. Itten taught the famous six-month Basic Course, not to mention a mystic religion, Mazdaznan, which involved meditation, a vegetarian diet, the wearing of a monk-like costume, deep-breathing and other exercises and considerable periods of fasting. The course itself included studies of natural objects and materials, contrasting their forms and textures, the analysis of Old Master paintings, to abstract from them principles of contrast in colour and tone value, rhythm and composition, as well as life drawing.

After the six-month Basic Course the students spent much of the next three years on theoretical work, including studies of nature, fabrics, geometry, colour and composition, constructions and presentations, materials and tools. Here, too, there was an emphasis on *abstraction*, as one can tell from the published courses of Kandinsky, Klee and others. At the same time, students designed and made things in the workshops which eventually included wood, metal, textiles, colour, glass, clay and stone. The students were meant to design for mass production but their prototypes, such as Marianne Brandt's famous teapot – a perfect hemisphere – were produced by hand, patiently formed by beating a sheet of silver. Such studies, as various students said, occupied only half the mind which left the rest free to contemplate other things, such as design.

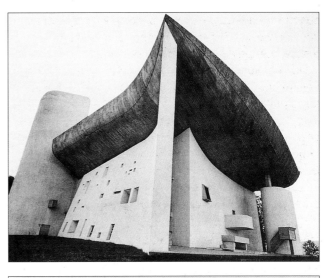

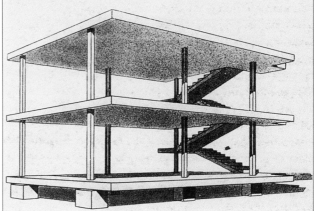

FROM ABOVE: Notre-Dame-du-Haut by Le Corbusier, Ronchamp, France, 1950-54; Dom-ino House, construction system by Le Corbusier, 1914

By 1920 the workshops were well enough established for Gropius and Meyer to design the Sommerfeld House for Berlin, bringing in the range of Bauhaus crafts. But there was still a mismatch between the theoretical and the craft teaching. Students as a whole found that the exercises in abstraction, which loomed so large in the syllabus, by no means equipped them to make designs. In a sense it was as if they had analysed form, colour, texture etc so thoroughly that they had no motivation for utilising them. Since they were not permitted to draw on designs they knew, they increasingly looked for a 'Bauhaus style' and found in *De Stijl*, Theo van Doesburg's magazine, work in painting, design and architecture, not to mention that of Dutch colleagues, such as Piet Mondrian, Gerrit Rietveld and JJP Oud. So well used was *De Stijl* that Gropius forbade his students to cut out the illustrations. Not surprisingly, Van Doesburg was immensely popular as a visiting lecturer and in 1920 the students petitioned Gropius for his appointment to the teaching staff. He moved to Weimar but Gropius refused; so Van Doesburg set up a 'pirate' course, for which the students had to pay, run from his own apartment.

And so the Bauhaus found its 'style' after all: the black lines and primary red, yellow and blue rectangles against a white background of De Stijl, which were increasingly reflected in Bauhaus designs, including some for an experimental house, 'Am Horn' at Dessau designed by Adolf Muche and built by Adolph Meyer in 1923, not to mention Gropius' own design for the new Bauhaus building in Dessau of 1925. This reflected an increasing split between theory and workshop practice in that the artists were housed in one building, the craftsmen in another, linked only by a bridge containing administration, including the Director's office over a road which had yet to be built.

By 1928 Gropius felt that the crafts had matured sufficiently for an architecture course of nine semesters to be started. He appointed Hannes Meyer, a Swiss architect, to run it and a year later, when Gropius resigned to go into full-time practice, Meyer succeeded him as Bauhaus Director. He rejected the Bauhaus style, specifically the cube with its 'yellow, red, blue, white, grey [and] black sides'. He was hostile to the painters as a whole and the way they dominated Bauhaus working. Some were forced to resign rather quickly and instead of their abstract, formal analyses Meyer grounded the course in psychology, sociology and economics. This seems to be the first appearance in any school of design of psychologists and sociologists, entirely at Meyer's initiative; although Gropius himself claims much of the credit in *The New Architecture and the Bauhaus*.

Meyer divided the course into two parts: theory and practical building; engineers were brought in to teach heating, ventilation, statics, building design, materials, daylighting and technical drawing. Practical craftwork included furniture from a Trade Union School which Meyer designed outside Berlin (1928) and for housing on the Törten Estate in Dessau. There were also prototype kitchens for the National Research Society.

But what had been a small Communist cell within the Bauhaus started to grow towards the end of the 1920s. Meyer himself was sympathetic and he was forced to resign in August 1930; making his way to Moscow. Mies van der Rohe replaced him as Bauhaus Director and he promptly closed the School, ejected the left-wing members and drew up new contracts with staff and students alike for a more authoritarian regime. Psychology and sociology were eliminated from the curriculum and replaced, in Mies' words, by: 'handicraft, technical and artistic training'. Students could bypass the Basic Course and, in the Second Stage, could enter directly into the Workshop on Principles of Building with no need to gain experience in the other craft workshops. They were taught building law, statics, heating and ventilation, materials, mathematics and physics. After this, Hilbersheimer taught apartment and town planning, including such things as orientation, the combination of tall buildings with low, specific types of houses and apartments, and the design of urban infrastructures. Mies taught the last three semesters; a studio class in which drawing was strongly emphasised and at least one project was a courtyard house. There were no live projects any more or any social content to the work.

By August 1932, however, the Nazis dominated the Dessau City Council and declared that the Bauhaus be closed and the building demolished. Mies moved what he could to an old factory in a Berlin suburb, but despite Mies' pleadings with the Nazis the Bauhaus was finally closed in April 1933.

ILLINOIS INSTITUTE OF TECHNOLOGY

Hochman has described in considerable and sometimes unsavoury detail Mies' operations in Nazi Germany. He was involved in exhibition design until the Nazis denied him even that. But by late 1935 he had already been offered a teaching post in California. He found the whole prospect of an American exile distasteful and declined; by July 1937, however, he was sufficiently desperate to accept an invitation from Mrs Stanley Resor, friend of Philip Johnson and Alfred Barr, to design a house for her in the mountains of Wyoming. Mies passed through Chicago on his way there and met with officials from Armour Incorporated, makers of Spam, who wished to add a School of Architecture to the Institute of Education they had founded there. Mies wrote a detailed programme for a Masters Course which was eventually accepted; his appointment as Director was announced in April 1938. In addition to setting up the programme, Mies of course became Campus Architect designing, among many other buildings, the Alumni Memorial Hall (1945-46), which was used for architecture and design until Crown Hall was completed (1950-56).

Mies' syllabus was divided into three parts: studies of *means*, of *purposes*, of *planning and creating*. By 'means' he had in mind materials: wood, stone, brick, steel and concrete; each treated in terms of its qualities as a material, the types of construction in which it could be used, its implications – alone or combined with other materials for the making of architectural form.

'Purposes' meant building types: dwellings, including houses of various kinds, hotels, clubs, resorts, dormitories and institutions; commercial buildings, such as stores, offices, display spaces, banks, restaurants and warehouses; industrial buildings for light manufacturing, heavy industry and assembly plants; public buildings, such as schools, libraries, churches, auditoria, theatres, museums, hospitals, transport buildings and government buildings. Students were expected to analyse a building's functions and to design not just the fabric of the building but also the furniture and fittings. They were asked to consider also the grouping of buildings, which Mies himself had displayed in the Campus itself, according to different social factors, such as dwelling, work, public administration, recreation and culture, as well as technical requirements such as topography, kind of development, hygiene and sanitation, and transportation.

Under 'planning and creating' Mies listed dependence on the epoch – the supporting and compelling forces of the times: material, functional and spiritual. His Ordering Principles included the mechanical, which could be too mechanistic, and the idealistic, which of course could become too idealistic. Then there was the organic – not in the sense of growing out of nature but of balancing Mies' mechanical and idealistic considerations. Mies' *Elements of Architectural Form* included walls and openings, surface and depth, space and solid, material and colour, light and shadow, lightness and massiveness. He saw 'form' as developing out of organisation and working methods, saw an overall 'obligation' to realise his particular version of 'organic architecture' and looked for architecture, painting and sculpture to be joined as a 'creative unity'.

There was much emphasis on drawing, including meticulously detailed perspectives of timber frame, brick and other forms of construction with, for instance,

Bauhaus, Dessau, aerial view. A direct translation into physical terms of the complex organisation of the school and a projection of its spirit into the new architectural language it was instrumental in creating

every brick joint drawn with a double line. As with the crafts in some of the Bauhaus workshops, this too left half the mind free for thinking about design. Equally meticulous drawings were required of buildings allocated for study in the history seminars.

Mies had the reputation of requiring students to work his way, arguing that if they did not wish to they could always go to another school. By the 1950s his architecture had been reduced almost entirely to towers with steel frames boxed in concrete for fire protection, and large-span, open pavilions. Most students conformed and continued to do so for years after graduation. There is much to be said for a school so strongly characterised, but some of us began to worry about the climatic performance of those buildings, with their tremendous solar heat gain, their heat loss and the massive inputs of energy required to make them habitable.

OXFORD CONFERENCE

There was a feeling towards the end on the 1950s that things were going badly wrong because much of the environment that was then being built was of very low quality. A group of intellectuals at the RIBA, led by Sir Leslie Martin and Richard (later Lord) Llewelyn-Davies, persuaded the RIBA to hold a conference at Oxford in April 1958. The last such conference had been held in 1924 and had resolved that, as far as possible, architectural education should take place, full time, in universities. However, as late as 1957, while 486 students graduated by the 'full-time' route, almost as many, 417, had worked by 'articled pupilage' and taken the RIBA's examinations externally. Much debate was concerned with entry standards then considered far too low; much lower than other professions required, such as medicine, dentistry, pharmacy, veterinary science. It was felt that higher-level students would encourage higher standards of education; theoretical and practical, they would diversify into the various specialisms that were increasingly needed. More of them would go on to post-graduate studies, and courses might even be shortened to leave more time for such things. Students of lesser calibre would be needed as technicians.

If courses were to be concentrated in universities or comparable institutions, then students could intermingle with students of other disciplines to their mutual advantage. Among other things, it would spread an understanding of architecture among future decision-makers. Architecture could also act as a bridge between the arts and the sciences, engineering, sociology and economics. These would inform the architecture course, not in any haphazard way but on the basis of theory, which was defined, for the purposes of the conference, as 'the body of principles that explains and interrelates all the facts of the subject'. What is more, as Sir Leslie Martin put it: 'Research is the tool by which theory is advanced. Without it, teaching can have no direction and thought no cutting edge.'

Part-time education presented many problems. One example was the way in which students, having prepared themselves as best they could for written examinations and some 32 drawings (their 'testimonies of study'), were failed by examiners in no position to tell them where they had gone wrong. The pass rate was some 40 per cent.

Although theoretical studies were emphasised, the conference also recognised the importance of practical experience to be gained preferably by training in an office. But time and again theory was emphasised: 'Knowledge is the raw material for design . . . It is not a substitute for architectural imagination; but it is necessary for the effective exercise of imagination and skill in design.' Lack of knowledge 'handicaps and trammels the architect, limits the achievements of even the most creative and depresses the general level . . .' Post-graduate study and research should be encouraged in the essential 'advancement of knowledge'. 'This,' says Sir Leslie, 'is the means by which the competence of the profession as a whole can be advanced.' This should include: 'the space and functional requirements of building types, studies of . . . day-lighting and town planning, the prefabrication and industrialisation of building . . . the special problems of tropical building . . .' Much of this work should be based on 'the inter-relation between architecture and social needs, the physics of environment etc.' Architects should work with engineers, structural, mechanical and production, with specialists in management and (work) study; with sociologists, psychologists, physicists, physiologists. Most architectural research so far had been in the field of history and of course this should continue. So the conference recommended higher minimum entry standards, the abolition of the RIBA's external examinations, the placing of a school in universities or institutions of comparable standard, the course to be full-time or possibly alternated with full-time office work, that students with these improved qualifications in architecture would be capable of, and encouraged to move into, other kinds of work, the essential nature of post-graduate studies and research.

It was shortly after this that I moved into architectural education and in 1967 I was asked to restructure the Portsmouth School which had been small, provincial and grossly underfunded. I decided that my model would be Mies, as it were in reverse; that I would develop a pluralist school in which students would be encouraged to develop in very different directions, provided that their work was convincing of its kind. I also took the Oxford view that we needed to build up the intellectual base while at the same time maintaining links with practice. It seemed to me too that if architecture needed injections of fresh ideas, which in my view it most certainly did, then those might best come from people outside the profession unwilling to take for granted what seemed to architects like 'received wisdom'. The School was staffed by ten architects and a structural engineer when I arrived and I was determined to broaden the base; more widely than at Oxford. Certainly we needed scientists, but we also needed artists.

Unlike anyone else, at least in Britain, I was offered ten new appointments on arrival and in the first few years we added to our staff, full-time or part-time, physicists, a mathematician, a materials scientist, a builder, a sculptor, a theatrical set designer, painters, a psychologist, an anthropologist, philosophers and of course architects of different persuasions, including an historian.

I also designed a framework for the course to coordinate the input from this very wide range. My division into architectural design, design science and the context of design has been used fairly widely in other places. There were two strands to 'architectural design'; the usual studio courses and lectures in theory, three years of which I personally presented, including the psychology of the architect, perception, the design process, communications, meaning in architecture and a history of theories from 1750 or so to the ever-shifting 'present day'. I also added a survey-course, albeit rather brief, from architecture in prehistory to 1750. Several projects emerged from this course, especially after some of it was published as *Design in Architecture*, including those ways of generating design which I called pragmatic, typologic, analogic and syntactic; not to mention those criteria for judging buildings: environmental filtering, symbolism, economic implications and environmental impact developed from the work of Hiller, Musgrove, O'Sullivan.

'Design science' naturally included construction, the theory of structures and the environmental sciences of heating, lighting and sound control. Most of these were taught by scientists or engineers, but they were expected to spend time in the studios, to learn at first hand, over their drawing boards, what architecture students really needed. They also set studio projects of various kinds and the first two years had students in laboratory courses learning, by experiments and surveys, how their experience of the environment around them could be related to what was measurable and therefore controllable. Yet the emphasis of these courses was by no means on calculation, it was, rather,

in developing the students' feelings for what the size of a column ought to be. We even said in our degree submission: 'We have never seen the examination room as a suitable place for the practice of arithmetic!'

By 'context of design' I meant the background of ideas from which designs emerge. We saw the most constant of these as the histories of architecture, art and urbanism, which were allocated considerable lecture and seminar time. Then, according to staffing at various times, we had anthropology, landscape, psychology, philosophy and urban geography.

These subjects also fed into the studios, especially in projects introduced before my arrival which came to be known as 'paradigms'. These were variations on the theme of: study an architect's work and working methods, analyse these and then design accordingly. Almost all these projects were highly successful with, in most cases, one of two results: a student continued working in that manner for some time before developing, as it were, 'out of it' or the student reacted strongly against it and in doing that, too, might well determine a personal language.

Altogether, the results were much as I had hoped with a marvellous variety in the work. In the early 90s, for instance, it was possible to see 'deconstruction' and full-blown Classical in the same studio. Our graduates, on the whole, brought a 'human' rather than a 'formal' approach to their work in which there were spectacular successes. Many of the well known Hampshire Schools were designed, in whole or in part, by Portsmouth graduates, putting into practice things they had learned in the School about passive energy systems; they have gained a great many awards and one was named, in 1994, as the BBC's 'Building of the Year'. Our graduates were able to work in this way because the County Architect, Sir Colin Stansfield Smith – now Professor at the School – is a 'pluralist' of a very similar kind.

I find it immensely intriguing that today's most adventurous architects, such as Frank Gehry and Daniel Libeskind, pay a lot of attention to the things we emphasised so much; acoustics, daylighting and so on. Libeskind with his many lighting models of his Jewish Extension to the Berlin Museum, Gehry with his lighting models of Vitra and Minnesota, and his extraordinary range of acoustic models for the Disney Concert Hall. *That* was the approach that we were trying to teach!

PRINCE OF WALES'S INSTITUTE

The newest School in Britain took its first students in 1992. It was set up by the Prince of Wales as his Institute for Architecture and his intention, right from the start, was to instil the values he had described in *A Vision of Britain*; with a Foundation Course based on the crafts to counter the mechanistic architecture he dislikes so much – to develop *human* values. Much of the Course is based on the crafts and there is very little 'theory', so the syllabus is much like that of the Bauhaus. The course contains a great deal of life drawing, painting and the study of traditional details, both in sketch books and by measured drawings. Rather than Bauhaus-like basic design the students learn the basis of drawing and design by the study of Celtic patterns and the geometry of Islamic tiling patterns. These have the advantage of requiring high precision in draughtsmanship while building such matters as colour symbolism, rather than Bauhaus-like abstract analyses.

These geometric studies are extended into three-dimensional structures; delicate assemblages of struts and cables and usable structures, such as hand-crafted park shelters in consultation with Imre Makovecz, a Mongolian Yurt etc. As at the Bauhaus, there are craft workshops in ceramics, clay modelling, metal working, stone carving and wood carving. Some of these are directed towards the study of architectural ornament, the way light falls on highly modelled surfaces and so on.

There are also projects at urban scale: the modelling to scale of historic places such as the Campo in Siena and the insertion of new buildings into sensitive sites, often with community consultation. There are, as everyone expected, studies of the Classical Orders, but these by no means dominate approaches to design. It seems that the emphasis on crafts encourages an 'Arts and Crafts' approach. That is certainly true of the major design-and-build projects in which any input from 'theory' is greatly discouraged. But there is no doubt that the discipline of craftwork on site gives the students insights into building achieved by few of their peers. In so far as history and theory are taught these are based on *A Vision of Britain* and an emphasis on spiritual values in, for instance, *Man, Building and the Cosmos*. Yet there are those involved with the Institute who argue that 'learning by doing' is the only way of mastering architecture. Perhaps there is something to be learned from the Lorenzo-Alberti debate! All in all though, the Institute seems a valuable addition to the ways in which architects can be taught.

OTHER APPROACHES

Of course there is more to be said, very much more, about other kinds of architectural education; about schools such as the Bartlett which after Oxford became almost entirely scientific, about schools such as the AA in which the presence of various people, namely Rem Koolhaas, Bernard Tschumi (also at Portsmouth), Zaha Hadid and others led to such a creative ferment that an

actual *style* was born. For that was the birthplace of much in 'Deconstruction'. But there was also the problem in the late 80s of 'creative entropy' when the various units seem to have absorbed so much from each other that with honourable exceptions a certain sameness crept in. There are schools such as Luton, emphasising technicalities and management procedures; there are also changes of emphasis such as that which occurred when the Bartlett had become more like the AA than the AA itself.

A UNIVERSITY OF ARCHITECTURE

The most ambitious scheme for the future, however, seems to be that of Tomás Taveira, the Lisbon architect who seeks to set up a University of Architecture. He finds himself as Dean of Architecture in a Technical University surrounded by engineers who have their own immensely successful ways of thinking which they apply to various kinds of engineering. But architects have their ways of thinking too which involve a firm rooting in culture and history; the obvious skills of drawing and designing; profound understanding of human values, namely spiritual, physiological, psychological, social; and the ability to 'juggle many balls at once' in the resolution of complex problems, fraught with ambiguities. They need a knowledge of many crafts, technologies, the ability to communicate with specialists in many fields and so on. Thinking, in Taveira's view, can be applied with equal relevance to all the visual arts – to theatre in its very many aspects, to film, to television etc. So Taveira is trying to set up a University of Architecture in which all these fields are represented and feed directly off each other.

DESIGN STUDIO
How relevant is this?

Very highly, or so it seems from Donald Schön's analysis of what makes architectural education so special. Like other observers from the human sciences, Donald Schön is fascinated by architects and their work, which he analysed, in considerable detail, in *The Design Studio* (1985). Schön sees this as the very model for education in all the professions, including medicine, law and even business. For like architecture these professionals also have to deal with: 'complexity, uncertainty, uniqueness and value-conflict'. They all have to learn, understand and incorporate material from the applied sciences which themselves are constantly developing. Indeed, such professionals all have to *integrate* their methods of working with what Shön calls 'reflection in action'.

For this way of working, says Schön, architecture is 'the very prototype . . .' The other professions have been 'selectively inattentive to artistry' whereas architects, whatever the technical complexities of their work, tend to make decisions on 'aesthetic' grounds. Shön by no means amplifies what he means by this but if one takes aesthetic to include *all* decision-making which cannot be rooted in objective, factual analysis, whether it be in wine tasting, investing in companies – or paintings – then no doubt he is right. Studio working, as he says, seems to be a 'reflection in action', indeed 'a kind of on-the-spot research' conducted within the very 'media' of architecture itself. Schön believes that this has its own 'standards of rigour' however different in kind these may be from those of the quantifying disciplines.

Architectural design is not simply a matter of solving problems. It is a question, first of all, of finding what the problems actually are. Architectural students, says Schön, constantly 'need to educate themselves to a new competence when they don't yet know what it is they need to learn'. So unlike other kinds of students: 'they must therefore take a plunge into *doing* before they know what to do', which, of course, is a special way of thinking, applicable – as Sir Leslie Martin said – to many fields indeed beyond architecture. So what a marvellous way to spend a career, helping young people to develop such ways of thinking.

Bibliography

Droste, M *Bauhaus 1919-1933*, Bauhaus Archiv-Museum, Berlin, 1990.
Hochman, ES *Architects of Fortune: Mies van der Rohe and the Third Reich*, International, New York,1990.

Geoffrey Broadbent is a leading/international authority on architectural theory and has been published extensively, as well as given lectures around the world. He recently retired as Professor of Architecture at Portsmouth University.

FROM ABOVE: Wren's monument obscured by the mechanistic architecture disliked so much by HRH The Prince of Wales; Bnu Building by Tomás Taveira, Lisbon, Portugal, 1983-89, a self-contained unit with an anonymous immediate location, without a special cultural quality

ONE, TWO, THREE: JUMP

BERNARD TSCHUMI

The history of architecture is deeply intertwined with the history of its educational methods, and today's changes at Columbia and in many other schools are part of a much larger evolution.

So I should like to raise the issue of architectural education and architecture in terms of the three great breaks or dissociations which occurred during the past two or three thousand years.

FIRST DISSOCIATION

From the time of the Pyramids to the end of the Middle Ages, the architect lived on the building site and rarely existed as an independent individual. There were no schools of architecture. In 1670, the first important split between architecture and construction took place. Colbert established the Académie Royale d'Architecture in Louis XIV's France, after commissioning Perrault to translate Vitruvius. The first School of Architecture was also created for political reasons, against the Guilds: divide and conquer through the split between theory and practice. The architect does not learn on the construction site anymore, he goes to school.

SECOND DISSOCIATION

After two hundred years the Beaux-Arts system is fully in place. Architects designed superb 'compositions' where the logic of two-dimensional paper aesthetics governs architecture. The logic of materials ceases to be the generator of construction and is replaced by the logic of rendering facades in watercolour. Viollet-le-Duc hid iron inside stone vaults, a process comparable to what architects are still occasionally heard to say today: 'I do not care how it is made as long as it looks the way I want' (ie painted plywood Ionic columns). American architects all go to the École des Beaux-Arts in Paris: Sullivan, Richardson, McKim, Mead and White.

Meanwhile, the US construction industry develops its own construction methods independently from the architects' input. This is the second dissociation, where architects have little control over the definition of building process. (In our litigious society, this is now translated in the USA by the fact that architects are not in

charge of 'construction supervision' anymore, but of 'contract administration services'.) Education flourishes. Schools of Architecture open everywhere. In the USA, it is first the MIT Architecture Department, immediately followed in 1881 by the School of Architecture at Columbia University, established by William Ware. Ware specifically insists on approaching architectural education from a *humanistic* rather than a technical point of view. Avery Hall opened in 1912, amid controversies between William Ware, the Director, and McKim, the campus architect.

Of course, the Beaux-Arts educational system with its emphasis on drawing and on Classical precedents is not the only pedagogical model. The Arts and Crafts tradition and the Engineering Schools each created their brand of architectural education. But in the USA the Beaux-Arts system was, by and large, the dominant model. Even the enormous influence of the craft and production-oriented Bauhaus was translated into Beaux-Arts' terms.

When Bauhaus' ideals and architectural modernism triumphed in America, with Johnson and Hitchcock's 1932 International Style exhibition, critics accused Philip Johnson of having stripped the Modern Movement from its social context. But it was probably the show's omission of the the Bauhaus' emphasis on construction methodology that will have the longer-lasting incidence on the making of buildings today. A school like Columbia evolved along similar historical lines. After the distinguished academic classicism of the pre-World War I era, with the leading New York professionals as its teachers, the curriculum was broadened dramatically in the early thirties with the advent of Modernism and the incorporation of studies in town planning.

THIRD DISSOCIATION

Almost exactly three hundred years after Colbert started the first school of architecture, all schools of architecture worldwide exploded. This is 1968. I shall not go back to the events that shook many schools a little over 25 years ago, but it is interesting to note that at Columbia they began with students' protests over the University building policies, with demonstrations against the 'bad Miami Beach decor' of one of its halls and above all the proposed construction of a large indoor gym in Morningside Park, at the edge of Harlem, at a time of tense social relationships between the two communities.

But it is on the educational aftermath of the 1968 events that I should like to concentrate. Of course, we then witness a new social conscience; architects establish advocacy planning and community workshops. But a new critical generation begins to develop. If on the wall of the Beaux-Arts' studios in Paris in the fifties, there used to be a sign saying 'Books are forbidden here', many architectural students now avidly read. From historical studies to the latest developments in post-structuralism, an intense questioning takes place. In the USA, the university context plays an enormous role. The architectural student is not isolated in a professional training school but is acutely aware of the forces around him and benefits tremendously from this academic context. Extraordinary work, often of an experimental nature, starts to emerge from the schools. To quote Rafael Moneo, my ex-colleague at Harvard, it is not the architectural schools that follow the trends set by the architectural schools. Multiple cross-overs between art, architecture, film and linguistic studies encourage complex architectural proposals, where 'theory' becomes a key word. The notion of 'theoretical practice', as represented by many of the younger practitioners today, has allowed an extraordinary development in the culture of architecture in the past ten years.

That leads me to that third dissociation. Theoretical practice does not build, it publishes. We increasingly witness within the ranks of architects themselves a split. This split is between the 'idea' architects, the media 'stars', the 'signature' architects, who do a well publicised sketch design, and the near-anonymous firms that do all the working drawings and pay liability insurance. Such a situation concerns me because we witness an historical evolution where the architect becomes more and more distanced from the forces that govern the production of buildings today.

First Dissociation:
Architects do not build, masons and carpenters do.
Second Dissociation:
Architects do not define construction methods, the industry does.
Third Dissociation:
'Design' architects do not prepare construction drawings. Job architects do.

Seen from 1670 onwards, this evolution would seem inevitable, accelerated in all its aspects by the extraordinary developments in computer technology that are currently completely transforming the theoretical *and* practical practice of architects *and* the construction industry.

The questions then are: What is our attitude towards this ever-increasing distanciation by architects from the actual fabrication of buildings and cities? How to turn such distanciation against itself? I should assert that the changing role of architects means that they might be less involved with the 'technology of construction', but they must be involved with the 'construction of technology' instead. They have to be instrumental in the construction of the new computerised technologies that are already transforming building and design processes. Moreover, the third dissociation does not mean that architects should simply retreat in a *laissez-faire* acceptance of today's conditions of design, but they should on the contrary design new conditions.

The design of new conditions for architecture of course means new attitudes towards the activities that take place in the architectural spaces they design: a new attitude towards programmes and the production of events, so as to reconfigure and to provide a rich texture of experiences that will redefine architecture and urban life. The challenge is enormously exciting. One, two, three: jump.

Bernard Tschumi is an architect in New York and Paris and the Dean of the Graduate School of Architecture at Columbia University. His most recent books: Architecture and Disjunction, Event Cities *(MIT Press) and* The Manhattan Transcripts *(Academy Editions) were just published on the occasion of his exhibition at the Museum of Modern Art in New York*

Pyramids of Mykerinus (Menkure; c2500 BC), Chephren (Khafra; c2530 BC) and Cheops (Khufu; c2570 BC), Giza. The supreme response to the vast landscape and the pharaonic will to immortality. The architectural eye of the Egyptians was keenly sensitive, and one would like to imagine that the visual interplay among the pyramids was consciously contrived, yet architects rarely existed as independent individuals

FRACTURES AND BREAKS

NEIL LEACH

I shall discuss fractures and breaks – fractures and breaks within an architectural tradition – and the need for new initiatives. I shall address the notion that education in architecture has been focused too much on the 'purely abstract intellectual architectural project'. I shall look first at the problem of craftsmanship, before moving on to look at how theory, and more specifically theory from *outside* architecture, might be able to offer a way forward for architecture.

That which I shall present will be divided into a retort and a report – a retort against certain developments which, to my mind, threaten to stifle architecture, and a brief report of an educational initiative from one school of architecture that seeks to open up the debate in theory.

RETORT

We owe our contemporary understanding of the role of the architect in large part to the early Renaissance and to Alberti in particular. It was Alberti's redefinition of the architect that inaugurated a *break* with the Medieval tradition. Alberti was keen to distinguish the architect from the craftsman. 'For it is no workman,' he wrote, 'that I would have you compare to the greatest exponents of other disciplines: the workman is but an *instrument* in the hands of the architect.'[1] Alberti then defines the architect as one who uses 'his own mind and energy'[2] to generate the forms that are realised by the workman in construction. Alberti's redefinition, then, of the architect as *homo cogitans,* as a thinking man, was in sharp contrast to the *homo faber,* the architect as craftsman, of the Middle Ages. It opened the doors for a more interactive use of theory in architecture. The art of building was to be informed by a conscious way of *thinking,* and a crucial reciprocity was established between theory and practice.

Recently, there have been moves in some quarters to return architecture to craftsmanship. While for some theory offers a way forward, for others architecture has been hijacked by theory. The latter calls for an architectural 'back to basics', a return to the 'simple' of building, a return to architecture as craftsmanship, a

return – in some senses – to the Middle Ages.

Such calls for architecture to be reduced to craftsmanship seem to conceal their own ideological imperative. They also fail to acknowledge the fundamental positivism of their position. Such claims appear to fall within what Lyotard has identified as 'the blossoming of techniques and technologies since the Second World War, which has shifted emphasis from the ends of action to its means.'[3] The question is now no longer 'why?', so much as 'how?'

For architecture to be reduced to craftsmanship would surely be a retrogressive step. Architecture must go beyond mere craftsmanship. Architecture must engage constructively with theory. This is not to say that architecture need not address the issue of craftsmanship, that it can *forget* its sense of materiality. Nor should it. It is through its very materiality that architecture achieves its authority. Architecture, as Derrida notes, 'forms [Western Culture's] most powerful metonymy; it gives it its most solid consistency, [namely] objective substance'.[4]

Alberti redefined the role of the architect during the early Renaissance. The Renaissance – as Hans Baron has described it – was a period of *crisis.*[5] In many ways our own time is characterised by a crisis. I do not refer here to the economic conditions, so much as to the *crisis of confidence* in the Modernist architectural project.

The responses to the faltering project of modernity have been many and various. Hal Foster has provided what is to my mind a very useful, if possibly simplistic, bracketing of these responses.[6] Broadly, these can be categorised in two ways: by a rejection of modernism and by a strain of resistance which continues to accept the trajectory of the modernist project, yet which attempts to operate a form of critical reappraisal from within, which, in his words, seeks to 'deconstruct' modernism.

The former, the *rejection* of modernism is best characterised stylistically by a return to a historicist language and the cynical incorporation of historical motifs on the facades of buildings. This commodification of architecture into a series of consumerist images fits broadly with what has been labelled by Charles Jencks as 'Post-Modernism', although this somewhat limiting appropriation of the term belies the more sophisticated understanding of Post-Modernism propagated by Lyotard, Habermas and others.[7] Post-Modernism in architecture is symptomatic, perhaps, of a general malaise, an incipient aestheticisation of the world, a move from a world of reality into a world of images. 'The so-called Post-Modern architects,' as Kenneth Frampton comments, 'are merely feeding the media-society with gratuitous, quietistic images, rather than offering, as they claim, a creative *rappel à l'ordre* after the supposed proven bankruptcy of the liberative modern project'.[8]

In the latter response identified by Hal Foster, the strain of resistance which largely continues the modernist project, yet exposes it to critical re-examination, seems to offer a more constructive response, a more positive way forward.

This seems to identify one way in which architecture can address the problem of modernity: by a critical self-examination. The crisis of modernity in contemporary architecture calls, in my opinion, for a radical *theoretical* reappraisal of the modernist architectural project. To misquote Adorno: 'Logically, the ageing of modern architecture should not drive architects back to obsolete forms, but should lead them to an insistent self-criticism.'[9] The question remains as to how this self-criticism might be performed best. To resort to architectural theory might not be enough, perhaps. The problem for architecture, to my mind, is a problem of tools. Not tools in the sense of the *craftsman's* tools, but tools in the sense of *theoretical* tools. Architecture, it seems to me, is deficient in the very tools that are required for this self-criticism; for too long it has been engaged in an hermetic discourse of self-legitimation. But where are these tools of self-criticism to be found? One place, I suggest, might be in the sophisticated theoretical discourses in other cultural disciplines. I see these other discourses not as a distraction but as a potential enabling mechanism for architecture.

Derrida's observation that architecture 'forms [Western Culture's] most powerful metonymy; it gives it its most solid consistency, objective substance' seems to acknowledge architecture's role as a cultural text. 'There is no outside-text', as Derrida remarked famously, meaning that all cultural artefacts are open to interpretation as texts. If architecture is to be perceived as a cultural text, then surely it can be understood to some extent – within the theorisation of culture in general, and surely theory in architecture can be related to theory in other cultural disciplines. At the same time, it is accepted that this interface is not that

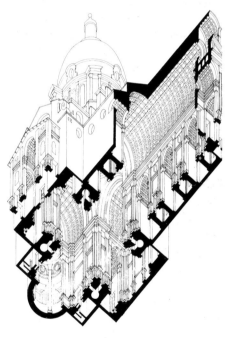

FROM ABOVE: S Maria Novella, facade, by Alberti, Florence, 1448-70. One of the most ingenious and far-reaching adaptations of an antique device (the supporting bracket of an entablature). Alberti concealed the sloping roofs of the side aisles with a scrolled gable, or volute, that was to become an omnipresent feature in architecture until the modern age; in 1471 Alberti remodelled S Andrea, Mantua, but died the next year before work had commenced. Although completed posthumously, it is considered to be Alberti's most complete work

simple. The mapping of other discourses onto an architectural discourse is not without problems. Nonetheless, something useful, I shall maintain, may often come from the space in between, from the dialectical opposition between architecture and other disciplines.

Curiously, the notion that there may be points in common between an architectural discourse and other cultural discourses was acknowledged even by Vitruvius.

> Indeed many if not all subjects have points in common with other disciplines, as far as theoretical discussion is concerned . . . Each individual art is made up of two components, the work itself and the theory (*ratio*) behind it. Of these one, the execution of the work, is the province of those trained in that particular field; while the other, the theory, is common to all learned people.[10]

Architecture makes use of debates external to architecture. In the design studio thinkers from Heidegger to Adorno to Deleuze, and even Popper, have been used to great effect. Within architectural theory it is difficult to conceive of a thorough understanding of Critical Regionalism, for example, that has not had recourse to the work of contemporary theorists of Cultural Difference, such as Edward Said and Gayatri Spivak.[11] In architectural history it is difficult to conceive of an unproblematic discussion that has not engaged with the work of contemporary theorists of history, such as Hayden White and Paul Ricoeur.[12] So too it is difficult to conceive of a rigorous, critical self-analysis within architecture without having recourse to the telling epistemological enquiries of Jacques Derrida and others, and without pitching architecture against the sophisticated critical discourses that operate in other disciplines. This, of course, may not be the only way of addressing the problems of contemporary architecture, but, in my opinion, architecture can only benefit from becoming engaged with other theoretical debates, and these other debates, I shall maintain, can provide architecture with the tools of self-criticism that it so urgently requires.

It has been suggested previously that education in architecture has focused too much on the purely abstract intellectual architectural project. I can only support this motion.

Architectural education, to my mind, has indeed focused too much on an abstract, intellectual, *architectural* project. Architectural education, I should argue, would benefit from broadening its horizons beyond its traditionally perceived limits. Hermetic debates within architecture need to be exposed to debates within other disciplines. Architectural education needs to be *infected* with other disciplines. Only in this way, I should argue, can an architectural discourse relate fully to debates in contemporary society, and only in this way can a rigorous self-criticism be undertaken.

I call for a *break* in tradition. Architectural education should not be limited to the purely *architectural* project.

REPORT

I now want to move on to a brief *report* of an educational initiative which attempts to address this break with tradition.

The idea of a certain universality of theory, that one discipline has points in common with the theory of another, and hence that the theoretical discourse in one discipline can inform the theoretical discourse in another, lies at the heart of an initiative set up at the University of Nottingham.

The School of Architecture at the University of Nottingham has recently forged a link with the School of Critical Theory. 'Critical Theory' refers to the theory of criticism and is an umbrella term covering contemporary theoretical debates in areas such as philosophy, gender studies, psychoanalysis, literature and other modes of cultural expression. The hybrid that has resulted from this link, a Masters Course in 'Architecture and Critical Theory', is an innovatory venture that aims to promote a heightened awareness of architectural theory and set it within a broader theoretical context. The aim is to focus on the origin and nature of debates in contemporary society and to make connections between developments in architecture and other disciplines. The intention is to expose architects to a range of debates to which, traditionally, architecture has not been exposed, and to introduce architects to a range of thinkers who are not normally considered within the traditional architectural education – thinkers such as Adorno, Benjamin, Habermas, Foucault, Baudrillard, Derrida, Freud, Lacan and so on.

The course cannot claim to be the first to introduce these debates into an architectural forum. Nor can it claim, I am sure, to be the first to have these subjects taught by experts from other disciplines – teaching on Barthes and Derrida, for example, is given not by architects but by lecturers from modern languages and philosophy. Our external examiner Christopher Norris is in fact a professor of philosophy from Cardiff, who is known in architectural circles for his work on Deconstruction.[13]

But the course can claim, I believe, to be innovatory in the direct links that it makes with other departments such as humanities departments, which, unlike planning, engineering and building science, do not traditionally have links with architecture. This strategy, this forging of links, is in line with the recommendations of the Burton Report that, 'schools [of architecture] should continue to explore and develop a range of links with other departments, including joint courses and inter-disciplinary studies'. These links take the form of shared lectures. Students from architecture are sharing lectures on Freud, Habermas and so on, with students from literature and other disciplines. Likewise, students from outside architecture are sharing lectures on contemporary architectural debates with students from within architecture. The mutual *polarisation,* the *cross-fertilisation of ideas,* that is likely to result from all this, I should argue, can only be of benefit for all concerned.

We have been pleasantly surprised, even amazed, by the ground-swell of interest in this enterprise. The success of the Nottingham experience demonstrates that there is a clear demand not only from those outside architecture to become engaged with an architectural debate, but also for those within architecture to trans-gress the limitations of a traditional architectural education.

All this merely backs up my earlier argument that architectural education has indeed been focused too much on an abstract, intellectual, *architectural* project. Architectural education, I should argue, would benefit from broadening its horizons beyond its traditionally perceived limits.

Architecture must *break* with tradition.

Notes

1 Leon Battista Alberti, *On the Art of Building in Ten Books,* Joseph Rykwert, Neil Leach and Robert Tavernor (trans), Cambridge, Mass, and London: MIT Press, 1987, p3.
2 *Ibid.*
3 Jean François Lyotard, *The Postmodern Condition: A Report on Knowledge,* Geoff Bennington and Brian Massumi (trans), Manchester: Manchester University Press, 1984, p37.
4 Jacques Derrida, 'Point de Folie – Maintenant l'Architecture', in *La Case Vide – La Villette,* London: Architectural Association Folio VIII, 1986, p9.
5 Hans Baron, *The Crisis of the Early Italian Renais-sance,* Princeton: Princeton University Press, 1966.
6 Hal Foster, preface to Hal Foster (ed), *Postmodern Culture,* London and Concord, Mass: Pluto Press, 1985, ppix-x.
7 On this see, for example, Lyotard, *op cit,* and Hal Foster, *op cit.*
8 Kenneth Frampton, 'Towards a Critical Regionalism: Six Points for an Architecture of Resistance' Hal Foster (ed), in *Postmodern Culture,* London and Concord, Mass: Pluto Press, 1985, p19.
9 Theodor Adorno, 'Reconciliation Under Duress', in *Aesthetics and Politics,* London and New York: Verso, 1980, p167; Adorno in fact refers to 'modern music' and 'composers', as opposed to 'modern architecture' and 'architects'.
10 Vitruvius, *De Architectura,* 1,1, translation by the author.
11 For the work of Said and Spivak, see, for example, Edward Said, *Orientalism,* London: Penguin, 1991; Gayatri Spivak, *In Other Worlds,* New York and London: Routledge, 1988.
12 For the work of White and Ricoeur, see, for example, Hayden White, *The Content of the Form,* Baltimore and London: The John Hopkins University Press, 1987; Paul Ricoeur, *Time and Narrative,* 3 vols, Chicago and London: University of Chicago Press, 1984-88.
13 Christopher Norris, *Deconstruction: Theory and Practice,* London and New York: Methuen, 1982; the interview by Norris of Derrida is published in *Deconstruction: Omnibus Volume,* Andreas Papdakis, Catherine Cooke, Andrew Benjamin (eds), London: Academy Editions, 1989, pp71-75.

Neil Leach trained at the University of Cambridge and taught both there and at the Architectural Association prior to taking up a lecturing post at the University of Nottingham, where he is course director of the MA in Architecture and Critical Theory. He is the co-translator with Joseph Rykwert and Robert Tavernor of LB Alberti's On the Art of Building in Ten Books, *and is currently working on a book about the interface between architecture and philosophy.*

TRANS-ATLANTIC DIFFERENCES

ROBERT MAXWELL

Eleven years of living and working in the United States have allowed one to see more clearly some of the differences, as well as many of the similarities, between the two countries, particularly in attitudes towards architects and architecture. There is a solid core of overlap, of common expectations, which is probably most clearly expressed in the Anglo-American empirical tradition in philosophy and science. The Ivy League universities are a repository of common traditions and allegiances, even to agreement on the proper look of a university: Ralph Cram, the principal architect of Princeton's campus, was sent to look at Oxford and Cambridge quadrangles before preparing his designs. Yet, in the day to day, the British resident's experience over there is of a different culture. Within the practice of architecture, adjustments have to be made even in the basic vocabulary. The young student arriving in the United States has to learn very quickly that a set-square is a triangle, an architrave a trim, a wash-basin a lavatory, a lavatory a water-closet, otherwise he will be off beam.

In the States, the career of 'Architect' is not generally looked down upon: if one's son or daughter elects to follow an architectural education, this is not a cause of panic. Education in the United States is still thought of as a passport to success in life, but not as simple training for a job. If we look across the system of architectural education, we find at present that out of a total of 100 schools of architecture, 60 provide a five-year professional first degree and over 40 provide a nonprofessional first degree. In the latter case, the student goes on to a second degree which contains the professional training. Although the five-year course is still predominant, it is found mainly in the large state universities and polytechnics, whereas the private sector, led by Harvard, is predominately devoted to the four-year liberal arts degree, with the professional training incorporated in a postgraduate Masters. The two-tier structure is seen as the more flexible and the more prestigious. But, even with the five-year course, there is still an expectation that many students will go on to add another degree, say, landscape, real estate development or whatever. The common expectation is that the students will progressively choose their career after beginning to study at a university, and not before.

For the more fortunate student, who wins a scholarship to a private university, the preference is for starting with a liberal arts degree (the undergraduate degree of Bachelor of Arts) and after gaining this the student has undoubtedly received a good general education and is in no way inhibited from going on to pursue graduate studies either in or out of a professional architectural course. In other words, architecture is not initially a technical subject of study but a cultural one, frequently linked to the study of art history. One useful byproduct of this arrangement is that not only are most architects well educated in the liberal sense before they take up a professional career, but a considerable number of educated people in society at large, who did not go on to become architects, know about architecture and are potentially enlightened clients. It is commonplace in the United States for students to transfer between courses and between universities and this is probably related to the greater mobility of families in general. It is also seen as normal to add degrees to one's resume. So, many trained architects go on to take up real estate or management. And in a liberal arts school such as Princeton, students can enter a three-year professional degree with a good first degree from any other university in *any* subject, just so long as they are good. The schism between arts and sciences simply does not exist over there.

In Britain, on the other hand, the educational system is not designed to postpone career decisions but to advance them. The high school student must decide on career directions before entering the last two years of study and must then select the examination track to be followed (that is, choose which subjects to take at 'A-level'). Once entered upon the five-year architecture course, it is very difficult to change subject, and the onus on the student is to prove competence, keep his grant and not show too much artistic or scholarly intent. Architecture schools in the UK are often linked to engineering, management or social science departments. Richard Llewelyn-Davies pioneered the two-tier degree structure in this country from 1962, with a theory based on the idea of freely choosing a personal curriculum, as was possible for students at Berkeley with its famous 'course-unit' system. Architects would thus be more diverse and less stereotyped. This structure has been generally adopted in Britain, yet the grip of the state bursaries is such that very little variation is possible in practice. Let us remember also that the only instance where government was prepared to allocate grant aid to a course of four years of study for the first degree, with progressive specialisation along the way – Social Science at Keele – has not been imitated, if only because it opened the door to longer and therefore more expensive undergraduate education. On the contrary, the government has been searching for evidence that would allow it to insist on shortening courses, particularly the five-year architectural professional degree.

My impression is that for all the distinction between first degree (with RIBA Part 1) and Diploma (with RIBA Part II), there is less flexibility than we might expect for the student to change schools between degrees. The five-year pattern still seems to predominate, since both parts are thoroughly professional, and it is hard to see them as following the principle of providing a general education first, followed by a professional training later. The sequence is so compelling that I call it the 'escalator effect': you do not have to do particularly well, just conform to the norm and you are carried up to the top floor. Moreover, conforming to the norm is easier if you adopt a high-tech hero, since what you are doing is clearly 'science' and so beyond criticism. The advantage of seeming to be on the science side is that you avoid being accused of self-expression or of looking to promote artistic intentions. Yet it is not clear that good architecture results from applying scientific principles to the management of design. The problem is not helped by the fact that building science has proved to have hardly anything of interest to say about the visible form of buildings. For example, energy conservation is assured above all by high standards of insulation concealed within the skin, not by a low-energy 'look'. But the British student who wants to justify a 'look' of some kind is forced to exaggerate technical aspects which can be presented as interesting, but not as self-expression.

But is the British architect not expected to be full of ideas too, to be able to make a contribution? Yes, but the scope of his art is seen to be far more limited by the duty to provide competent and well crafted buildings. In Britain, if the door knobs fall off, or the roof leaks, this is taken as a major flaw in the architecture. When, as a student at Liverpool University, I showed an

appreciation of the ideas of Le Corbusier, as did most of my generation, the faculty had an immediate response: do not waste your time, do you not know that all his buildings leak? It is true that Le Corbusier has a lot to answer for in terms of bad buildings and bad imitators, but his ideas became part of the myth of Modern architecture and thus an inseparable part of modernity itself. The high-tech school, so successful as establishment architecture in the UK today, is undoubtedly based on an extension of the functionalist approach that Le Corbusier promoted so energetically.

In the British response to an architecture of ideas, there is an immediate fear of the high cost of ideas, and even more a moral reprobation of an art that is practised for the benefit of a professional career but paid for by the client. This moralism looks with suspicion on any kind of building that is not understood as a practical answer to practical problems. As a result, British architects tend to identify very strongly with the ideal of a technically competent architecture, where everything special about the design can be justified as the result of practical considerations and never attributed to anything as inherently arbitrary as an artistic impulse. To avow artistic intentions, in architecture, is a sure way of arousing suspicion that the architect intends to make free with the client's money for his own purposes, whether megalomaniacal or merely personal. Artistic intentions, if they exist, have to be dissimulated or at least played down. Hypocrisy enters in.

Another way of protecting or concealing artistic intentions is to present them as the result of following an age-old technical tradition, one confirmed by centuries of use and enjoyment, and this is the argument put forward by the Classical Revivalists. Buildings should not be egregious statements of new technical possibilities, part of an increasingly dubious and violent future where civil virtues are in decline, but should be part of the stable structure of continuity that helps to bind society together and retain existing values. Common sense becomes the preponderant value. Buildings and streets make up a system of land use which is so complete and extensive that it cannot be exchanged suddenly for a new 'system', as was proposed by the modernists after the Second World War. The existing environment consists for the most part of buildings that are nondescript and part of the background, and architects should be prepared to design modestly and allow their buildings to merge into the background, unless there is a social reason for them to stand out. The built environment has evolved, like the natural environment, and should be protected and changed only after careful consideration. This point of view has already made inroads in the utopian vision of a rational society, as the popularity of 'environmental impact' studies confirms: it gets more and more difficult to build a new motorway. New buildings, then, where they represent important institutions, should be distinguished not by their material construction but by their attention to social propriety. They should 'work' for people, which means they should look familiar and reassuring.

In a strange way, therefore, British architecture tends to polarise into two opposing camps, both of which rely on a technical argument and reject any idea of a free artistic impulse. On the one hand, the high-tech school advocates technical innovation and the use of new materials and techniques that may involve risk but will be seen as progressive. Architecture should be something up-to-date, state-of-the-art, equal to the modern world of lasers and computers. This approach goes down well in Britain, and the high-tech school is replete with knights and beloved of the Establishment. On the other hand, Prince Charles has championed the cause of a traditional architecture that works because it follows well tried and tested methods and avoids unnecessary risk altogether. In both cases, it is a practical argument that is emphasised and personal expression that is played down.

In America, on the contrary, no architect can rise into the big time without promoting an image of personal success. But equally, no architect can gain his client's confidence without giving attention to the bottom line – the end cost that permits a cool assessment of value for money. American design is therefore dominated by a down-to-earth realism. Clients may occasionally want to put up an extraordinary building that will present their business as first in the world, but this building is more likely to do so by being higher than anything else around than by being technologically advanced. The reality of controlling expense is to build rapidly and reduce the element of labour costs. In practice, this means a steel frame, from which everything else is hung. What shows in an American building is not the system of construction but an image of the success of the client, and this image may be of any style thought appropriate. Polished granite and polished plate glass can be alternated to convey Gothic or Classical, homely or exotic, as required.

Michael Graves' Portland Building made a virtue of this by alternating punched and strip windows to outline the profile of a giant keystone, thus making an ironic statement about the very act of constructing 'architecture'. This flexibility is not confined to the Post-Modern school, but extends to all schools. Richard Meier's whiter-than-white buildings, derived from the twenties style of Le Corbusier, are constructed in exactly the same way, with an outer skin of enamelled steel panels hung from the constructional frame to assure a self-cleansing, permanently youthful appearance, appropriate to the concept of modernity as Le Corbusier defined it; and indeed better than Le Corbusier could achieve it, since he preferred exposed concrete as an expression of the building's reality, and concrete does not tend to stay white. Meier therefore uses Modern building science not to pioneer new methods of construction but to assure a more competent desired image.

In the United States, no design will be accepted unless it conveys an image, makes a statement. But it had better also come inside the budget and be built on time. To spend extra money on pioneering new construction, or in simply celebrating construction, would seem naive; Sir Norman Foster's Hong Kong and Shanghai Bank, where the visible form derives directly and extravagantly from the structure, seems to Americans to be a *very* expensive way of conveying an image of the success of the institution.

In conclusion, American architecture expects to serve the client by looking right, by presenting the right image. British architecture reaches behind the client into principles that will justify the result, not as arbitrary self-expression but as a simple necessity, the result of applying scientific principles. The architect wraps himself in moral certainty. The education in each country is geared to the expectations of society, and each country gets the architecture it deserves. In neither case, I should claim, are we free of illusion. In spite of the hype, much American architecture is extremely cost-efficient. Much British architecture conceals prejudice and ideological fervour and unadmitted artistic intentions. Its your guess which attitude is the most free of hypocrisy.

So far as architectural education is concerned, I should prefer to have less ideological fervour and more understanding of the value of good design. Good design cannot be equated simply with cost-effectiveness, still less with design management. But good design *should* indeed be cost-effective and well managed. It is not enough to *look* efficient, it should *be* efficient. What it should look like is another thing altogether. What it should look like is fresh, unusual, encouraging. It is too bad if it has been decided *in advance* that it should conform to a norm, whether that is to anticipate the technological future or simulate a lost paradise of belief. It should have something to do with the human spirit and its need for assuagement in a world that is increasingly riven by differences in belief. In this direction, I have been advocating a return to rationalism, not as an end, not as nostalgia, but as a way forward. This means redefining functionalism as an aspect of human culture, not as technology or tradition.

How a building 'works' in practice is the product of its material formation and its spatial organisation. Most architects will describe their work as the moulding of space. It is natural that this should embody everything to do with the feeling of the space, not only its shape, its functional potential, but also its appearance and its stimulus to the spirit. Our education should begin by recognising the highest aspirations of the architect, not business efficiency alone.

If architecture can attain the status of High Art, it will have to encompass something more than 'workability', the more so since the efficiency of a plan tends to change with time and with different users. Architects themselves are not certain how much they should address themselves to their immediate audience, or to some ideal audience, or to posterity. All artists have this problem. The success of a play is judged during its run. Some of the best plays, as literature, have had the shortest run. So there are intangible aspects about buildings which can be left as incidental or explored for their value to the human spirit. We need to recognise that architecture in the past has always been an integral part of society and of cultural values. It should be so again. In this respect the British have something to learn from the United States. Our education should recognise these aspirations not assume that architecture is merely technique. It should also be art.

That said, it has to be recognised too that many teachers have gone overboard in the pursuit of the spirit, to the extent that all the old common-sense ideas are thrown out. The aim is to measure up to the idea of the iconoclastic artist, the genius of the avant-garde, whose ideas are both shocking and inspirational. A great deal of what I see in design studios today, on both sides of the Atlantic, is trying to be conceptual art, using ideas that were high in conceptual art circles some 15 years ago. This may be good for the ego, it is not good for the human spirit. If time at school is spent on art training, the young architect has to begin all over again when he enters practice. We have to recognise that today ANYTHING can be art, but not everything that is art is architecture.

Architecture is an art, enclosing building science, design management and cost control and reaching out to an expression of the human spirit. To see it as anything less is to deprive society of its values. To be able to teach it requires first of all that we recognise what architecture is and what the mission of the architect should be.

Robert Maxwell is Emeritus Professor of Architecture at Princeton University. His latest book is Sweet Disorder and the Carefully Careless – Theory and Criticism in Architecture.

FROM ABOVE: The act of constructing 'architecture' as evident in Public Services Building by Michael Graves, Portland, Oregon; High Museum by Richard Meier, Atlanta, Georgia

PARADIGMS LOST: PARADIGMS REGAINED

THE PARADIGM PROJECT AT PORTSMOUTH

BARRY RUSSELL

Architectural teaching prides itself on its wide ranging approach, and architectural teachers see themselves as tolerant of almost any project method.

There is, however, one type of project that can fiercely divide loyalties and engender hot debate. It is a project which uses the systematic study of precedent as an explicit aid to design, and in a studio context. Its recent origin was, I believe, at Princeton in the sixties and with Philippe Boudon in Nancy in 1971 under the title 'Design in the Style of' or, more correctly, 'A La Manière', and from this it will be no surprise that, in principle, it uses an École des Beaux Arts method of formally studying precedent.

Although precedent studies were powerfully used by Alan Balfour, when he taught at Portsmouth (fresh from Princeton) in the late sixties, it was Ruslan Khalid, almost 20 years ago, who introduced the 'Design in the Style of' project. It was clearly redefined and sharpened by Tomas Llorens (the Spanish philosopher and critic), when he taught with us, into the Paradigm Project, and with this title it has since survived many transformations under different hands, namely Chris Abel, Nigel Mills, Dick Bunt, David Parham and for seven years myself. For a project to endure this long is, in my experience of schools of architecture, unique.

The use of precedent study, together with the assumption that design strategies can be directly researched and then applied, in a unified studio project, has been surprisingly controversial. It has also been a powerful context in which to pursue the debates and changes of recent years. For those steeped in ritualistic modernism, anything redolent of overt copying was and maybe still is, anathema. Although judicious stealing (I prefer to call it learning) from precedents, however recent, is a central part of the creative process, this must not apparently be made explicit.

The thorough knowledge necessary was, by some, said to destroy creativity in the student who must be encouraged to pursue innovation at all times. Innovation of course is one of the main planks of modernism, both formally and technologically, and thus the notion of a teachable body of knowledge became implicitly ignored. Does this explain the profession's largely dismissive attitude to research, knowledge and skills?

Other disciplines such as medicine and law, however, would find it bizarre that innovation was expected while the study of precedent was discouraged. How can the one occur without the other?

The project takes the view that the ideas of architects (or group) and their implementation in the architecture form a whole. Also, that the ideas, the formal design strategies and their technological realisation can be shown to have consistencies and patterns and that these can be studied, understood and applied. In this context, an informed acceptance or rejection of ideas can take place and real creativity begin.

These patterns, or nets of relationships, are paradigms, drawing on the notion put forward by Thomas Kuhn in his book 'The Structure of Scientific Revolutions', where shared examples provide models from which spring coherent traditions in science – the laws, theories, application and instrumentation of what he called 'Normal Science' and which change dramatically when *Paradigm Shift* occurs. Ironically, for us, Kuhn took his idea from the world of the arts where developments are clustered into style categories.

A central feature of the project is that it explicitly integrates history, theory, formal strategies and technology with the act of design in a studio project. The project works at its most potent when individual paradigms are intentionally structured to illustrate larger paradigms, a narrative of ideas or events: for example, early modernism, modernism and classicism – or clustered around theoretical positions such as archetype, organic, Deconstruction, or Globalism and Regionalism.

At Portsmouth the project consists of three parts:
Part 1: Study of a specific architect's philosophy, ideas, precusors and design strategies, by groups of two or three students. These are presented in a continuous seminar so that ideas and themes can be made evident.
Part 2: Study of a specific building by that architect, as a paradigmatic case – a representative instance

of a concept. Again, in groups, the students, with models and drawings, show formal characteristics and, importantly, how it was constructed and performed, since, as Focillon pointed out in 'The Life of Forms': 'technique is the poetry of action'.

Part 3: A design project in the spirit of the subject studied, where clear use has to be made of the ideas by each student. In using the ideas, strategies, the design devices, the student begins to understand them and their limitations and to interpret and transform them for their own purposes.

The explorative research nature of the project engenders high enthusiasm and intense debate among both staff and students at every stage.

From this sample idea we have, at Portsmouth, developed a subtle pedagogical tool. I shall draw your attention, without elaboration, to a few of the issues raised by the project:

(1) Who, or what categories shall be studied? It can embrace the whole of architectural history, specific aspects of it or sets of ideas, and this in itself is controversial.

Try naming your five most important architects and asking others if they agree! Try proposing a specific narrative framework and await the critical response!

(2) The limits of knowledge. In spite of the explosion in architectural publishing in recent years, the lack of thorough information on even well known buildings (with a few exceptions) is always a surprise to students. What does it say about our ability to teach the subject?

(3) Being specific. The project insists on a thorough, critical study of the ideas and work, if it is to be applied, something most students find difficulty in engaging.

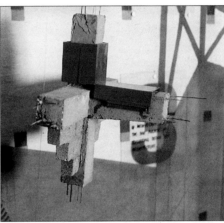

(4) It encourages an adventurous approach to research, with now no architect safe from their fax machine! Visits, phone calls and letters are of course fair game; but to receive a good fax response from the Venturi or Takamatsu offices (as we did) is enormously encouraging to students.

(5) The detailed building study insists that students look beyond the glossy photographs, minuscule plans and obligatory eulogies to piece together a deeper understanding of their chosen building. The power of photography is such that when students discover that early Richard Meier houses are of timber not concrete they exhibit astonishment or even disbelief. And they are surprised and encouraged when they find that a seminal work such as Rietveld's Schroeder House uses traditional construction techniques.

(6) It unites and extends architectural knowledge often seen in compartments; history with technology, analysis

FROM ABOVE: Display of project on Bernard Tschumi: Part (b), study of building, Folie N5 at Parc de la Villette, added to Part (a) study of and architect. By D Ainsworth, P Whelan and S Whight, 1989; Bernard Tschumi: Part (b) study of building, Folie N5 at Parc de la Villette. Construction detail model. By D Ainsworth, P Whelan and S Whight, 1989; Bernard Tschumi: Part (c) design 'In The Spirit of', Folie at La Villette. By Sandra Woodsford, 1990

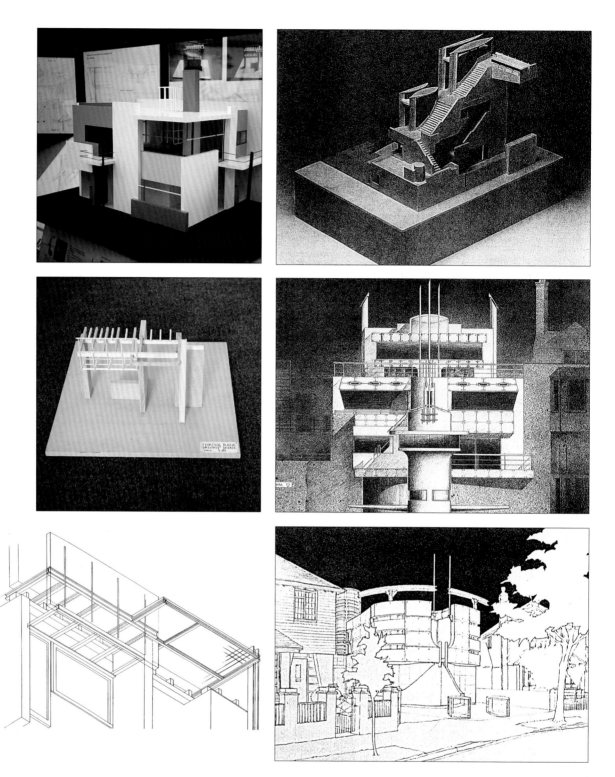

FROM ABOVE: Gerrit Rietveld: Part (b) study of building, Schroeder House, Utrecht. Model and Gerrit Rietveld: Part (b) study of building, Schroeder House, Utrecht. Model of balcony 'floating plane', southeast elevation. Showing the elaborate traditional construction used, from information provided by the Rietveld Museum. By H Adams, R Maguire and A Meredith, 1990; Schroeder House, worm's eye view showing the structure of the floating plane. By H Adams

FROM ABOVE: Shin Takamatsu: Part (b) study of building, Syntax Building. Model of part, from published material and drawings provided by Takamatsu office. By D Evans and D Galvin, 1990; Shin Takamatsu: Part (c) design 'In The Spirit of', Sailing Club in Old Portsmouth. By D Galvin, 1990; Shin Takamatsu: Part (c) design 'In The Spirit of', House in Portsmouth. By D Evans, 1990 with the act of design, even methods of drawing with ideas. Cultural context becomes vitally important.

(7) Preparing formal presentations to their peer group is both demanding and rewarding, with a whole day becoming an exciting – even theatrical – debate, as the narrative of ideas unfolds. It can also be memorable fun as was Le Corbusier's work presented as a trial, Meier's as a cooking recipe and Venturi's as a striptease – something to do with decorated sheds as I recall.

The paradigm approach has now been used throughout the school to teach theory, urban design, construction, landscape and, more recently, used in conjunction with computer analyses. Most significantly, it has been carried to other schools. It has provided a continuous context for the probing of architectural ideas, for students and staff to position themselves in the fragmentation that has followed twentieth-century modernism.

Of course, the paradigm notion itself can be seen in a Deconstruction context, as a carrier of conventions. However, it is one of the strengths of the project that it can also be used to question conventions, to respond to shifting imagery and new alignments. But all that is another story.

Barry Russell is an architect who has taught at Portsmouth School of Architecture, England, for some years, and in the USA and Malaysia. He is the author of Building Systems, Industrialisation and Architecture *and numerous papers.*

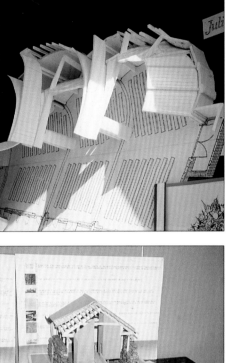

FROM ABOVE: Alvar Aalto: Part (b) study of building, church at Vuoksenniska, Imatra. Model, the complex construction of the curvilinear 'thick' wall which takes the moving partitions. By T Chapman and J Jones, 1990; Sverre Fehn: Part (b) study of building, Museum at Hamar. Model, relation of new and existing construction, 1991; John Outram: Part (b) study of building, Harp Group Headquarters, Swanley, Kent. Model, relation between the existing frame and new construction, 1987

A REGRESSIVE APPROACH

COLIN STANSFIELD SMITH

What has happened to Regionalism?
Regionalism has a bad name. Bosnia springs to mind and Quebec. And even burnt out cottages in Wales. That is politics. In architecture, Regionalism is at best an irrelevance, at worst a regression. In England it became fatally entangled with Prince Charles' Gothic Exhumation, a romantic nationalist yearning for a return to the craft culture of yore. Why then bother to talk about it again? Mainly because a surprising number of students are passionately interested in the subject. Why? Where is this interest coming from?[1]

So let's be regressive . . .

What does Regionalism mean to me?
Hampshire, a region, could claim that it has made a genuine attempt to create something regional rather than ideas of contextualism and typology mustered to combat the spread of universal space and the loss of identifiable space.

Giancarlo de Carlo in Urbino gives more than a few clues. He talks of 'reading' a place – he uses a sort of physiognomic archaeology. Knowledge of a place is more than its physical and factual characteristics. To know a place is to know about its intangible qualities – its myths, legends, its sense of occasion, even its politics, its wit, its humour, its art, but essentially its human chemistry. Giancarlo lived and worked in Urbino and that is a compelling story, particularly when one understands the willingness of how he invites participation while reconciling a rich crumbling urban heritage with the vitalising programme of a university – this transcends architecture and becomes holistic environment.

For me, Regionalism is living and working in and with a place, having to evolve and develop, sense its change, maintain and sometimes manage regional knowledge. It is not about 'home style' or hit and run architecture; it is about vernacular, provided it is imbued with scholarship. There is certainly no prescription of Contextualism; there is no limitation of talent, of patronising only local talent to induce an incestuous self-consuming mediocrity.

For me it is the touch of Grassi and Scarpa that integrates the contemporary inspiration with the preciousness of surviving antiquity. In Hampshire we have always imported talent and players to be the relevant catalysts – Cullinan, Hopkins, Aldington, MacCormac, each one of them adding to the cultural chemistry, but always extending their commission with an understanding of their architecture.

Perhaps what I am giving you is a job description for a County Architect – now an almost extinct species. Hampshire, a county at the edge of extinction. A county as a regional administration entity older than this country – rate saving, rural, Right wing.

So let's be regressive again . . .

When I first read Frampton's chapter titled, 'Critical Regionalism' which he added as a sequel to his book *Modern Architecture*, I almost felt in those first few paragraphs that he was addressing me personally as County Architect of Hampshire. In the sixties, Hampshire more than any other county had devoted itself to a procedures systems approach to solve its building problems. It had found a complacency in universal answers and standard repeats. As a practice in the late seventies and eighties we had already anticipated a regional culture and formed a vision for a design chemistry on an incremental project-by-project basis – a counter to the phenomenon of universalisation (Ricouer's subtle destruction of traditional cultures).

But Regionalism is about something else.

In Hampshire were the ingredients of a potentially delicious architectural and educational experiment.

Firstly there was a large, responsible public sector client covering an urban, suburban and rural environment with two cities, an ancient capital, two new towns and a beautiful coastline. A county rich in heritage and history, a county with an ancient landscape.

This client is concerned about the effective and efficient use of its buildings where, in Francis Duffy's terms, space planning and the management of space over time becomes of paramount importance for a prudent landlord. It would be in constant need of advice and ideas; it would need to be persuaded to experiment, to investigate, to analyse its own programme and develop opportunities, to ask innocent questions of ecological and conservation import about its own responsibilities; to promote civic pride exceptionally in Hampshire. For all this, it would need the intellectual resources of a university.

Secondly, the public practice associated with this region with a responsibility for a large estate of enormous diversity which represents a cross-section of the nation's general fabric ranging from historic buildings of the status of the Great Hall in Winchester to the great bulk of its buildings built since the Second World War. This estate could be a vehicle for research and environmental understanding that would need reorganisation and rationalisation. An estate that must be flexible, dynamic and ever-changing and that consumes nearly fifteen per cent of the County's total budget.

Such a practice would remain small enough for each project to be indulged and played on its merits, but always seeking a partnership with the best talents in private practice. It would be expected to recruit young energetic newly qualified students.

Thirdly, a school of architecture. A single school in a whole region – a school that sat confidently as 'the jewel in the crown' of the university which forms part of the inner fabric of a city and enjoys the potentials of a 'City within a City'.

So the notion of these three elements acting in partnership was a starting point. They would be interdependent and symbiotic where the department would form the practice unit and training ground for the school; it would share a design culture with the school which would offer research and experimental analysis and a recruiting base for the practice; and this region would enjoy the benefits of this developing environmental ambition. Resources would be shared on a knock for knock basis.

Ironically, there is a renewed interest in professional ethics and social responsibility in 1994 just at the time when the review of local government may well snuff out this newly kindled social vitality, with its recall of Giancarlo, (Aldo van Eyck), Herman Hertzberger and Scharoun in Berlin.

But, inevitably, there was a downside to this vision. As we all know there has been a loss of belief in the social mission after the 1960s. So it was inevitably difficult to persuade the school to identify with public practice and the stigma that it represented. Its impoverished physical environments were an embarrassing legacy and seen as an alienated public estate. In addition, creativity and design in the public sector had

been reduced to a series of stereotypes subject to guidelines, procedures, regulations, where prescription guaranteed mediocrity. So the purpose of Hampshire practice in the seventies and eighties was to reverse these attitudes, to achieve and earn architectural and design credibility.

This brings me to the schism between practice and academia. How uncomfortably the practitioner sits in academia – I speak now as an academic astride a schizophrenic divide of misunderstanding and alienation. It is not that long ago when the New York Five were in full flight and that Gwathmey and Meier were spoken of *sotto voce* as the lightweights because they had going practices and made money out of architecture. Design influences in schools have for a long time been from architects who do not build. As a practitioner one is made to feel an accessory to an unpalatable ethos, a regime that one should have conspired against or at least declared one's guilt. There is resentment or jealousy from both sides. And yet both need each other.

To design is to decide, 'the agony of deciding'. Designing buildings is like locking oneself into a determinist framework when one wants to go on endlessly with a play of options. As I metamorphose into an academic I can feel this discomfort of terminating the ever-continuing hypothesis 'what if' because some inconsiderate client wants his building now.

The fascination for me in the Eisenman shifting oscillating grids is the suggestion of a perpetual questioning, a gossamer and lacework of ideas, a veil, a yashmak, but also a deceit because one can pretend that the drawing is an end in itself, that the drawing is architecture.

Let me be regressive again . . .

My own personal tutor and mentor and subsequent hero during the fifties and sixties was Leslie Martin. His keynote paper at the Oxford conference was a watershed. It was a watershed for mainstream Modernism and for architectural education, status, but also for public sector practice. It had a relevance for all schools. He was promulgating the state of the art, such as it was, of architectural education that people understood. There was a common baseline for debate. There seemed to be general principles that were applicable to the whole of the profession. There was a collective universal view and that view was that architectural education had to be more science based. There was a need for more measurement and calculation, a need to apply technology and science with rigour. Technology had assumed a legitimising role in modernism; that science and technology were at the heart of enlight-

ened progressive architecture. There were also assumptions about a belief and a continuing tradition of
Functionalism.

A range of specialisms was introduced into the cur-
ricula covering every aspect and facet of engineering
from the social to the environmental – the legacy of that
is reflected in the growth of science based institutions
all having autonomies in their own discipline and a
responsibility for their educational programmes.

The consequence for the environment as well as/or
for architecture was the loss of an holistic culture. The
problem for education twenty years later was how to
reintegrate these specialised fragments. Effective multi-
disciplinary working was seen as exceptional rather
than the norm in spite of the fact that most public sector departments represented all these disciplines. With
the blinding wisdom of hindsight there was an amazing
realisation that architecture had to be taught by architects. But what sort of architects? Is there not another
innocent presumption here? The vocation and skill that
matters in academic life is teaching. Some academics
whether specialists or architects are 'pied pipers', are
enormously talented as teachers, and by the same
token some are *not*.

After thirty years, the response to Leslie Martin's proposals is less than benign. For me, however, the changes of mode and mood in the mid-1990s does not
release us from the obligations and responsibilities that
Leslie Martin pinpointed if we are not to become peripheral. We cannot enter the 21st century and think that
we can get away with the partial solutions of the 20th
century. No building of the Modern Movement has ever
really been celebrated for its functional performance. In
a subversive way we take an anecdotal pride in the
failure of our heroes' buildings. (Evidence of their wit in
retorts to disaffected and long suffering clients with
leaky or nonweatherproof buildings). Buildings designed and built after the Second World War have left a
liability that will exhaust the endeavours of generations
of building managers and surveyors. This liability
disinherits and preempts the birthright of successive
generations of architects. Possibly, the most interesting
fact about building in the 20th century is this massive
incidence of failure and the shift of resources from new
build to refurbishment.

(We talk of the 'Domesday sequence' – a 20th-
century phenomenon, pernicious structural failures like
concrete cancers – HAC, calcium chloride, box plywood beams, gang rail trusses, cavity wall failure, or
the dangers and costs of eliminating asbestos. Fire,
health and safety, access for the disabled, retrofit and
refurbishment have dominated our programmes for two
decades. This, of course, is exacerbated by the growth

of users, expectations and lack of tolerance of building
performance, utilitarian investment, impoverished
thinking.)

Unlike Leslie Martin's captive audience there is no
universal view in the nineties. We live now not in 'Modern' but in Post-Modern times, the age of pluristyle,
form as parody or pastiche, art as quotation; it is the
era of culture as world fair. Everywhere, politics and
culture and certainly architecture have become just
spectacle. Everything is everything and nothing at the
same time. We expect our academics and architects to
be our priests, prophets, philosophers, social and
moral historians.

Each school, whether of its own choosing or the
victim of circumstance, has become individual and
particular – a caricature of itself – where its philosophy
is developed sometimes as a result of external events
and the impairment of resources. Each school has a
different starting point. There is a pretence about a
core curriculum, about a contractual obligation.
Schools now play to their strengths and gloss over their
weaknesses.

Education is not now a shared experience although
we pretend it is. In the current mode of education it is
about competition, having an edge on your rivals –
exploiting one's talents because we are all competing
for the same market. The consumerist model is pur-
veyed with relish. We are told quality is customer orien-
tated and if you have an advantage or privilege you
exploit it, you do not share it. Both this university and
practice take quality management systems very seriously. Accreditation means survival.

The universities' and the schools' customers are its
students – more and more they will determine the
nature and scope of their own education.

This has been a century of intellectual terrorism.
There is always the presence of our own skeleton in the
cupboard. Most of our heroes, artists and intellectuals
have had strange flirtations with this mad ideological
world. Pound had played with Fascism, Heidegger with
Nazism, Brecht with Stalinism, Sartre with Marxism.

You will wonder what Hampshire's skeleton is? What
did more damage *The Diary of an Edwardian Country
Lady* or *Das Kapital* by Karl Marx?

Is it any wonder our students prefer to identify with
architecture of the Holocaust or nihilism. They chose
the apocalyptic subjects like Stonehenge. They prefer the
Buddhist retreat at Holy Island – 'a world on the edge'.

The idea of finding architecture in an ordinary building is still a chimera.

It is fashionable to preach the death of art, of art history, of history itself, of the author, literature, the novel,
but also the architect because such a death should

permit the rebirth of architecture. The mood is ritualistic.

Is it surprising? For in that outside world the abuses of the profession are grotesque. As with other professions, ethics and morality are discounted, ignored or spurned. To be project managed is to realise that the architects' contribution is no more important than any other member of the building team. To be invited to compete in a prestigious national competition is salutary and expensive, and if you do not win, demeaning (and sometimes if you do win, even worse).

The despair and depression is wholesale.

Every school's focus must be its degree and diploma courses. But its final professional qualification offers a very special relationship with practice.

Through such an enterprise this schism will be solved. The Continued Professional Development market represents a solution for both, provided of course the school has the will, resource and credibility. During a recession, practice has the time opportunity (if not the resource) for its own retraining, re-education. This is, surely, the platform for research. This is the invitation to achieve the presence of practice in the school.

Note

1 Quote taken from Susannah Hagan, *Architectural Review*, February 1994.

Sir Colin Stansfield Smith is an RIBA gold medallist, Hampshire County Architect and Professor of design at the University of Portsmouth.

FROM ABOVE: Cow plain, Queens' Middle School; Woodlea Primary School, Whitehill, Bordon

THE TEACHING METHOD

MORE QUESTIONS THAN ANSWERS
GIOVANNI SALVESTRINI

The 'Teaching Method' raises topical questions which refer to the present situation of Italian schools of architecture.

Until last year, an extremely low teacher:student ratio existed (for some first-year architectural design courses as low as even 1 to 250), the student's initial heterogeneity, owing to free access to the university and to the lack of any selective admission procedure, prevented any working method based on direct student experimentation and on continuous contact between student and teacher.

From this year, schools of architecture are gradually introducing, by law,[1] studio teaching into first-year courses (the suggested ratio is 1 teacher to 50-80 students maximum).

So we could put a question to the Italian Ministry of Universities: what is special about studio teaching?

The use of the traditional trial-error teaching method is not sufficient even for teaching architectural design in a studio with a few students in which the teacher gives too little importance to design theory – or if he/she views the studio 'as a poor replica of an architectural office'.

In order to teach architectural design, the ability to do a good project is not sufficient; one also needs to explain what architectural design is and how one designs. In order to learn design, carrying out a project is not enough.

In the studio, we often get the students to do a project, without considering the complexity of design, as a decision-making process requiring a gradual training in order to approach the numerous choices it implies. A training in which relevant steps, in the project, have to be emphasised; while attention must be drawn to methods and available techniques, which should also be considered in their historical context.

It is not important to do this in a studio, particularly when there are no more than 80 students and you are helped by a teacher of history and by a teacher of technology. As in my studio, in which this training does not envisage a guided development of a complete architectural project of a building; rather it is based on a language allowing the design process to be described according to its main critical steps and to gradually learn problem-solving by using particular methods/tools.

The peculiarity of architectural design as a process is constantly underlined. This process is made up of strictly intertwined, though self-contained phases. In order to achieve each of them, operational and critical tools have to be used and known; data can thus be checked and compared and a project decision taken.

Phases range from interpreting housing needs to identifying and quantifying available resources; from choosing a housing pattern to organising the size of built and open spaces and relating them to the scale of housing units and of micro-urban fabric, and eventually to evaluating the impact of a chosen solution on housing costs and the quality of dwellings.

To obtain more concrete results, all steps characterising designing and decision-making processes are simulated in exercises dealing with the theme of housing, which provides an opportunity of applying ideas and operational tools to each phase of the process.

Students therefore analyse a whole range of case-studies consisting of residential unit projects representing a range of housing patterns. Case-studies allow critical analysis and interpretation of design solutions adopted by architects (all experienced and of proven skills), in order to satisfy specific users' needs.

This process of interpretation also illustrates the role which (social) history of architecture, architects and architectural theories can play, and to learn to fully exploit all subjects studied in the curriculum.

Students, through exercises, are continuously encouraged to undertake two parallel steps: first, to reconstruct by formulating assumptions based on case-study observations, decisions architects took in each step of 'their own' design process; second, to measure the efficiency of their decisions compared with a 'standard quality' proposed by teachers via a reference model, consisting of housing requirements of a residential system.

Following these steps, students are asked to introduce changes and make them accordingly. In this first approach to architectural design, the complexity of design process is gradually grasped by simplifying themes and breaking down problems. The great importance attached to method facilitates the creation of a sound background of critical tools, which may in turn be fruitfully used in subsequent, more complex design experiences.

This approach is therefore different compared with those who consider architectural design as a single phenomenon and sole reference.

The final results of the studio are not spectacular. The efficiency of this method can only be evaluated by checking whether the students have acquired a few attitudes like:

– setting the correct approach to design programmes;
– choosing and using disciplinary and extradisciplinary tools that are most convenient to each step of design process;
– interpreting and comparing choices and design solutions taken by architects, in order to find the best project, satisfying some given needs; and
– integrating all disciplines parallel to architectural design and considering them not separate and instrumental, but part of a whole.

In order to obtain these results more 'design' is needed in design teaching and students must be allowed to do a sort of self-training. This paradox can work also at the beginning of architectural design training. More 'design' in design teaching means:

– to teach all students a common language (meaning by language the words and concepts that describe the steps of a design process), the design tools and methods;
– to convey one or more design culture(s) by conceiving the architectural design and its theories;
– to create learning conditions in which students can develop both their attitude to criticism, interpretation and choice at every design step and their individual originality and creativity; and
– to allow students to carry out self-training, which means showing them our own pedagogical rules.

Note

The new code of the Italian Faculties of Architecture explains:

> Teaching of the Diploma in Architecture is organised into a formative part devoted to the learning of theories, methods and disciplines, and a theoretical-practical part devoted to learning and training the 'know how' in the field of the professional activities.

For this second part in the Faculties are established the studios as teaching structures with purpose: the knowledge, the culture, the practice of design . . . In the studios will be assured a personalised relation between learners and teachers . . . Therefore, each studio will be of no more than 50 students.

The studios are (in the 5 year Diploma programme):
– architectural design   (4 studios);
– architectural construction   (2 studios);
– urban design   (1 studio);
– monuments restoration   (1 studio); and
– diploma   (1 studio).

Each studio will have 180 hours per year (120 for the main discipline and 60 for interdisciplinary activities).

At this moment in the first year course of the Turin Faculty of Architecture there are ten architectural design studios of 80 students each.

References

M Baffa, A Bazzi (eds) *Come si Insegna Progettare? Qestioni di didattica del progetto*, CLUP, Milan, 1988.
G Ponzo (ed) with M Ceppi, E Monzeglio, G Salvestrini, *Progetto casa e Dintorni, materiali e metodi per la progettazlone della residenza*. Quaderno 3-Ed. Levrotto & Bella, Turin 1992.
N Teymur, *Architectural Education*, Question Press, London 1992.

Giovanni Salvestrini is currently at the Dipartimento di Casa-Città, Politecnico di Torino, Italy.

ARCHITECTURE AND THE QUESTION OF TECHNOLOGY

DALIBOR VESELY

There is a strong feeling that the multitudinous traditional ways of making and creativity are slowly being absorbed into one dominant way of making and thinking. This process of homogenisation is not new, but it has reached unprecedented levels today. To see the difference, it is enough to recall the nature and the depth of discussions, in the early decades of the present century, about creativity in different domains of culture, about the relation between art and science or technology, about the nature and status of the applied arts, industrial design, and so on – in such movements, for example, as the *Werkbund*, *l'Esprit nouveau*, *l'Architecture vivante*, Futurism, Constructivism etc. While some awareness of the distinction between invention, creativity and pure production remains, it is no longer clear how this distinction should be established; that may be one of the reasons why the current debate is mostly confusing, unsatisfactory, and frustrating.

The topic of this debate, to which most other questions are usually reduced, is the merit of technical efficiency versus that of aesthetics. Even issues of cultural meaning or social and political relevance, or issues that directly affect the long-term well-being of our society, are often discussed in such simplistic terms. It is not too difficult to discover that this oversimplification has its roots in the dogmatically accepted belief in the universality of technical (instrumental) thinking. As a result, not only technical thinking itself but also a technical way of making have become the standards against which any kind of making is measured. This tendency is usually referred to as the technical or technological imperative. We hear often about the inevitability of technological development and progress, about the historical destiny – the 'mission' – of technology. Despite the growing number of sceptical voices and despite the amount of literature devoted to the question of the technological transformation of modern culture, our understanding of the nature of technology remains surprisingly limited. One of the main obstacles to a better understanding is our inability to discuss technological problems from a non-instru-

mental point of view. In the current scientific parlance, this is often considered to be non-scientific – a verdict that seals the issue and encloses it hermetically in a vicious circle of understanding/non-understanding. A typical example is found in the recent attempts to study the problems of the natural environment by extending the existing technological knowledge into wider fields without changing the primary criteria, conditions and goals of research. The illusory nature of such studies and their inevitable limits have been very clearly summarised in the following analogy:

> With its seemingly unlimited growth of material power, mankind finds itself in the situation of a skipper who has this boat built of such a heavy construction of iron and steel, that the boat's compass points constantly at herself and not north. With a boat of that kind, no destination can be reached, she will go around in a circle, exposed to the hazards of the winds and the waves.[1]

Instrumental thinking tends to impose its hegemony by creating a world that it can fully control. Control of that nature requires not only a special kind of knowledge but also a particular kind of will. And the knowledge that meets the conditions of the will to control is 'knowledge as power'.[2] Because this kind of knowledge must be subordinated to the will, we can speak here simply of a 'will to power', which as a consequence becomes a 'will to will'. It is well known that knowledge as power represents the essence of modern science – its metaphysical foundation – but it is also the essence of modern technology.[3] This leads to a deeper insight into the hegemony of technical reason and into the nature of the vicious circle of our 'understanding' of technology. The difficulty in breaking that hegemony – and in understanding that technology as the fulfilment of the will to power is not unconditional – is well summarised by Heidegger:

> Because the will to will absolutely denies every goal and only admits goals as means to outwit itself wilfully and to make room for its game, the will to will may not appear as the anarchy of catastrophes that

it really is. However, if it wants to assert itself in beings, it must legitimate itself. The will to will invents here the talk about 'mission'. Mission is not sought with regard to anything original and its preservation, but rather as the goal assigned from the standpoint of fate, thus justifying the will to will.[4] The need of the will to justify its role and its fulfilment reveals that the will itself is not absolute, that it is always situated and cannot completely disguise its own 'situatedness'.[5] References to mission and fate are a clear manifestation of a deeper intentionality and deeper historical circumstances, in which the will appears as a historical possibility, but always in contrast with other possibilities. If the will represents a movement towards the appropriation of power, culminating in modern technology, the other possibilities represent a movement towards participation that has most consistently been preserved in the domain of the arts. The existence of other possibilities – and their replacement by simple will – must be taken as a point of departure for any understanding of the apparent fatality of technological progress and of the belief that this kind of progress is our historical destiny. It is true, as we have seen, that such a belief belongs to the essence of modern technology; but it is also true that, in itself, this kind of belief is nothing technological: Because the essence of technology is nothing technological, essential reflection upon technology and decisive coming to terms with it must happen in a realm that is, on the one hand, akin to the essence of technology, and on the other, fundamentally different from it. Such a realm is art.[6]

That art is akin to, but at the same time fundamentally different from, technology as a result of historical development, in which the two domains originally shared a common ground but became differentiated later into the arts and technology as we know them today. Art originates in *techne*, which in its Greek sense is a knowledge related to making and is always known in its final sense as *techne/poietike*. *Techne*, as a relatively new kind of knowledge, superseded spontaneous knowledge and intuitive skills, which demanded a close contact with objects and tasks but could lead to the discovery of what is common and permanent in all of them. This emancipated knowledge teaches us a general lesson about things and can be used *a priori*, without direct reference to the things themselves. As a project of possible knowledge, *techne* receives most of its knowledge from accumulated experience but elevates it to *a priori* knowledge that can be taught.

What exists *a priori* and can be taught was for the Greeks a *mathema* – hence mathematics as a special form of such knowledge. *Mathema/*mathematics is the true origin of the transformation of *techne* into technique and finally into modern technology. In the Greek experience, however, *techne* was still far from becoming such a project. It was a drama situated between the new possibilities of knowledge and the intimate understanding of the inner possibilities of nature (*physis*). *Techne* was not yet seen as a human possession but as a power of nature, which humans could possess only to a limited extent. This may explain why:

> the first man who invented art [*techne*] beyond common sense was looked upon by his fellow man as a wonder, not only because there was something useful in this discovery, but also because he was thought wise and superior to others.[7]

The fact that *techne* is only a transition to technique is reflected in its relation to making (*poiesis*). Broadly speaking, making means to bring into being something that did not previously exist. *Poiesis* takes place not only in human effort but also in nature: 'All things that come into being are generated, some by nature (*physis*), others by art (*techne*).'[8] Art originally received its legitimacy and meaning from the universal divine order, which was seen as the product of an ultimate craftsmanship. 'When a thing is produced by nature, the earlier stages in every case lead up to the final development in the same way as in the operation of art, and vice-versa.'[9] In this rather dense formulation are already present all the future definitions of art as reality that complements nature, as a completion and fulfilment of nature's inner possibilities, or as imitation of nature. The imitation of nature, in particular, is a creative process that contains a large residuum of mystery. The Greeks were very much aware of it and referred to it as chance (*tyche*). Aristotle made this very clear in a well known passage: 'Art dwells with the same objects as chance . . . chance is beloved of art and art of chance.'[10] And he wrote elsewhere: 'Some hold that chance is the genuine cause of things, but one that has something divine and mysterious about it that makes it inscrutable to the human intelligence.'[11]

It should be emphasised here that making is based on productive knowledge but that such knowledge is never complete. It always depends on a prior understanding that has its origin in the spontaneity of making. The inscrutable element in making to which chance refers has its main source in *mimesis*. Because *tyche* is inscrutable to our intelligence, *mimesis* is equally so. In principle, it is possible to say that *mimesis* is a creative imitation where something that exists potentially is recognised and re-enacted as something actual. For example, movement can be recognised and re-enacted as a significant gesture; sound, as song or music; visible reality, as image or picture; and ideas, as an articulated and structured experience. In its most original sense, *mimesis* is a re-enactment of elementary order:

> Testifying to order, *mimesis* seems as valid now as it was in the past, insofar as every work of art, even in our own increasingly standardised world of mass production, still testifies to that deep ordering energy that makes our life what it is. The work of art provides a perfect example of that universal characteristic of human existence – the never-ending process of building a world. [12]

The role of *mimesis* in the process of making reveals the mystery of order as a tension between the potential and actual existence of order, which in its ultimate form always points towards the ultimate order – the cosmos. It is in that sense that the re-enactment of cosmic order can be seen as the most primordial form of making. [13]

The mimetic mode of making, which precedes the formation of *techne*, takes place most often in the domain of ritual. This is apparent not only in such rituals as dance or music but also in the rhythm and movement of the process of making itself, thus showing that the making of order and the making of things belong together. In both cases, the result of the mimetic action becomes a vehicle for participation in the overall order of things. The participatory meaning of *mimesis* and ritual – the need to come to terms with the universal order of reality – is challenged and, to a great extent, upset by the tendency to replace participation by the appropriation and manipulation of the order-creating powers. This tendency has its origin in the efficacy of traditional ritual, often wrongly identified as magic. It is obviously a great mistake to see magic where we are dealing only with the efficacy or instrumental aspect of traditional rituals. [14] It is well known that certain gestures or objects used in rituals may have the power to produce certain desirable results, but this does not mean that they can be described as magic or as primitive techniques. The power to influence the order of things in a culture that does not yet see a difference between the natural and the supernatural always depends on the reference to reality as a whole, which cannot become a domain of manipulation:

> There is an important difference between two kinds of actions, actions done by man and actions done by man in the belief that their efficacy is not human in any reducible sense, but proceeds from elsewhere. Only the second kind of action can be called any sort of a religious rite. [15]

The difference between the efficacy of ritual and magic is manifested in the nature of magic itself. Magic differs from all other forms of religion in that the desire to dominate the world belongs to its essential nature.

The emancipatory, appropriative tendency of magic, in contrast to the participatory nature of ritual, could become an important phenomenon only under certain historical conditions because

> the domination by will has one essential condition: before the world can be thus controlled it must be transferred inwards and man must take it into himself. He can actually dominate it only when it has in this way become an inner realm. For this reason all magic is autism, or living within oneself.' [16]

Historically, this became possible for the first time and in any real sense during the Hellenistic period, when the disintegration of the cultural and political institutions of the *polis* led to the disintegration of traditional corporate rituals and left man to his own resources and in relative isolation. 'Magic is commonly the last resort of the personally desperate, of those whom man and God have alike failed.' [17] The emancipation of magic was closely linked to the growing interest in other esoteric disciplines (such as astrology, alchemy, or theurgy), as well as to the new interest in mechanics and technicity in general.

In the introduction to his book on mechanics, Pappus of Alexandria recognised the link between mechanics and magic quite explicitly:

> The ancients also describe as mechanicians (*mechanikos*) the wonder-workers, that is the magicians (*thaurnasiourgos*) of whom some work with air as Heron in his *Pneumatica*. [18]

It was under such circumstances that *techne* came to exist as technique in its most elementary form. This is confirmed by, among others, JP Vernant, who, at the end of a long study on the possibilities and limits of technical thinking in ancient Greece, came to the same conclusion:

> Only in the work of the Alexandrian engineers, especially Heron, is there any evidence of interest in the instruments and machines as such, and only here was their construction undertaken with an attitude that we can describe as truly technical. [19]

What makes this attitude truly technical is not only a new type of knowledge, but rather a new interest and will. In a typical Hellenistic definition of a machine, we can see that 'machine is a continuous material system . . . moved by appropriate revolutions of circles which by the Greeks is called *kiklikekinesis*.' [20] However, that circular movement is not a purely mechanical phenomenon; the text points to its origin in the regularity of the celestial movement, which is also imitated in ritual and dance but is represented here in a more tangible form by the body of the machine.

The incomprehensibility of the movement of nature, manifest most explicitly in the movement of the celestial bodies, has been identified by modern anthropology as the deepest motif of technicity and described as a 'fascination with automatism'.[21] The nature of this fascination is a continuous attempt to grasp what is most incomprehensible through something that we understand and can construct and manipulate. One can also describe these attempts as a 'technisation' of the original mimetic reenactment and participation. The machine is a tangible model of such a process and, as a consequence, is also a model of the inscrutable cosmic order. A model is comprehensible because we have made it. It is surprising to see how close the Hellenistic authors themselves came to such an understanding:

> All machinery is generated by nature and the revolution of the universe guides and controls it. For first indeed, unless we could observe and contemplate the continuous motion of the sun, moon and the five planets; unless these revolved by the device of nature, we should not have known their light in due season nor the ripening of the harvest. Since then our fathers have observed this to be so, they took precedence from nature, imitating them and led on by what is divine, they developed the necessities of life by their inventions.[22]

It is at this historical stage that technique becomes, at least potentially, a methodical operation that can be carried out in such a way that it can accomplish a particular predictable end. Unlike *techne*, which is always rooted in the concrete life of the *polis*, magic and technique are, to a great extent, emancipated from the political and cultural context. In the ethical sense, they represent individual or group egocentrism, based on the acquisition of power and on domination. The emancipation of magic and technique from the ethically oriented life of the *polis* creates a situation of new freedom in which there is no room for good or evil and for the sense of guilt or sin. It is in such a situation that the question of truth is replaced by the question of practical achievement. Because this is true for both magic and technique, it is very difficult to draw a clear line between them. On the other hand, it is possible to say that magic recedes into the background, leaving a certain residuum of its original power in the more rationalised forms of technique. It is for this reason that it would be more appropriate to speak of an element of magic than about magic itself in the development of modern technique. And it would also be more appropriate to speak about a technical tendency in the domain of the existing arts (*artes technai*) than about technique when we refer to the act of making or production. This would certainly simplify the confusing and very often misleading discussions about the role of magic in the

formation of modern technology.[23] We have to keep in mind that the traditional understanding of art includes every kind of making – from the making of shoes or tools to arithmetics and geometry in the *quadrivium*. The difference between the arts was their involvement with matter and manual labour and with their theoretical status, which was most often expressed only through adjectives – the mechanical arts (*artes mechanicae*), usually situated at the bottom of the hierarchy because of the labour involved; the liberal arts (*artes liberales*), which include the *trivium* and the *quadrivium*; and, finally, the theoretical arts, sometimes known as *scientiae*, consisting of theology, mathematics and physics.[24] That the arts represented not only experience and skills but also an important mode of knowledge, is reflected in the ambiguity of their relation to science.[25]

The sciences that contributed to the formation of modern technique and eventually to technology were mainly astronomy, optics and mechanics, known as *scientiae mediae* (the 'middle sciences'). The reason for that designation was not their 'mixed' nature, as is sometimes thought, but their position halfway between metaphysics and physics.[26] The *scientiae mediae* should be seen as a branch of mathematics – physical mathematics – that prepares the way for the development of mathematical physics but is, in principle, radically different from it. It is important to bear this in mind, particularly in view of many current interpretations of Renaissance perspective and mechanics. These interpretations do not always seem to recognise the fundamental ontological difference between the indirect and direct 'mathematisation' of reality. In the domain of Renaissance art, mathematics plays a role of approximation, mediation and symbolisation. It still represents, on the one hand, the essential (ie intelligible) structure of reality (being) and, on the other hand, the visible manifestation of such structures. It is the mediating and symbolic role of mathematics – and not only its precision – that gives it such a prestigious place in early modern thinking. The process of the indirect mathematisation of reality – the main characteristic and contribution of the middle sciences – can be seen particularly clearly in the role played by medieval optics in the development of perspective as well as in the mechanical inventions of the sixteenth century. The attempts to bring the physical reality of vision and movement into the sphere of mathematical reasoning were, for a very long time, faced with a paradox of apparent success and real failure. Each successful step in mathematisation revealed a new area of reality that would resist completion of the process. This was expressed very often in the frustrations of sixteenth-century artisan-'engineers', who became only too aware of the gap that separates speculative mathematics from the concrete reality of the artisan. The concepts with which the mathematician works 'are not subject to those impediments, which by nature are always conjoined to the matter which is worked on by the artisan'.[27] It is for these reasons that Renaissance perspective and mechanics cannot be seen as true sciences in the modern sense. The middle sciences, like the arts, can be called sciences only by analogy. True sciences are concerned with universal reality and require absolute proof. Perspective and mechanics, on the other hand, are concerned with particular situations, with human works and operations and with contingent things. If we take into account how perspective and mechanics were really practised, and not just how they are presented in textbooks or in projects, we may see them as arts, deeply influenced and informed by science. But unlike the sciences or the emancipated techniques, the arts deal with direct experience and with the probable. They belong to the primary mode of embodiment – to the visible world, which is the ultimate criterion of their meaning, relevance and success. Indirect or partial mathematisation could not change these conditions.[28] This also shows the clear limits of the mathematisation and technicisation of the traditional arts. As long as the arts were situated in the life of nature and society, they could not become a subject of mathematical understanding and control, and to that extent their technicisation remained inevitably partial and limited. Only a total mathematisation of reality could remove these limits.

It was in the second half of the sixteenth century that such a project became, for the first time, a real possibility. The initial inspiration came from the middle sciences, where the old and jealously guarded boundaries between mathematics and physics were crossed.[29] However, the most decisive changes took place in the domain of mathematics itself, particularly in the sphere of algebra, which had developed into a 'universal mathematics'. This was complemented by similar changes in the domain of metaphysics, where the prima philosophia became a 'universal science'. Universal mathematics became the mathematical equivalent of traditional logic. Because universal mathematics operates with the pure essences of things, which are taken for simple magnitudes, the formal essence becomes identical with pure mathematical essence/magnitude.

It is under these conditions that universal mathematics can claim to cover the same area of knowledge as traditional logic – in other words, the area of all possible knowledge.[30] The new idea of all possible knowledge is very different from traditional dialectical or demonstrative knowledge. It aims to explain things only in terms of order and measure, regardless of their

material and qualitative determination. It was because of the universality of such a claim that universal mathematics earned the title, as long ago as the sixteenth century, of 'queen of sciences' (regina scientiarum), sometimes elevated to scientia divina or ars divina.[31] These lofty definitions would obviously not be convincing without some supporting evidence that must come from the understanding of the physical world. In a similar way as in mathematics, the development of knowledge in sixteenth-century physics went through a radical change. The traditional distinction between divine and human knowledge was weakened to such an extent that it became possible to speak about physics and metaphysics in the same language and in terms of the same principles.[32] The affinity between the metaphysical interpretation of physics and universal mathematics was reflected in the new understanding and use of scientiae mediae and, in particular, of mechanics. It is very important to realise that, contrary to a widely held opinion, the usefulness of mechanics was secondary to its primary meaning – the understanding and representation of movement in the created world.

The continuity of movement between the celestial and terrestrial domains played a critical role, first in Aristotelianism and later in scholastic metaphysics; as we know, it was the latter which played a decisive role in the formation of modern mechanics.[33] It is only with great effort that we can understand today the complexity and importance of movement (motion) in the seventeenth-century vision of reality. The enigma of creation, the manifestation of the divine order in the terrestrial world, and the continuity of this order were all related to the phenomenon of movement. Movement was seen not as a universal principle of reality but also as the efficient cause of everything that persists in life. The divine origin of movement was not yet in doubt, nor was the tradition in which divine reality manifested itself as an eternal truth that could eventually be grasped as mathematical truth. Descartes made this clear when he wrote:

> Mathematical truths which you call eternal were established by God and depend on him entirely like all other created beings. Do not hesitate to assert and proclaim it everywhere that it is God who set up these laws in nature as the king sets up laws in his kingdom.[34]

Attempts at understanding these laws were strongly influenced, if not determined, by the new idea of knowledge – knowing by doing or by construction. In other words, universal reality can be known by the art whereby it was made. In Descartes' own words, 'God's will, understanding and creation are one and the same thing; none is prior to another, even conceptually.'[35] The identity of understanding and creation was the last condition needed to open the door for mechanics to become the critical discipline in the formation of science and technology.

It is important to see that it was not utilitarian and purely technical interests but a metaphysical quest that gave mechanics such a privileged position. It was in the domain of mechanics that the mathematisation of physical movement could be investigated or explored and finally accomplished. The tendency to treat physical reality and movement as inevitable and potentially mathematical was most certainly motivated by the growing desire to discover more tangible links between human and divine reality – which, in Galileo's time, meant more tangible links between physical and mathematical reality. In Galileo's *Dialogues*, we find the following statement:

I still say with Aristotle that in physical matters one need not always require a mathematical demonstration. Granted, where none is to be had, but when there is one at hand, why do you not wish to use it?[36]

What can possibly motivate such a wish? Galileo himself answers this question:

As to heaven, it is in vain that you fear for that which you yourself hold to be inalterable and invariant. As for the earth, we seek rather to ennoble and perfect it when we strive to make it like the celestial bodies, and, as it were, place it in heaven, from which you philosophers have banished it. Philosophy itself cannot but benefit from our disputes, for if our conceptions prove true, new achievements will be made.[37]

It is well known that the key to Galileo's achievements is the mathematical demonstration performed in a domain that had traditionally been considered to be only contingent. This demonstration, which was radically new, can best be described as a dialogue between an *a priori* mathematical formula and idealised physical reality. In this dialogue, the mathematical formula, used as a hypothesis (as an argument *ex suppositione*), is followed by an approximation and anticipation of the physical results.[38] On the physical side of the experimental dialogue, phenomena are simplified through abstraction to the point that the approximate mathematical form is free of all difficult material impediments and circumstances. When Galileo speaks about the conditions of the free fall, he comes to the following conclusion:

A more considerable disturbance arises from the impediment of the medium by reason of its multiple varieties, this is impossible [to subject] to firm rules, understood and made into science. No firm science can be given of such events [as] heaviness, speed and shape which are variable in infinitely many ways.

Hence, to deal with such matters scientifically, it is necessary to abstract from them.[39]

Galileo's experimental method and its potential rigour include a zone of deep ambiguity that can only be eliminated when physical impediments can be successfully abstracted. But this is not always possible – certainly not in the same degree. To that extent, Galileo's mechanics remains a promise and, even in its best moments, a rigorous hypothetical discipline rather than a rigorous science. It contains an enigmatic element that will never be completely eliminated. The enigma has much to do with the process of mathematisation and, in particular, with the nature of the experimental dialogue. Paradoxically, the main source of the enigma is the nature of experimental reasoning, which substitutes an implicit demonstration for an explicit one. In the implicit demonstration, it is not necessary to take into account or to know all the circumstances, conditions, and causes of a particular phenomenon or event (irregular movement, for instance). What is not necessary to know remains enigmatic because, when it comes to understanding, this negligence also remains unknown – and therefore enigmatic.

It is for these reasons that it would be more appropriate to see the experimental dialogue as the result of intellectual craftsmanship rather than a rigorous philosophy of science. As a consequence, the *topos* of the workshop or laboratory is a more appropriate vehicle for understanding the nature (essence) of modern technology than the *topos* of study. The laboratory is a place where nature is systematically transformed into mathematically idealised models. In a world that has been transformed into a laboratory model, construction and making become the privileged form of knowing.

As ideal places for the conduct of experimental dialogue, the workshop and the laboratory represent a new, secondary mode of reality where new rules of knowledge can be developed and cultivated. Unlike traditional knowledge, which was cultivated in a dialogue with the primary conditions of reality, the new rules are articulated in the relatively closed world of the experimental dialogue. The imaginary nature of this new world is well described in Descartes' own words:

For a short time, therefore, allow your thought to leave this world in order to come to see a wholly new one, which I shall cause to be born in the presence of your thought in imaginary spaces.[40]

As for the nature of knowledge or science that can be developed in the new 'imaginary spaces', Descartes again tells us what is possible and what is also seriously anticipated:

By science I understand skill at resolving all questions and in inventing by one's own industry everything in that science that can be invented by human ingenuity (*ars inveniendi*). Whoever has this science does not desire much else foreign to it, and indeed is quite properly called *autarches* – self sufficient.[41] The science invented by human ingenuity is a construct. It is a productive science, motivated by an ambition to be nothing less than *creatio ex nihilo*, traditionally linked only with divine creativity. However, what is traditionally true for the divine is now considered to be also true, or at least possible, for man. In other words, we know, and can create, at least in principle, exactly as God knows or can create.

This new, unusual confidence has its origin in the drastically simplified representation of reality, which became possible because of the deep metaphysical faith in the mathematical nature of reality sanctioned by divine presence. The result, most likely unintentional, was a method for the construction of productive knowledge, based on the unlimited possibilities of experimental dialogue. '"Idea" was the term I used because it was the familiar philosophical term for the forms of which the divine mind is aware (*formas perceptionem mentis divinae*).'[42] In terms of our own interpretation, however, the idea also represents a new type of knowledge – a primary force of production and the origin of modern technology. The unlimited possibilities of invention opened through experimental dialogue have their source in the infinity of will, which for Descartes is a single analogy of the human and the divine. The full meaning of the infinity of will is 'most visibly displayed in the programmatically anticipated infinity of artifices through which the new sciences are to prove their credentials.'[43] In the openness to future possibilities lay the foundations of the ideal of progress and, on a deeper level, the intra-mundane eschatology of modern technology.[44] The convergence of the infinity of will and the infinity of artifices completes the ambition to understand given reality as *a priori* and whole, and from a clearly defined position.

> Applying knowledge through construction to the whole world was as inevitable as it was dangerous. It was dangerous because it makes mankind be like God, knowing good and evil. Many seventeenth-century philosophers shunned its inevitable consequences, but only a few had the courage to deny categorically that this kind of knowledge reveals reality.[45]

In a sense, that is still true today. We do not yet fully understand the real nature of the experimental knowledge on which modern technology is based because it is difficult to follow the transformation of reality and the nature of the representation in a picture (model) from

which all but efficient causes have been eliminated and where the qualitative diversity of phenomena has been reduced to a mathematical interpretation of matter in motion. There is quite clearly a gap between the domain of situated knowledge and productive knowledge. This gap, which represents a radical discontinuity with the natural world, reduces the gnostic value of productive knowledge and makes it merely a technical tool. The fact that a technical tool can represent the most sophisticated achievements at the same time is demonstrated, for example, by nuclear research and its results or by the aspirations of current genetics or electronics. From the very beginning, however, the overwhelming success of productive knowledge was limited to phenomenons susceptible to mathematical treatment. This has also determined the selective and uneven development of modern technology. Architecture itself can serve as a very good example here.

The area where technology had the greatest influence was in the calculation of structures; this, as a consequence, led to a more inventive use of certain materials and new types of construction. But as we know, extending the role of instrumental thinking in architecture was a very slow procedure. It is perhaps not surprising that it was only in certain, rather limited areas that technicisation had some success. Factories, railway stations, exhibition halls, and generally structures that could be treated as an engineering problem can be seen as good examples. On the other hand, there were whole areas that proved extremely difficult to mechanise. These were mostly areas of greater complexity or areas dominated by values more deeply rooted in cultural tradition. Because of the particular development of modern European culture, the public domain became rather indifferent to private interests and could therefore be simplified, and as a consequence became rather anonymous. It was for these reasons that technology could be applied more easily in the public domain. As a result, the modern city shows more clearly the true impact of technological thinking than do private homes or residential areas.

In contrast to the earlier, rather slow and partial improvements, the transformations that took place during the nineteenth century were, for the first time, truly systematic and comprehensive. What made these transformations fundamentally different was the possibility of interpreting whole segments of reality in terms of self-referential models and systems. 'System' was not a new term, but it had already received a new and very different meaning during the seventeenth century. It was at that time that a system ceased to be a representation of the essential structure of the given reality and instead became a simulated equivalent – an *a priori* instrumental representation with the ambition to become a universal matrix. That ambition could not be fulfilled everywhere but only in those situations where it was possible to represent the given reality through a model and its purely formal language. Because the formation of systems followed the paradigm of the laboratory experiment, the principles of non-contradiction and sufficient reason – the only criteria of experimental reality – also apply to the instrumental representation of any reality that might eventually be represented in that manner (ie as a system). The intrinsic conditions of a particular system cannot determine how far it can be extended and what kind of reality can be incorporated into the instrumental representation. This always remains an open question that can only be decided in light of the actual conditions of specific cases.

An example may show this more clearly. The development of railways in the last century – and, in particular, their extension into the cities – stands in sharp contrast not only to the surrounding landscape or urban fabric but also to the earlier forms of transport, such as roads or canals. Unlike roads or canals, built in an open dialogue as comprehensive systems from the very beginning, a comprehensive system requires an *a priori* plan in which everything is designed beforehand and in the language and logic of the system chosen. This must be done in such a way that nothing outside the system can interfere with its coherence and its working. In the case of railways, this amounted to nothing less than creating a relatively complete and autonomous reality within the given world. As a result, the movement of trains, the functioning of stations and signals, etc. must be predictable and reliable.

The relative perfection of a system is not unconditional, however. A whole set of conditions must be met if the system is to exist and work. The first is the spatial environment in which everything that we make must be situated. The second, closely linked with the first, is the cultural environment in which every system must be absorbed, incorporated, and reconciled with everything that is already there. Only under such conditions can technological production be creative in any way. However, the distance or gap that, in most cases, separates the systems produced from the given world illustrates how limited is our understanding of their conditional nature, how strong is the faith in their autonomy, and how difficult it is, therefore, to bridge the gap. The gap is very often discussed as a problem of adaptation. But what should adapt to what? Today, it is rather taken for granted that the given world should adapt to the imperative of technological possibilities. This shows the limit of our understanding of what is really taking place,

what is the nature of the given reality, and what technological interference and manipulation really mean. It is this lack of understanding that is the source of the confused belief that we live in a 'technological world'. And yet, to understand what is the true nature of the world in which we live is probably the most difficult task. We certainly live in a world that is profoundly influenced and shaped by technology. But this is very different from living in a technological world, if we understand by 'technology' what has been established in this paper. What is at stake here is not a semantic difference but the very nature of our current civilisation, which we may or may not understand. If we do not understand it, we will never be able to see the ambiguity, tension, and very often deep conflict that exist between the being of technology and the being of the world. In that case, we will also be unable to recognise that ambiguity, tension and conflict are, in fact, essential characteristics of the world in which we really live.

Only when we take into account the reality that is not directly affected by technology – the primary conditions of our embodiment, the finitude of our life, and so on – can we understand the true nature of the so-called 'technological world'.

Notes
1 Werner Heisenberg, 'Rationality in Science and Society', in *Can We Survive our Future?* edited by GR Urban, London: Bodley Head ,1971, p84.
2 This was programmatically formulated for the first time in the well known passage of Francis Bacon's *Instauratio Magna* (Sp. 1; 132 [V, 21]): 'I am labouring to lay the foundation not of any school of thought, but of human utility and power.'
3 'The basic form of appearance in which the will to will arranges and calculates itself in the unhistorical element of the world of completed metaphysics can be stringently called technology', Martin Heidegger, *End of Philosophy*, London: Souvenir Press, 1975, p93.
4 Ibid., p101.
5 This is particularly apparent in the situatedness of will in the context of time, formulated for instance by Nietzsche as the attempt to overcome time through the 'eternal return'.
6 M Heidegger, *Vortrage und Aufsätze*, Pfullingen: Neske, 1959, p43.
7 Aristotle, *Metaphysics*, Loeb edition, trans. H Tredennick, Cambridge, Mass.: Harvard University Press, 1933 *et seq*, 981b14.
8 Aristotle, *Physics*, Loeb edition, trans. Rev P Wicksteed and FM Cornford, Cambridge, Mass.: Harvard University Press, 1937 *et seq*, 199a7.
9 Ibid., 199a9.

10 Aristotle, *Nichomachean Ethics*, Loeb edition, trans. H Rackham, Cambridge, Mass.: Harvard University Press, 1926 *et seq*, 1140a20.

11 Aristotle, Physics, 196b5.

12 Hans-Georg Gadamer, *The Relevance of the Beautiful,* Cambridge, UK: Cambridge University Press, 1986, p104.

13 Examples that may illustrate this point can be found in ancient Near Eastern cosmogonies and in the Greek understanding of creation, as well as in the articulated cosmologies and in the role of the craftsman as *demiourgos*, which also correspond to Heidegger's understanding of metaphysics.

14 'For a science of religion which regards only instrumental action as meaningful, magic is the essence and origin of religion'; W Burkert, *Greek Religion*, Oxford: Blackwell, 1985, p55. 'Science views religion and its manifestations according to its own image and regards everything which refuses to succumb to its techniques as "magical" and primitive'; R Granger, *The Language of the Rite*, London: Darton, Longman & Todd, 1974, p90.

15 R Granger, *Language*, p78.

16 G van der Leeuw, *Religion in Essence and Manifestation*, Gloucester, Mass.: P Smith, 1967, p548.

17 ER Dodds, *The Greeks and the Irrational,* Los Angeles: University of California Press, 1968, p288.

18 Pappus, *Greek Mathematical Texts*, Loeb edition, v.2, trans. Ivor Thomas, Cambridge, Mass.: Harvard University Press, 1939 *et seq*, p 61.

19 JP Vernant, *Myth and Thought Among thc Greeks*, London: Routledge & Kegan Paul, 1983, p295.

20 P Vitruvius, *Ten Books on Architecture*, book XCII, Loeb edition, v.2, trans. F Graniger, Cambidge, Mass.: Harvard University Press, 1931 *et seq*, p275.

21 Arnold Gehlen, *Die Seele im technischen Zeitalter*, Hamburg: Reinbeg, 1957, p15.

22 Vitruvius, *Ten Books*, book XC14.

23 See, for example, the discussions that followed the explicitly formulated opinion about the role of magic in the development of modern science and technology by Frances Yates, recently summarised by BT Copenhauer in *Reappraisals of the Scientific Revolution*. Edited by DC Lindberg and RS Westman, Cambridge, UK: Cambridge University Press, 1990, pp261-303. A similar difficulty seems to arise in discussions about the relationship of art and technique before the seventeenth century, particularly during the late Renaissance. The most interesting here are the discussions about the contribution of such personalities as Leonardo da Vinci and his role as artist, engineer, or scientist.

24 For a more detailed discussion of the nature of the arts and their status in the Middle Ages and in the early modern era, see PO Kristeller, *Renaissance Thought and the Arts*, Princeton, NJ: Princeton University Press, 1980, 163ff; and *The Seven Liberal Arts in the Middle Ages*. Edited by DL Wagner, Bloomington, Ind.: Indiana University Press, 1986.

25 It is characteristic that the arts have been very often referred to as science (*episteme*), not only in classical but also in medieval scholarship. This is illustrated in the well known debate, at the end of the fourteenth century, on the completion of Milan's cathedral, where the main question raised is known as *ars sine scientia nihil est*. For details, see JS Ackerman, '"Ars Sine Scientia Nihil Est": Gothic Theory of Architecture at the Cathedral of Milan' in *The Art Bulletin* 31,1949, pp84-111.

26 In the classical ontology, mathematics (and geometry in particular) is seen as a mediating link between metaphysics (theology) and physics, just as the soul (*psyche*) is a mediating link between the intelligible and the sensible realities.

27 Buonaiuto Lorini, *Della Fortificazioni*, book V, Venice, 1575.

28 Further illustrations of the limits of mathematical mechanisation and the discussion of the achievements of Leonardo da Vinci can be found in EJ Dijksterhuis, *Mathematisation of the World Picture*, London: Oxford University Press, 1961, pp37-50.

29 RE Butts and JC Pitt, *New Perspectives on Galileo*, Boston, Mass.: D Reidel, 1978, p187; WA Wallace, *Galileo and His Sources,* Princeton, NJ: Princeton University Press, 1984, pp126-149.

30 F Vietta, 'Introduction to the Analytical Art' in *Greek Mathematical Thought and the Origin of Algebra*. Edited by J Klein, trans. E Brann, Cambridge, Mass.: MIT Press, 1968, Appendix.

31 Ibid., p181.

32 Like universal mathematics, *prima philosophia* refers ultimately to the principle of non-contradiction and sufficient reason. The new algebra of a metamathematical kind and physica of a metaphysical kind have the same characteristics.

33 Étienne Gilson, *Études sur le role de la pensée médiévale dans la formation du système cartésien*, Paris: J Vrin, 1967; and Wallace, *Galileo*.

34 Descartes, Letter to Mersenne, 15 April 1630, in *Philosophical Writings*. Edited and trans. E Anscombe and PT Geach, Edinburgh: Nelson's University Paperbacks, 1954, p259.

35 Descartes, Letter to Mersenne, 27 May 1631, in ibid., p261.

36 G Galilei, *Dialogues Concerning the Two Chief World Systems*, trans. Stillman Drake, Los Angeles: University of California Press, 1967, p14.

37 Ibid., p38.

38 'I argue *ex suppositione* about motion, so even though the consequences should not correspond to the events of naturally falling heavy bodies, it would little matter to me, just as it derogates nothing from the demonstrations of Archimedes that no moveable is found in nature that moves along spiral lines. But in this I have been, as I shall say, lucky: for the motion of heavy bodies and its events correspond punctually to the events demonstrated by me from the motion I defined'; cited in Butts and Pitt, *New Perspectives*, p234.

39 Ibid., p232.

40 Descartes, *Œuvres*, tome XI, Paris: Tannery, 1975, p31.

41 Ibid., tome 111, 722.

42 Descartes, *Philosophical Writings*, Objection V, p136.

43 DR Lachtermann, *The Ethics of Geometry*, London: Routledge and Kegan Paul, 1989, p140.

44 J Ladriére, 'Technique et eschatologie terrestre' in *Civilisation, technique et humanisme*, Paris: Aubier-Montaigne, 1968.

45 A Funkenstein, *Theology and the Scientific Imagination*, Princeton, NJ: Princeton University Press, 1986, p327. Among those who had this courage are Malebranche and the *occasionnalistes* (Guelinkx, for example), and, most explicitly, Leibniz.

Dalibor Vesely, architect and art historian, was born in Prague, studied in Prague and Munich, taught at the Architectural Association and from 1978 at the University of Cambridge, Faculty of Architecture and History of Art, where he teaches studio and a post-graduate programme. He is also visiting professor in Princeton and Harvard. He has written on poetics or architecture, problem or representation and is currently working on the conflict of the symbolic and instrumental representation and the problem of artificial intelligence.

ARCHITECTURE: A SOCIAL PHILOSOPHY AND A SPATIAL SKILL[1]

PIERRE PELLEGRINO

The first reading of any object is semiotic – we recognise it as being an object of a certain kind, of a certain period, by a certain designer and so on . . . So, space, surface and structure are analysed here within the semiotic categories: pragmatics, syntactics and semantics. This enables us to penetrate much further than mere aesthetic analyses of architecture as space.

G. Broadbent, 'On Reading Architectural Space', in: *Espaces et Sociétés*, no 47, L'Harmattan, Paris, 1985

INTRODUCTION:
EPISTEMOLOGY AND SEMIOTICS OF ARCHITECTURE

What is the object of architecture? How are we to distinguish it from that of other disciplines? What enters into the semiotics of that object?

Materiality *per se* cannot specify the object of knowledge. What is built is not the only object of architecture. Its reality varies widely according to the point of view from which it is perceived and the knowledge which can be brought to bear in criticising it.

If not through its materiality, is that object distinguished through its form? Is it through a rigour of form that architecture recognises its product? Or, on the contrary, is such rigour the expression of a geometrisation of thought that would trivialise architecture?

What takes shape in architecture? What does architecture unify in its project? Form imposed on content: what relationship does it express between external appearance and internal presence? How, in giving an architectural form to its presence, in a way that goes beyond the mirror of appearance, does human society perceive itself?

Is the imaginary of architecture a register of figures, like a lexicon of strange things that would be consulted in the course of a creative activity? Or is it that which fills a mythical universe with figures? Is it in itself an imaging activity, finding in an image not the reflection of a reality but the means of penetrating it more deeply? If it is in opposition to an existing reality, does it aim at the *atopos*, an absence, or does it attempt to draw the contours of a dreamlike 'elsewhere', or of a project that might become a reality in the near future?

The work of the imagination is undermining our culture, producing a distortion that ultimately destroys the very signs of that culture; the means of expression are becoming saturated and losing their efficacy, to the point where the very perspective in which we view our surroundings, our world of objects, is called into question. This questioning will be fraught with anxiety until such time as we discover ways of giving expression to the newness of our vision. To give expression is to formalise the unformalised, to structure it so that one meaning makes sense in relation to another; so that the meaning which originates in our senses finds, hidden in our uncertain wanderings, a way out to the surface of the opus that unveils its form intact in yet another embodiment.

The architect does not approach his project without a culture that has undergone architectural debate. That culture not only influences material aspects of the project by interpreting a reality *in praesentia* but also has an impact on the choice of references to other architectures considered *in absentia* to be similar in their projection of reality.

The criticism addressed to architecture is mainly concerned with its integration in the world of human amenities. Discussions always end by questioning, more or less explicitly, the very definition of architecture in terms of the responses it makes or does not make to the social needs of human beings. The grounds adduced for such criticism range from a lack of form and utility to an excess of them.

Between form as appearance and form as a principle of existence lies a universe of discourse in which distance and closeness, difference and similarity, significance and silence are the object of the project. Often its goal is to turn architecture into a 'social art' in which 'speaking from the standpoint of architecture', judging and referring to certain models means dealing with the presence of 'man' in the world as the scale and relevance of any architecture.

Semiotics of architecture, seen as the investigation of structures of meaning, and semiology, seen as the investigation of the production of meaning, are applied to architecture. Since architecture controls, and is controlled by human forms of perception and modes of cultural interaction, it has to be analysed not only from a functional but also from a social and historical point of view. The satisfaction of particular historical, social and functional requirements through varying techniques of construction can, in specific local contexts, engender new architectural codes.

If space is to be the object of semiotics it must be studied as an expression of meaning, determining discrete and combinable units of meaning. It must first be studied as the form of the content, the structuring of its substance. Its manifestation in the form of signification, of differences connoted and portrayed in a representation, is a second phenomenon that also lends itself to semiotic study: the study of a process relating it to virtual units, namely the units of a preliminary or possible system.

The Saussurean conception of the relationship between signifier and signified and Hjemlslev's concept of connotation are used to clarify the various approaches to the description of meaning production developed in the theory of architecture. In this way, architecture can give an explanation of the functionalist, emblematic, communication-oriented, modernist and post-modernist approaches to the world.

FORMS AND FIGURES OF ARCHITECTURE: TYPES, PATTERNS AND EMBLEMS

Architecture re-examines notions such as distinction, etiquette, style and face, which may be helpful in studying the relationship between the partitioning of human space into areas and the distinguishing marks of its use: social, geographical, historical and so on. In other words, architecture sets out to study the significant attitudes that a given society develops towards spatial subdivisions when they are transferred to the plane of language.

The culture of urban space has some specific qualities that are expressed in architectural marking and cutting, as well as in painting, design, city planning and city renewal operations. This meeting proposes to examine the superimposition of signifying mechanisms and their linkings, the derivation of signs and their fitting into a spatial synthesis.

The articulation of the existent, regarded as denoted or represented, with what can be imagined of it because of its connotations is one of the possible lines of approach to such a synthesis. Another possible approach is the articulation of the reductive procedures that suggest the complexity of a reality, these procedures being analogous to those which govern the fitting of particular categories into more general ones.

Yet another approach might be the spatial interplay between the enclosed form and the expressed form, the game of veiling and unveiling, where space, being a relationship rather than a quantity, creeps in between expression and content, taking advantage of its status as a form of expression. Veilings and unveilings present certain kinds of behaviour which urban culture recognises as forms of distinction, style, etiquette or self-presentation. These forms can be examined in their dependence on categorisations of the universe, on models of expectations and response norms, or on the interpretation of context and the formation of an adequate representation. Other approaches are also possible, but all should seek to understand a space which features the play of mobility, creating synthesis in the relationships between forms.

Styles pattern archetypes of housing and make them reality in types of dwellings: types which thus find their value in periods of reference. Among the types of dwellings supplied in each style of building, some are selected by social categories that make them emblems of their presence in relation to others in the built-up area. But styles are not mere elements of the labelling of the external facades of housing; they also provide models for living inside the dwelling. By breaking down and reassembling these models, the occupant personalises his dwelling. The occupant's social personality, making play with their interfaces, expresses itself through the masks on the urban face of housing.

The problem is to reconcile value and meaning: that is to say, to determine how a social form can contain a universality. In terms of spaces, it is a matter of potentiality, of a dimension as much virtual as real, and never realised completely.

Within what constitutes the dominant space, there is a contradiction. Social formations, states, are competing to redefine themselves and to impose themselves on the scale of the contemporary fluxes and of the networks that traverse them. This contradiction is reflected in a struggle between social classes for classifications. Housing is one of the dimensions of those classifications.

ARCHITECTURE, SPACE AND SOCIETY

Contemporary space is surreptitiously transforming itself in many dimensions: spatial redefinitions, changing interdependences, different emphases, new configurations and new relationships between appearance and substance, newly defined movements and other imbalances. These transform space, but do so in different ways according to their scales of reference.

How can we visualise tomorrow's space without

reducing it either to a mere imposition of new barriers in a general movement of introspection and a logic of juxtaposition, or to the imposition of an undefined and unlimited flux in a polyvalent world and a logic of exclusion?

Although other disciplines conceive space only as the emergence, the expression, of a structure existing entirely apart, architecture considers that social space constitutes a relevant sphere of determination not only through the oppositions it reconciles but also through the groupings it determines and the relationships it organises.

The transformation of contemporary space is the transformation not only of the territory and the buildings in it but also of all signs of the spatial units, forms and relationships which basically constitute structures and interactions and conversely are framed by them. From this point of view, the presence and absence of sites, with their look, their consistency, their articulations and manifold disarticulations into 'spatialities' of distinct scales and relevances, are significant.

For ages past, occidental civilisation has been continuously spreading over the world, continuously conquering new territories. The relationship with space, aided by technological development, has tended to reduce distances through the reduction of travelling times (transport systems) or the concentration of activities in one place (urban density).

Nowadays, the growth of telematic culture is leading this sequence of developments to the point of reversing direction. Through changes in perception and representation, the relationship with space is changing both quantitatively and qualitatively. The spatial medium, presupposing marked decentralisation, is transforming the scales of relationships with otherness, the other being everywhere and nowhere in the immediacy of an 'elsewhere' and in the standardisation of the 'here' and the 'everywhere'.

Within the relationship between mobility and identity, spaces, as represented by actors, refer to scales by a dialectical process of inclusion and exclusion. These scales are relevant to an explanation of movements and fluxes and to an explanation of collective forms of identity linked to spatial mobility.

Urbanisation, periurbanisation and the bypassing of traditional rural areas are induced by increasing mobility and testify to new territorial compositions. But construction and deconstruction (representation by the combination of elements rather than their separation, by recollection rather than by projection, etc) are equally the signs of new forms of identity marked by the alternation of departures and arrivals.

Contemporary public space is changing from its

legitimising function, which affirms the permanence of group values, by featuring rapid exchanges, long-distance communications and mobility-plays that affect all social actors. This transformation not only creates a risk of anomic disintegration of the subject, but also makes it possible to bring into play the quest for polymorphic identity, which seeks its stability in the interplay of different components of social networks.

The meaning of public, community and private space is to be found at multiple levels of spatial and temporal scales and in a new relationship between integration and differentiation that reorganises the sharing and communication of values. Thus, all dimensions of social, economic, cultural and political life take a spatial form and, in this way, reveal the social construction of a society.

Nevertheless, space is not just a simple reflection. We have also seen how far society itself is modulated by the forms of space, its organisation and the way people find their places in it. Space is a matter of making new figures and of creating new relationships.

A PROBLEM STATED

Towards the end of the last century Viollet-le-Duc, in the thirteenth of his 'Discourses on Architecture', affirmed that:

> If, then, architects do not wish to be classified in 1900 among the lost species that have passed into the condition of extinct historical individualities, like astrologers, alchemists and armour-clad men-at-arms, it is time they set resolutely to work, for the old mysteries they rely upon are beginning to be seen through . . .[2]

What had happened to architecture that one of its most ardent defenders should see fit to make such a prophecy of imminent disaster? What had the architects, the builders of palaces and stately homes, done that in the nineteenth century their profession should be under threat? Viollet-le-Duc made himself pretty clear: architectural learning could no longer rely on old mysteries! They would be unmasked as mountebanks' tricks.

INTELLIGENCE AND ARCHITECTURE

And yet architectural treatises were many and had been written, as century followed century, for a long time past. When we go back to the founding texts of the European architecture of the last 2,000 years, or at any rate to the earliest text still accessible to us, the ten books of Vitruvius' *De Architectura*,[3] we find a very precise definition and an explicit construction of architectural lore.

In the first of his ten books, Vitruvius addresses the prince – the Emperor Augustus – to inform him of the purpose of his work, which is to acquaint him with what architecture is, to 'make' that 'science intelligible' to him, so that he may judge for himself the beauty of the buildings he orders to be erected.

We then learn that 'this science is acquired by practice and by theory'. The practice consists in the execution of designs, 'whereby the matter' of architectural works 'is given suitable form'. The theory 'explains and demonstrates the fitness of the proportions of the things it is desired to make', the relevance of the measurements given to the various parts of the edifice planned. Architecture cannot do without theory or practice.

We also learn that architecture 'is a science that should be accompanied by a great variety of studies and knowledge, by means of which it judges all works of the other arts that belong to it', to the point where 'most cannot comprehend that the understanding and memory of one man should be capable of so much knowledge'. All sciences, however, have 'a communication and link between them . . . universal science is composed of all these sciences', so that it is enough for the architect to know the 'consistencies . . . between certain things that are common to all the sciences, one of which helps in learning another more easily'.

This is a piece of extremely rigorous epistemological thinking, placing architecture at the heart of what at the time was regarded as universal science; but architecture is allotted a place, that of a branch of learning which today would be defined as learning of a generalist kind. That applies, at least, to the theory, since for Vitruvius a practice belongs especially to him who professes a particular art, whereas theory in architecture is 'common to all the learned'.

And theory in architecture, according to Vitruvius, is a semiotic theory inasmuch as 'in architecture, as in any other science, two things are noticed: that which is signified and that which signifies'. Still more precisely, it is a theory based both on a metasemiotic system, in which the thing signified, the thing stated and spoken about, is the object of the architectural design, the building, a tool possessing a certain utility for those who use it –

Signifier design of the building	Signified metasemiosis of the building	
	Signifier building	Signified building

– and on a connotative representation in which the thing that signifies is the design of the object of architectural learning, 'the demonstration given of it by reasoning, supported by science'.

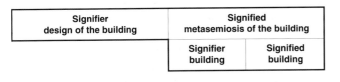

FROM ABOVE: Open-sided market hall; section through a Venetian palace. The polymathic Viollet-le-Duc defends architectural learning and the concept of the architect as educator and communicator, disseminating information and knowledge through the art of building. The famous angled cast-iron columns of the open-sided market hall support heavy masonry above, thereby creating a more or less unencumbered space at ground level and introducing the idea of pilotis

Signifier design of the reasoning		Signified connotation of the reasoning
Signifier reasoning	Signified reasoning	

For Vitruvius, what signifies in architecture is not the building *per se* but the secondary representation which architecture gives of the connection that the edifice may have with things other than itself: certain items of knowledge, a branch of learning, certain values, its meaning.

The significant connection between what architectural reasoning signifies and what is signified in the edifice which it builds is thus designed, marked in the building as a 'right measurement' of objects 'in relation to their use'; architecture is then 'constituted' by operations of mensuration, the ordering, disposition, rhythm, proportion, fitness and distribution of the parts of the edifice. And theory of architecture is a theory of the meaning of the measurement signified in the edifices it produces.

But the meaning of the measurement is not limited to a use value of the building; it is thematised synthetically as the 'meeting' of the sturdiness, utility and beauty of the edifice. Sturdiness demands that 'nothing should be spared' in choosing the best materials and digging firm foundations, and hence it results as much from an economic principle of investment as from the quality of the materials. Utility refers back to the disposition of the edifice and the integrity of each thing which, set in its place, must have everything that is 'proper and necessary' to it; it stems from respect for the needs of the human body, but also for established social customs. Beauty is achieved in the shape of the edifice through the right 'proportion' of all its parts; it depends on geometry, but also on the taste for 'elegance' and on seeking for the 'agreeable', for cultivated aesthetics.

THE SEARCH FOR CONTEMPORARY SOLUTIONS

This cognitive system was challenged in the nineteenth century. What upheaval of learning took place at that time to cause Viollet-le-Duc to fear for architecture's very existence? The people were making themselves heard and the industrial revolution not merely 'imposing its products', as our author perfectly understood, but also imposing its intensive methods of production and the sciences that made them possible: not only the natural sciences – physics, biology and chemistry – but also the work sciences: economics, psychology and sociology. The quantities to be produced were at the centre of research and scientific thought.

A rift was appearing in what had formerly been ordered as a 'universal science'. On the one hand, the natural sciences were developing through the study of an object defined in its own substance, the material reality of things; on the other, the work sciences, which pretty soon came to be called the human sciences, were taking as their object not the materiality of things *per se* but the practical knowledge an actor might have of that materiality according to the point of view which he held and which he shared with others: a practical knowledge made up of values, wishes and needs.

Architecture thus saw its principle of unity exploded: architecture which had to measure not only the materiality of the buildings it erected but the uses to which their recipients might put them according to the conventions of their period and rank. Faced with the now acknowledged impossibility of a universal science purporting to embrace everything on one and the same principle, some architects attempted to maintain their hold over the production of buildings by abandoning all theory and taking refuge in the area of practices in order to claim a position as 'orchestra conductors'.

In reality, from formalism to functionalism, the successive schools of modernity took to shuttling helplessly between two levels of the conception of architectural space, which was henceforth split up. Between what signified and what was signified, the demonstration of 'reasoning', even aided by science, no longer held unconditional sway; between the level of the signifier and that of the signified, an epistemological cut no longer permitted strict deduction.[4]

The objects to which architecture proposed to give measurement no longer took on meaning only in certain customs hallowed by immutable social norms, but were relevant enough to be planned in some cases and not in others, depending on the (numerical or metrical) quantity of the substances in which they were built. There was no longer any theory of the 'right measurement' that was *a priori* automatically valid both for the materiality of things and for the meaning they had for those who used or abused them.

Measurement itself, having become as much a means as an end, was changing its dimensions. It was no longer solely a matter of ordinal variables, hierarchies and right relationships fixed in proportions that enabled us to notice them; it was the means of drawing nearer to knowledge of what was not yet known because it was connected with masses of information of a kind not immediately perceptible, with quantities linked to phenomena of scale. That is certainly why architectural theory, enriched by its past, is today in mid-redefinition, seeking new instruments of knowledge and applying itself to territories of new scope.

PROSPECTS

In our culture it has become necessary to base our

conception of the world not only on universal categories but also on experience, on the assessment of facts and on taking into account phenomena of scale and the quantitative facts that transfuse them. Architecture itself, as a principle of begetting, builds its learning and its projects on the basis of facts gleaned by experience. Whereas in the past the architect addressed himself to the Prince in order to acquaint him with universal measurements and sound proportions, in present day the architect addresses himself to the people, showing that he has experience. But that experience is not based on tradition alone; it measures its effects in modernity.

For this very reason, even more than in the past, an overall theory is necessary to the development of architectural learning. In order to measure the effects of contemporary experience, it is necessary to be able to compare the objects of that experience and the conditions of their making and use, which vary with the places where they are planned, the economy current there and the people who live there. The meaning of an architectural object is not given, but projected.

Signifier form of architectural knowledge		Signified object of architectural project	
Signifier reasoning	Signified reasoning	Signifier building	Signified building

The relationship between what the forms arising out of architectural learning signify and what is signified in the project is of the order of the probable correspondences. These are projected correlations between magnitudes measured in architecture and magnitudes analysed in other sciences, especially physics, which calculates the stability of the edifice from the strength of the materials assembled, and the human sciences, which assess the amenity of the housing supplied in terms of the value it has for particular users.[5]

Architectural learning is not positivist but seeks to define itself among the sciences of the artificial, where what is involved is an epistemology of knowledge of the transformations undergone by the material reality of things. But whereas the engineering sciences, approximate branches of knowledge, test measurements and dictate standards defining suitable correlations between the economics and the physics of what is to be built, architecture, a projected branch of knowledge and a creative act, works on surpassing the standards and emphasising unexpected rhythms and correspondences.

In architecture, practical knowledge and poetical knowledge are conjoined; and, while not all those who use the language of architecture to grasp the world they live in are necessarily poets, the mere fact of living in a product of architecture is an exercise in that language, just as reading a text implies a command of the language in which it is written: a command that is not necessarily as learned as the writer's, but sufficient for the writer to be to some extent understood. And so everyone learns a little about how to write; the Prince is no longer the sole reader of architecture.

It is not writing that has disappeared in the transformation of languages, but the scribe, whereas he had an exclusive function, a function of trust, to perform in the days when the man in the street could neither read nor write. Perhaps one day the profession of architect will disappear as Viollet-le-Duc feared it would, at least in its present form. Architecture will not be condemned on that account; provided it managed to absorb some exogenous items of knowledge essential to dialogue with the analytical sciences, it might even become the living language of transformation of the world we live in.[6]

Notes

1 English translation by HS Burrows.

2 Viollet-le-Duc, *Entretiens sur l'architecture*, 1846-1904, republished Mardaga, Brussels, 1977.

3 Vitruvius, *Les dix livres de l'architecture*, c80 BC, French trans. by C Perrault, 1673, republished Balland, Paris, 1979.

4 The articulation between the form of architectural expression and the form of the content of the product of architecture could no longer be left to a single logico-deductive calculation (stone edifices age well, this edifice is in stone, this edifice will age well), but required a statistico-abductive calculation (stone edifices age well, I want the edifice I am planning to age well, it is highly probable that I should do well to choose to build this edifice in stone) – a calculation in which creative invention emerged from significant differences between probable cases (I can also conceive that it could happen that this edifice, even though built in stone, might age badly on the chosen site, and I can also conceive that this edifice might be built of other materials and age well).

5 In evaluating the object of an architectural project, history is not left behind, for it dictates a judgement based on the measurements supplied to it by other sciences and submits to that judgement the beauty of the objects weighed by its critical thinking.

6 The general teaching of architecture needs to be based on an architecturology that combines an epistemology of practical knowledge of the transformation of masterial reality into architectural edifices with an epistemology of poetical knowledge of reality; all poetical knowledge is knowledge of the transformation of a language that enables us to grasp a reality.

Pierre Pellegrino is currently Professor at the Centre de Recherche en Architecture et Architecturologie, École d'Architecture, at the Université de Genève.

TREE OF THE SKETCH
BIRGIT COLD

TREE OF THE SPEECH
(T Nørretranders, 1991)

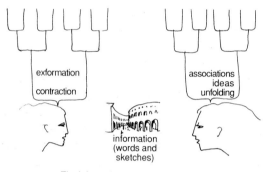

exformation
contraction
information
(words and
sketches)
associations
ideas
unfolding

The information gets deeper the more
exformation is produced and thrown away

As information, a message and a sketch may be compared. All the decisions which are made to find the
suitable words or lines require choices, which means
that something is left behind unspoken, invisible, but
still part of the process. Nørretranders calls this 'silent
language' exformation.

Visualising concepts and the environment by making
sketches is universal. The importance and value of the
sketch are, however, assessed differently at different
times. In former centuries, sketches and drawings were
looked on as necessary exercises for the final design of
a building, painting, play or piece of music.

The awareness of the value of sketches is now stron-
ger because of the interest in creative processes, in
which quality emerges.

THE SKETCH AND THE POEM
When we searched for the dog,
we did not find it
neither indoor nor outdoor.
When we searched for the happiness,
we found the dog
under the staircase
(Annie Riis, 'Runder', 1986)

In a poem and in a sketch, each word and each line are
chosen to represent 'a world of ideas and experiences'.
The interpretation and the understanding depend on
the cultural access to this silent and invisible everyday
world. It is the vision of what is not said or drawn, the
absence of words and lines, which make 'the receptive
mental tree' grow large. The poem of Annie Riis gives a
reflective key to everyday expectations, as the sketch
of Saul Steinberg presents an ironic and common key
to the development of the modern city.

THE SKETCH
The sketch is communication
– between 'me' and 'I'
– between **me** and **you**
– between **student** and **teacher**
– between **architect** and **client**

The internal communication between 'me and I' takes place between 'directness, naiveté, belief, inspiration on the unconscious side – me – and illusion, persuasion, professionalism, bluff on the conscious side – I'. (W Orskov, 1966)

Reading and interpreting sketches make you recognise what you have 'chosen to emphasise': the features, the space and the light. To open up to the phenomena and to make 'the unconscious stream' flow between the senses, the mind, the hand, pen and paper, a deep concentration and a conscious attitude towards the power of this unconscious cooperation is necessary. Exercising this 'internal cooperation' is crucial in the design process.

THE SKETCH
The sketch is a moment of life in a place

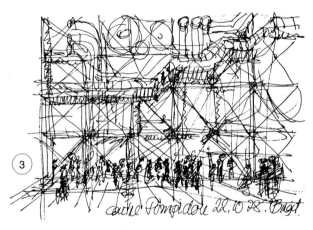

Exercising the awareness and the visual attention is the premise for building up a repertoire of architecture and places.

Studying the local environment (as the Vienna students are doing under Rob Krier), travelling and visiting new and ancient architecture, places of everyday life and monuments, are very important parts of the architectural education.

Making sketches is one and perhaps the best way of increasing awareness and concentration, and strengthening the memory for building up this repertoire. Such a repertoire is necessary to draw on in the creative design process.

THE SKETCH
Sketches and pictograms summarise
large amounts of information in some short
'exformation-rich macrostates',
with a small amount of nominal information.

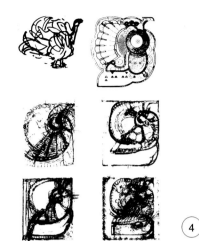

Architectural sketches as well as architectural drawings are abstractions. They have different functions, information and appearance.

An interesting question is whether the sketches, as 'exformation-rich macrostates', are closer to the perception of the real environment than the drawings, as 'information-rich macro- and microstates'. Perhaps it is so, because we normally perceive only the macro features and the spectacular or the diversities from our expectations, which is precisely what sketches do.

THE SKETCH
The sketch is **a promise of the completeness**

The strength of the sketch as a working method is the openness, the unfinished, the incompleteness, the suggestions, which may give a promise of 'the divine solution'. Architecture students at the Faculty of Architecture in Trondheim design a small museum for selected pieces of art in their second year. Before the students have taken the design decisions, they are asked to present nine sketches from 'a walk in the museum', showing the space and light they want to create. The sketches are presented on 12 x 12 cm cardboard-like playing cards. A tenth card shows the walk. This is an unpretentious way of communication that stimulates the progress in the discussions between the student's 'me and I', and between student and teacher. In the spirit of Gordon Cullen's serial vision the same exercise is used, when visiting architectural places.

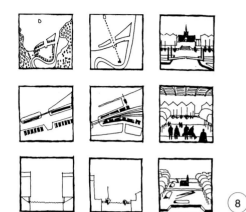

(8)

THE SKETCH

Our memory is limited by the amount of unities it masters,
– not of the information the unities represent
(T Nørretranders, 1991)

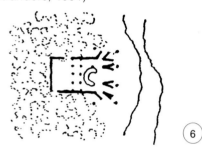

(6)

Symbols help us in remembering a lot of information, even if we cannot have more than seven things in our head at the same time
(GA Miller, 1956)

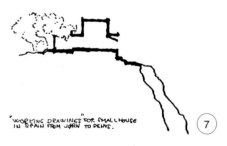

"WORKING DRAWINGS FOR SMALL HOUSE IN SPAIN FROM JORN TO PENNS."

(7)

Symbols are like the Trojan Horse,
they smuggle information into the consciousness,
like soldiers were smuggled into Troy
(T Nørretranders, 1991)

THE SKETCH AND THE PICTOGRAM

They concentrate on 'the essence'
– a macrostate with a high degree of entropy (many possible microstates)
– 'everything which is not present, hasn't disappeared either'
(T Nørretranders)

When students work together, and in discussions between student and teacher, the sketch invites participation and development. The 'invisible' challenges and stimulates the creative process.

Series of sketches point to possibilities, main choices and interpretations of the subject and the place in question. The nine pictograms describe the main ideas in a Norwegian architectural competition: 'The City seeks the water', 1993.

THE PICTOGRAM

Pictograms communicating the essence and the main features are a way of controlling the total context.

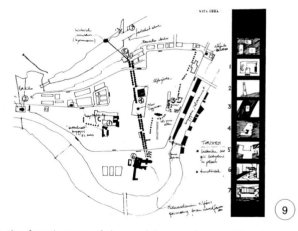

(9)

In the fourth year of the architectural education in Trondheim, Sabine and Geir made urban design proposals for the inner city of Trondheim. In a series of pictograms they show the main ideas.

I am aware that focusing on the significance of sketches and pictograms as a learning and teaching method may be rooted in the belief in 'cultivated simplicity' as a fundamental conception. Perhaps a Scandinavian puritanism mingled with classicism and functionalism, a 'less is more' perceived as a virtue.

THE PICTOGRAMS

for the Norwegian Winter Olympic Games, 1994, are
- playful and active
- historic like rock engravings
- original and natural 'as Norwegians'

In the creative process the sketches represent 'the labyrinthine search' for ideas. The talent and the skill to make the lines expressing the ideas are crucial to all visual arts and crafts.

THE SKETCH AND THE PICTOGRAM
as a learning and teaching method

The aim is to develop all the potentials of a student.
The method should help
- to develop the awareness
- to see and choose 'the essence'
- to communicate with yourself, and your ideas
- to develop, cultivate and understand ideas
- to communicate concepts in a process with people
- to play and have pleasure

(10)
Le Corbusier

The use of the computer in the design process is growing fast. The computer is more accurate, faster and combines separate information as desired. The computer as a sketching tool has been developed, but the machine, the hardware and the man-made programmes are barriers in the creative process compared with sketching on paper. The difference between

sketching and visualising ideas on a computer is the involvement of the directness, the preconscious, producing and throwing away exformation during the sketching process. The main reason for encouraging hand sketching is the importance of learning and knowing how 'to catch, keep and create' environmental impressions and conceptions directly in time and on the spot.

LET US SKETCH

References
T Nørretranders, 'Mærk verden, en beretning om bevisthed', Gyldendal, Denmark, 1991.
A Riis, 'Runder', Aschehoug, Oslo, 1986.
GA Miller, Psychological Review, 1956.

Illustrations
1 S Steinberg, Graph Paper Building, 1950. H Rosenberg's text, Whitney Museum of Modern Art, NY, 1978.
2 J Utzon, Own house in Mallorca, 1971 and Church in Bagsværd. Living Architecture, no 8-89, Denmark, 1976.
3 B Cold, Centre Pompidou in Paris, 1978.
4 R Pietilä, Tampere Main Library. Living Architecture, no 6-87, Denmark, 1979.
5 Second year student: Museum for selected pieces of art, The Faculty of Architecture, Trondheim NTH, 1990.
6 & 7 see J Utzon.
8 B Cold, E Hiorthøy, A Øyasceter, R Hafstad, Nine pictograms from the Architectural competition 'The city seeks the water', 1993.
9 S Eri, G Hermansen, Students project, 'Vita Urba', Places in Trondheim. Faculty of Architecture, NTH, 1990.
10 Le Corbusier, 'La Maison des Hommes', Paris, 1936.
W Ørskov, Aflæsning af objekter og andre essays. Borgens forlag, København, 1966.

Birgit Cold is Professor at the Department of Architectural Design at The University of Trondheim

CONCEPT FORMATION IN A STUDIO PROJECT

CORINE DELAGE AND NELLY MARDA

The issue of architectural cognition, the way architectural concepts are formed in students' minds and how students develop an understanding of what architecture is, are important aspects which need to be addressed. This account stresses that the 'having' or 'entertaining' of a concept is not an all-or-nothing affair but a developmental process. Thought consists of concepts. A concept is not an isolated, changeless formation but an active part of the intellectual process constantly engaged in serving communication, understanding and problem-solving. The prerequisite under which architectural concept formation or concept learning occurs is a grasp of the nature of representation. The visual expression in architecture is fundamental for its understanding. Both verbal expression (talking) and visual representation (making) are concrete expressions of architectural thinking and both interact with each other transforming our concepts about architecture.

We shall present the studio teaching method developed over the past three years mainly in the first year at the University of Greenwich School of Architecture and Landscape in order to initiate students to architectural concept formation.

The teaching method implemented is based on the experience that students can think and develop thought processes about many aspects of the world but cannot yet think spatially and architecturally. Architecture has two levels of expression: verbal/conceptual and visual/ representational. The assumption is that learning architecture is like learning a language and that at the beginning of the learning process *thought/architectural concepts* and *speech/visual forms* develop along different lines, independently of each other up to a certain point in time. At this point these lines meet, where upon concepts become visual and forms conceptual.

The method consists in developing these two aspects separately in the student's work until there is a conscious correspondence between them. A student has to learn how to talk about his models/drawings in a coherent way, as well as to express his concepts through drawings and models. The method stresses the need to develop both levels (visual and conceptual) simultaneously.[1] Schematically, one may imagine concepts and representations as two intersecting circles. In their overlapping parts, concepts and representations coincide to produce what is called architectural thinking.

One can say that the processes leading to architectural concept formation develop along two main lines,[2] that also correspond to two forms of mental activity. The first relates to the 'complex concept' formation based on bringing things together under a common 'family name'. This corresponds in linguistics with the plane of the syntagm.[3] In the articulated language, this space is linear and irreversible and refers to relationships of combination. The second is the formation of 'potential concepts' based on singling out certain common attributes of objects and creating classifications. This corresponds in linguistics with the plane of system. The first line is bringing things together through relationships of combination and the second one through relationships of similarity.

On the syntagmatic level, the theme of 'transformations' is quite abstract and provides endless ways of combinations throughout the design process. This opens up a field of experimentation in the use of different techniques in order to research spatial qualities. The students are encouraged to work by using different visual techniques like photography, photocopy, tracings, castings, models for their transformations. The syntagmatic level is the level of the visual transformations and it creates relationships between the different images. This level relies on part-whole relationships in an ordered, extended context and constitutes the exostructural/relational context of the objects.[4] To this level belong the different contextual issues (in relation to a site) and nonarchitectural objects (ie mechanical, electrical, painting) that the students have to choose and transform.

The systematic level is actually the level of selection, substitution and similarity, which is the level of abstraction and of architectural concepts. This level relates to the concept of endostructure,[5] applying to the determinate form of the object, which in this case is the architectural space. Concepts like boundary definition, inside-outside, transparent-solid, sequence and depth, scale and structure belong to that level.

The studio project is working on the levels of syntagm and system at the same time, thus allowing the formation of architectural concepts to take place. The interaction between the two levels is possible through the use of metaphor. The planes of syntagm and system correspond with the concepts of metaphor (of the systematic order) and metonymy (of the syntagmatic order) used by Jakobson.[6]

Jakobson concludes that not only language but all sign systems are organised in terms of metaphor and metonymy, and that stylistic and discursive devices and genres derive from the differential positioning and emphasis of messages according to these two poles. It is obvious that neither of them can function on their own since both syntagm and system are necessary to all discourse. Syntagm cannot 'progress' except by calling successively on new units taken from the associative plane (system) through the creation of metaphors.

In linguistics, metaphor[7] presupposes the establishment of a tension between two terms in the sentence through the violation of a linguistic code. The metaphorical statement then appears as a reduction of this tension by means of a creative semantic pertinence within the sentence as a whole. The emergence of sense is accompanied by a transformation of the referential dimension, endowing metaphor with its power to re-describe reality. The nature of this transformation, which affects not only metaphor but literary works in general, is clarified by the concept of the text.

In architecture one can say that the pole of exostructure/relational context relates to that of metonymy in signs; and the pole of endostructure/morphology relates to that of metaphor in signs. The way that architectural space presents itself to our representation is neither endostructure nor exostructure. It is a meeting ground, or interface, of a particular and special kind, which affords us a view of the space under both its endostructural and exostructural aspect. In order to make an object stand out from its metonymic context, and become an architectural space, one has to engage in a metaphoric shift. To do so is to topicalise and focus certain features of an architectural concept (endostructure). In this way, metonymic combination and metaphoric selection interact in the construction of architectural space.

In order to make a visual image stand out from its metonymic context the student has to engage in metaphoric shift. He has to focus on certain architectural features like boundary definition, inside-outside, etc. For instance, a mapping of movements on site is trans-

lated into a space – music notation becomes a space.

The use of words is an integral part and it facilitates this process. The introduction of the use of a specific 'word'[8] during the design process is of great importance for the project. It helps the student focus on the conceptual level and helps him translate his idea on the visual level. The relationship of the visual expression to the 'word' undergoes changes through a continual movement back and forth. In that way the 'metaphoric twist' between the syntagmatic and systematic plane is something which happens through the use of the word.

The level of the interaction between the syntagmatic and systematic planes and the use of metaphor does not have the same intensity all of the time. Currently, one can see two main trends on the level of architectural concept formation that exist in studio teaching at Greenwich and in architectural education. These trends are not mutually exclusive:

(a) In the first approach, the visual understanding of architectural space is arrived at through the transformation of visual materials, generated by the student's first-hand experience or intuitive perception of the world (ie everyday objects, mechanical objects etc). The formation of architectural concepts is helped by an experience of the site and by the introduction and transformation of concepts borrowed from extra-architectural 'worlds' or events (ie the world of Modern art, of theatre, etc). This approach works mainly on the relational context of architecture (exostructure) using metaphor to engage with architectural concepts and it is contextual, experiential, individual and expressive.

(b) In the second approach, the visual understanding of architectural space is arrived at through the transformation of geometrical configurations and forms. One would study not just the elements of architecture but the mechanisms of transformation of those elements in order to understand how changes in the structure or programme must affect the form. It deals with the syntactic rule systems of form and organisation in architecture. Considering form in its syntactic capacity, one sees it to be ordered according to specific laws internal to architecture and not derived from notions which are borrowed from other disciplines. Here, the approach works mainly on the morphological level (endostructure) and is self-referential and systematic.

Sometimes the process used by the tutors does not consistently belong to one of the two approaches but uses both in an interactive way.

Architecture is not only about forms or concepts but

about their interaction. The way that architectural space presents itself to our representation is neither endostructure nor exostructure, it is an interface between the two. The way the students engage with it is by making and verbally expressing their thoughts. Architecture in this process is not seen as a philosophical pursuit or as a craft. It is placed in an interactive process that relies on the tension between the two poles.

Notes
1 Lev Vygotsky, *Thought and Language*, The MIT Press, 1986. According to Vygotsky, thought and speech have different roots. In the speech development of the child, we can certainly establish a preintellectual stage, and his thought development, a prelinguistic stage. Up to a certain point in time, the two follow different lines, independently of each other and then they meet, where upon thought becomes verbal and speech rational.
2 ibid, pp 96-145. Vygotsky distinguishes several phases within each concept formation line.
3 Ferdinand De Saussure, *Course in General Linguistics*, Fontana/Collins, 1974, pp 122-127, and Roland Barthes, *Elements of Seriology*, Hill and Wang, New York, 1986, III Syntagm and System, pp 58-88.
4 Chris Sinha, *Language and Representation*, Harvester-Wheatsheaf, 1988, pp 174-175. Dealing with the problem of representation in language he brings forward the concepts of endostructure, applying to the determinate form of the isolated or particular object; and of exostructure, referring to the behaviour of the object in relation to other objects. The pole of endostructure/morphology in objects relates to that of metaphor in signs; and the pole of exostructure/relational context in objects relates to that of metonymy in signs.
5 ibid, pp 174-175.
6 Jakobson Roman, *Two Aspects of Language and Two Types of Aphasic Disturbances,* Jakobson and Halle, 1956, pp 54-82. 'The aspect of the linguistic code of governing relations of *selection*, *substitution* and *similarity* between linguistic signs was designated by Jakobson as its metaphoric pole, indicating that metaphoric figures depend for their interpretation upon these relations. The aspect of the code governing relations of *combination*, *contexture* and *contiguity* was designated metonymic, indicating that the device of metonymy relies upon part-whole relations in an ordered, extended context.'
7 Paul Ricoeur, *Hermeneutics and the Human Sciences*, Cambridge University Press, 1982, Introduction pp 12-13 and Earl McCormac, *A Cognitive Theory of Metaphor*, the MIT Press, 1985.
8 Lev Vygotsky, *Thought and Language*, The MIT Press, 1986, see chapter 7 'Thought and Word'.

Corine Delage is currently Subject Leader for Architecture at the School of Architecture and Landscape, University of Greenwich, having practised architecture and landscape in France, the UK and the USA. Nelly Marda is currently doing a PhD research on architectural education at the Bartlett and is teaching at the School of Architecture and Landscape, University of Greenwich.

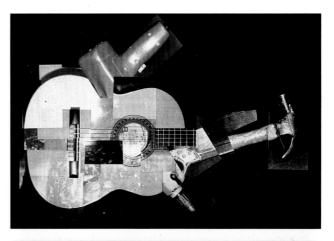

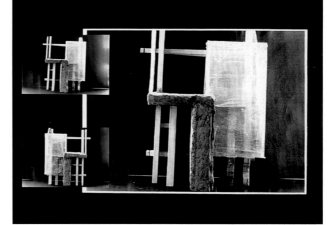

PAGE 64, FROM ABOVE: An example of the use of a 'word', in this case 'defense', within the design process; the use of the 'word' 'defense' as an integral part of the design process. 'The relation of the visual expression to the "word" undergoes changes through a continual movement back and forth. In that way, the "metaphoric twist" between the syntagmatic and systematic plane is something which happens through the use of the word . . .'; FROM ABOVE: Through the transformation of visual materials, generated by the student's first-hand experience of the world (musical instruments, everyday objects, etc), the visual understanding of architectural space is arrived at; student's work illustrating the transformation process, opening up a field of experimentation in the use of different techniques in order to research spatial qualities

ARCHITECTURAL EDUCATION IN THE SLOVAK REPUBLIC

JARMILA BENCOVÁ, MARIÁN ZERVAN, MONIKA MITÁSOVÁ, DANIELA GINDL, DAGMAR PETRÍK, MAROS FINKA AND ROBERT SPACEK

EDUCATION OF BIZARRE

Jarmila Bencová and Marián Zervan

It is possible to find historical documentation about the constitution of cultures and the substances given to its existence by the organisers, as well as naïvists, anarchists, totalisers, kings, jesters and their diverse relations.

Architecture as the microcosm of culture has mirrored this relationship in a different way. From the beginning there coexisted the norm-setters, rationalists, ruralists and dadaists, arrièregardists, eclectics, avant-gardists and futurists. In addition, those who were 'classical' and 'bizarre'. We can find identical structures in the spread of these types. Structure has its poles, axes and centre point. A dynamical diachronic axis is represented by the poles of anarchists and totalisers, arrierregardists and avant-gardists. A stationary synchronic axis is demonstrated by poles of organisers and naïvists, ruralists and dadaists. In the centre is polarity of the king and the jester, the classicist and the bizarrist. It is possible to say, very simply, that poles are manifestations of radicalism and that in the centre is based the dynamical equilibrium.

Architectural education expresses striving after the reflection of whole structure, but most of the time there is a tendency to prefer a synchronic axis. Education obviates radicalisation of styles, movements and orders as well as agreeing with academic essential practices.

Is this an acceptable form of academic radicalism in the education of the architect? Many architects pretend acceptability, but undoubtedly it is one kind of the cultural deformation. How is it possible to reach the diversity of culture and its diverse creators in architectural education? From our point of view it is possible when we dynamise the centre point of the structure, because of the meeting of all external amplitudes, without any deformations. That means a recreation of the cultural model of the king and the jester. This model has faced the inner-relationship and the reversibility of the powerful authority and weakness of 'high' and 'low', earnesty and laughableness.

The king is the embodiment of the dominant princi-ples and recourse of the culture, while the joking jester impersonates the clean but distorting mirror. The wit, joker or jester is also an interpreter, a mediator of radical opinions. Each full-value culture intentionally cultivated this 'king-wit' model. Totalisers have been threatened as laughing was too dangerous for them.

Likewise, anarchists took away the jester's influential position by the dethroning of the king. For norm-setters, the jester is but a mentally non-normal. The free place for a jester is naïvité, but here is lost the original sense of his existence. There is nobody who should be mirrored as the king does not exist.

Are there some indications of operation of this model which can be applied to architecture? It is possible to see them in the grotesqueness of serious buildings like the medieval cathedral, also in anthropomorphisation, likeness, illusionism, miniaturisation or popularisation of the high-style architecture. In the sphere of education, the medieval guild is a good example, where craftsmanship has been handed down without losing the dimension of the comical ceremonial aspect, also the 'Cabinets of Bizarreness' were based right inside the kings' castles. The architectural king has always been on top – architecture and its diverse wit form the term 'bizarre' architecture. Not only because of Charles Jencks' book, but the term 'bizarre' also includes many meanings (flaw, failing, defect, different, peculiar, strange, sinful, ill and lively) and really should be subsumed as radicalism and naivité together with a jester acting.

In the history of architecture we can find periods in which top architecture dominates and, in opposition, epochs with a hypertrophy of bizarre. Education of architects, placed on the synchronic axis, has mostly in its programmes classical 'kingly' forms of architecture, while its bizarre modifications are seen only as eccentric mistakes and anomalies of the concept. The extreme gradation of the obvious is solved over caricaturing, even to the point of being turned upside down.

The task of bizarre interpretation is the notification of temporality and the limits of essential practices without any question of the radicalism, if nothing more.

A NON-ARCHITECTURAL STUDIO AT A SCHOOL OF ARCHITECTURE

Monika Mitásová and Marián Zervan

Current discussions reflect the fact that education of architects should be somewhere between philosophy and craft, between speculation and practical knowledge.

By Vitruvius' experience the knowledge of an architect is born from the *fabrica* and *rationatio*. Since Vitruvius, *fabrica* is seen just as handiness, and theory is seen as something out of the world of the practice. Even if Vitruvius had tried to put the recommendation of erudition in various theoretical and art disciplines, through these two poles he had noticed the fact that parallelism had different historical modifications which were dependent on types of historical cultures and schools. Fundamentally, what has been illustrated by the questions at this seminar remains unchanged.

From the medieval guilds to the Bauhaus there has been a renaissance of the guild-system, declared by Walter Gropius as the existence between the natural unity of the craft, art and theory. Since then a strategy for overcoming indicated duality has been looked at but without any succession, because nobody has thought seriously on the matter: the split of liberal arts and the mechanical dates back to the Middle Ages. It is probably better to talk about the verification of the slow progress of the differentiation process in this case, than about some 'original unity'.

The European educational systems of the Art and Architectural School, based on this estranged coherence, did not realise how to escape the speculations about the relationship between philosophy and craft.

When changes are allowed, they are mostly general. In ancient times, where this polarity of theory and practice originated, we also find the universally accepted interpretation of the word architecture and architect. This interpretation prefers craft without any mention of philosophy, as an architect is seen an *arche tekton*.

Heidegger in his work has showed that before philosophical and architectural systems came into fruition, from the phenomenon of polarity, there was also an understanding of *theory* and *techne*.

Techne from this point of view had not only been the algorithm of steps and manipulations, which resulted in the determination of the artwork or object, but was also the renewal of the poetic dimension. Plato had connected the terms *techne* and *episteme* because both of them expressed the same meaning; a meaning which is close to recognition, revelation, disclosure. Also, Aristotle had differentiated these two terms into the realms of mediation, the truth cognition. By building a house a man disclosed the relationships between place, material and construction and included them within distribution, disposition. By this discovery he had brought it into the realms of the cosmos – truth contained in art creation (design).

The process of discovery has often been more important than its results. Theory was not just a speculation which broke away from practical life, it was an introduction of the primary, the initial thing to human sight.

The word 'theory' originates from the Greek verb *teorein*, which arose from the two radicals *tea* and *orao*. *Tea* means 'the point of view', 'aspect' or 'form', whereas *orao* expresses the process of seeing, the 'way of looking'. *Teorein* therefore means that way of looking in which the true form of an object can be seen – a revelation – the initial Order of the world.

Is it possible to teach this initial sense of the process of building, which is probably the original dimension of architecture? If yes, how should it be carried out? We thought it was possible when we placed architecture over the polarity of philosophy and craft, that means to find out, again, the origin of the dimensions of *techne*.

In the area of 'philosophication' of the craft, results are not only presented, but also the way of asking questions. The connection between asking and craftsmanship highlights the basic, simple relationship of men and objects. What is functional on functions? What is structural on constructions and what is forming on forms and why? Finally, who should supervise this kind of asking studio? Is it the architect?

DILEMMA OF UNIFORMITY AND DIVERSITY IN THE CONTEXT OF PROXIMATE SPACE

Daniela Gindl, Dagmar Petrík and Maros Finka

The concept of Regionalism is usually connected with the physical-geographical boundaries of space. In spite of that, the interpretation of these architectural concepts derives from the system of the used formative elements, genres or types.

When analysing the coherence of their choice we can find out that it is not possible to explain their presence by physical-geographical determination. The multi-stratification of the architectural space inspires us to think of untraditional interpretations of the topics of Globalism and Regionalism or Localism.

In human history there is no more suggestive proof that space is the result of human culture than the result of its brutal and rational 'humanisation' and transformation into a multipartial organism of a city. Nowadays, we feel that Descartes' disexorcism of new space resulted in the technocratic, one-sided optimism which became the force of Western civilisation development. Near-sided rationality leads us to the closed street. The planned control of space is changing to the unplanned defeat of man and devastation of his place

The basic negative aspect of the technocratic purposeful way of space and place organisation is its abstraction and deformed simplification which does not take into account the unique individualism of personality or the collective memory of community. In addition, personal reflection, actual experience and cultural perception of a place and space offer infinite possible ways of organising the living space, as they have a determining and productive influence on the way of their adoption and human transformation.

Based on Ch Norberg Schulz's typology of spaces we should like to show how a different approach towards this topic can cause a shift in the comprehension of architectural space creation. This is consequently reflected in the architectural teaching methods.

The basic approach is an untraditional interpretation of the quality of 'local space'. This quality is a dynamic phenomenon of proximate space. The basis for defining this space can be seen as a man who controls his proximate space by his consciousness with the use of a logical scheme created during his lifetime. Those are his 'backgrounds' for the identification of space organisation or for his activities when organising his space.

As an American of Chinese descent, Yi Fu Tuan in his thoughts, including concentration of the Eastern culture traditions with the view of the modern world man, states that the primitively developed consciousness of space and place during human lifetime is getting broader, enriched and transformed, and after reaching the top it is once again collapsing. Explanation of this process and inspiration for further thoughts we find in the functioning of synergic law of quality, a rise and gradual increasing of organisation of the systems, from chaos through complicated structural systems of organisation to chaos of new quality-determinative chaos.

In the frame of this chaos each of us is the centre of his own world. The space surrounding the man is perceived through the prism of logical schemes. His origin is found in his consciousness on the basis of personal experiences from previous interactions with space or as a product of collective unconsciousness (archetypes in Jungman's comprehension, ideas on space order etc).

Furthermore, the spatial experience is not necessarily caused by direct interaction of a man with space; it can be substituted by cultural experience or through media.

By transferring the place of settlement (not by mechanical mobility of a man in space), the fluent flow of proximate space in the frame of global space is reached. This leads to the dynamic transfer of meanings which are bound to the concept of local space.

Along with this, the flow of proximate space comes to its expansion in the global space (when this part of global space, which was originally a part of proximate space gets outside its boundaries, and the other way round, the other part comes into the proximate space). This is caused by the development of man's mobility and media communication which enables the fluent flow of proximate space in the frame of global space. At the same time, the new confrontation of that part of global space which is included in the proximate space of man with his logical schemes and patterns transforms the contents and the meanings of the place as a local space. When using the logical schemes in the space unstructured by the different meanings, the man perceives space as an organised one, even if its physical structure has not been changed.

In the process of perception there was only a shift from the cognitive space. This space is the individual model of the space transforming the personality and the cultural strata in the consciousness and unconsciousness.

The perceiver is creating, in the frame of global space which is getting into his proximate space, a new cultural stratum. This stratum can connect smoothly with the new continuity of the residual of those parts of the global space, which were in his proximate space in the past. At the same time, it can, in harmony with genius loci in the proximate space of the newly concluded part of the global space, create a new quality.

The man as a carrier of new meanings of the local space is therefore becoming a bridge releasing the existence of quality of 'local space' from its connection with the real physical-geographical boundaries of space.

The activity following, after adopting this position, is the effort of the man to declare, by changing the quality of the physical structure, the appurtenance of the given part of global space into his proximate space, thus controlling it (eg China Town in New York).

It is therefore possible to comprehend the cultural transfer of the meaning 'local space' into the new physical-geographical contexts and their reality as a contribution to the increase of global space diversity. This approach also opens a new point of view of diversity in architectural space, which is important when searching for a counter-balance between those results of global processes leading to the individuality suppression in the role of the creator and in the role of the user of the architectural space, or to the seeming deformation of the place phenomenon.

Our untraditional interpretation of the relationship between global and local (regional) space through the proximate space wants to emphasise the permanent danger of the analytically oriented science, which is enlightening the knowledge in the partial fields and darkening people's living space in its complexity, synergic relationship and intuitive coherence.

Such an approach is symptomatic not only for architectural practice but also, unfortunately, for architectural education. It has impact on the structure and the content of theoretical and practical subjects as well as on the teaching methods of studio work.

The violent enforcement of rationality and one-sided analytical/technocratic approaches can lead to a loss of man's actual multidimensionality, to the suppression of his emotionality, intuition and creative individuality.

VARIETY OF UNITY IN ARCHITECTURAL EDUCATION
Robert Spacek and Marián Zervan

Vitruvius has left us one of the key questions of the architectural education. In general, it is most probably one of the basic questions in the educational process. We could call it a problem of the rate of specialisation and universalisation. Apart from dividing architecture into technical realisation and theory, he has connected with it quite a number of various disciplines, from drawing through mathematics, medicine, astronomy to history, law and philosophy.

Afterwards, he is questioned on whether a man is able to adopt and memorise so many disciplines. In the polemics with Pythos he states that only some people are so gifted, but in spite of that it is inevitable to give all the possible knowledge to the architect, even if only on an average level. The known examples follow: an architect does not have to be a musician like Aristrachos – but music should not be strange to him; he does not have to be a general practitioner like Hippocrates – but he cannot ignore medicine; and he does not have to be a painter like Apelles – but it should not happen that he cannot draw and paint.

Vitruvius, on one side, emphasised that the architect should have been universally educated, but at the same time added that his knowledge would not be equal to the specialists' knowledge. Nowadays, we are fully entitled to ask: in which disciplines does the architect's specialisation consist and in which the other specialists are not able to compete?

With all the cultural-historical changes and modifications Ch Norberg Schulz can still see it at the same level or even more pointed. He also supposes that the profession of an architect must be based on the universal education. It does not mean that he must necessarily know all the current and historical facts which have happened to mankind. In our century, the number of architectural disciplines has undoubtedly been broadened, and it is almost impossible to have a proper survey of them. Even if Ch Norberg Schulz compares with

Vitruvius, he tries to put a certain hierarchic system of education based on the integral theory of architecture, enabling the methodological limitation of the branches and topics of the architectural creation, the types of problems and tasks and the differentiated repertory of the means – the question of specialisation and universalisation has been left open. Along with the obvious effort to provide the unity (specialisation) of education with the basic types of tasks, which are of the synthetic kind during the whole process of education in dimensions of a form, technique and semantics (universalisation), the question of the architectural specialisation has remained unanswered. It is possible to suppose that Ch Norberg Schulz would answer it in a different way to Vitruvius as he follows the idea that the objective of architecture is to solve the cultural and social problems rather than to build houses based on knowledge.

The regulations of the Council of the European Community on the architectural qualification from 1985, or the principles and standards of RIBA, indicated clearly enough the multilaterality of architectural education. It is natural that the solution/realisation of these problems is up to various educational systems, schools etc.

The institutions solve the educational system by traditions and actual orientation. The result is special courses (and essential practices) and universal courses without any deeper relationships between them. Universal courses cannot reach the central point of the architectural expertise.

The problem disclosed by Vitruvius cannot face the inner participation of universality in specialisation. Vitruvius' question should be deconstructed. Deeply inside of the cultural consciousness is the image of the architect composed of the images of craftsman, scientist, physician etc. Each of them is the owner of 'magical' and 'ritual' practices; thanks to them they are unlimited and incomparable. This universality is the threat of losing character of profession. An architect is like a philosopher: 'he knows all but nothing'.

The change of the cultural and social sense of architecture is the last consequence of our reformulated question. The obedient servant of the social and economical demands turns unnoticeable to the indicator of events accepting all responsibility, so that professional limit could become an advantage, which is comparable to the one guaranteed by the specialisation of the profession. In both cases, one-sidedness continues.

The authors are currently at the Department of Human Studies and Theory of Architecture, Faculty of Architecture, at the Slovak Technical University.

CAN WE DESCRIBE HOW WE DESIGN?

MICHAEL BRAWNE

I shall try to be precise, though it is frequently hard to do that. I want to start from two very simple assumptions. The first is totally obvious: that most of our environment is designed. The second assumption is that this activity of designing is particularly important in schools of architecture not just because architecture has to do with design but because in teaching we actually believe it to be important. Go to any school of architecture and discover how the marks are distributed. You will find that in ninety per cent of the cases more than half the marks go towards design. Now if that is so, there is another underlining assumption behind that which was mentioned yesterday, and that is that architecture and particularly architectural design is actually capable of being taught. We are not talking about people's inborn ability, that it is all in their genes. No! we assume that something can be undertaken to bring out what is in them, that we have to go through some kind of a process and that they turn out to be better designers, more competent designers, perhaps more imaginative designers, at the end of their education than they are at the beginning. If we do not believe in that then it is unlikely we were actually here or that we are taking whatever we are being paid honestly.

It is therefore interesting to me to discover whether we can describe or find some kind of an explanation, some kind of a theory, a theory in the sense of it being explanatory, a theory of explaining a series of relationships, which can apply to the design process (at least not necessarily design itself but the design process because that is probably what we try and teach in schools of architecture). I think there have been a number of attempts to do so or at least to find generalities which begin to say something about how you might approach the idea of designing. A number of theories exist and you could argue that they are competing theories, and at least in that sense that they do not explain the totality of the process adequately.

The idea of typology seems to me a possible way of thinking about design, a way of classifying. There is a type, a kind of ideal that makes me recognise theatres from other building types. But it is a rather flawed idea

because there is a great deal of building which is very hard to classify, so maybe the idea of type is not quite as clear as one might suspect. There are also many buildings which were originally designed for one purpose, and now without much change serve quite another.

When I was being taught at the Architectural Association in the late 1940s and the early 1950s, it was assumed that what you needed to do was not to look for types but to look at the brief. As John Summerson in his description of the roots of architecture explained, it was grounded in a social definition of what was needed, which was the brief. Behind it was the assumption that the task could be analysed in sufficient detail and described verbally and numerically. And this, of course, is based on the whole idea of determinism and of course behaviourism. I am glad to say that supposition has died some years ago.

There are naturally alternative ways of looking at the question; ways which do not seem to stem from outside architecture like typology or the brief devised by a client but from within architecture. For example, the opposite of the idea of a brief would be Mies van der Rohe's notion of universal space, that one could build space which was allegedly anonymous. The view that all sorts of activities could take place in such a space is again somewhat discredited.

The Kahnian differentiation between served and servant spaces is a variant which proposes two categories of space. When the number is increased further we come close to Christopher Alexander's *Atoms of the Environment*. Interestingly enough, nobody, including Christopher Alexander, has yet been able to design on the basis of the pattern language. Alexander, himself, acknowledges this.

So are there some other facts? Let me digress for a moment and suggest to you that there is one which I personally find extremely attractive, and once again it goes outside the realms of architecture to the philosophy of science and the work of Sir Karl Popper. Because he deals with science it does not necessarily mean that it is not applicable to architecture. Though I would in no way, and this is extremely important and very easy to misunderstand, suggest or claim that architecture is a science. Popper has a line of demarcation between science and non-science and it is in no way the case that only those statements that are in science are either worthwhile or true. Those in non-science are just as true. The only significant difference is that science is always potentially falsifiable, not true but potentially falsifiable. Now architecture is not potentially falsifiable so I believe. Popper suggests that the way in which scientists attack problems starts with something that enables a problem, P_1, to be recognised for a variety of reasons, including the failure of the current answer to deal with the observed phenomena. I believe that in architecture we start with a very similar kind of assumption of what constitutes a problem except that it is posed as much by ourselves as by external circumstances. Given this problem recognition we then go to a hypothesis or a tentative solution which then goes through a process of error elimination and ends up not as a solution but as P_2, as the problem for subsequent action. By that I mean two things, that P_1 to P_2 can be seen as a short-term sequence which is actually happening as you are dealing with the design problem and you continually iterate that from P_1 to P_2 from P_2 to P_3 and so on. (Always going through this sequence.) But it is also a long-term sequence in the sense that the building stock which has been created as P_2 has been designed after P_1 and hence influenced our whole perception of what P_1 will be the next time around. We cannot purge our minds of all the existing buildings in the world, in our immediate surroundings, yet they influence our perception of P_1. Now it seems to me that a number of things follow from that. If it does describe the design process then educationally a number of points in it become important.

Students need to come to terms with their own recognition of what the problem is as well as understand that at any particular time there is a perception of what the important problems are. The definition of P_1 is extremely related to time. We then need to help them to come to a hypothesis, the TS process. Most significantly of all, perhaps, we must go through with them to ease the error elimination process and to recognise that P_2 is only a temporary solution and that the iterated process continues. Perhaps it also has an implication on the way in which we look at architectural history. If P_1 is always related to time T and so is P_2 then perhaps the whole of history is a series of such hypotheses and not some kind of Darwinian rising curve of evolutionary progress; the Parthenon on the Acropolis cannot be said to be better or less good than let us say Ronchamp, also an ecclesiastic building on a hill, just because there is a time difference. Most important of all

is the attitude to model selection within a school. I would go back to my own time as a student; members of staff officially said you must not look at magazines because you will cloud your vision, your personal imagination, presumably, by seeing these other examples.

If you assume that the P_1, TS, EE, P_2 sequence has any relationship to fact and that architectural design actually happens this way, then of course you need an extremely large vocabulary and an extremely wide understanding of what other people have done in order to recognise both P_1 and TS.

Finally, Isi Metzstein was somewhat understandably critical of schools of architecture being in universities. I think what he also felt was that schools of architecture were aping or trying to be like other departments in universities. I would almost argue the very opposite notion, that what we should be saying and what is true is that we in architecture have a method, a process, which is not only applicable to architecture but also elsewhere. Because what design does is to forecast an event on the basis of past experience. And that is true of many other fields of endeavour, for many intellectual processes and all kinds of creation.

Juries, critiques and reviews have a great deal to teach other subjects, as to how to follow the teaching and learning process.

Michael Brawne taught at the University of Cambridge and was then Professor of Architecture at the University of Bath until 1990. He has practised independently since 1963 designing museums, libraries and university buildings.

Project for office building for Friedrichstrasse by Mies van der Rohe, Berlin, 1921. A glass envelope designed before the technology of controlling the internal environment was fully developed, which through its powerful imagery became a much-copied model

GLOBALISM V REGIONALISM: THE *OTHER* TAJ MAHAL

ANDREW BALLANTYNE

The 'versus' which separates Globalism and Regionalism in the title acts as a wedge driven between the terms to set them in opposition to one another. In fact, in buildings there is not always an opposition between the terms 'global' and 'regional', as for example in the culture of the travel agency, which generates and distributes images of instantly recognisable buildings from around the world, and uses them as icons: the Taj Mahal, the Empire State Building, the Forbidden City, Sydney Opera House, the Pyramids, the Parthenon. All of these are used to stand for regional identity in a global culture. They have a presence in global awareness, but they signify difference, otherness, the glamour of the alien. If they were not in some way radically different from what could be had at home, then there would be no point in travelling to visit them; so these buildings particularly represent the regional in a global culture.

The following text illustrates the point. It enacts a conversation between two individuals who belong to a global culture, turning their minds to consider the regional. Their voices alternate:

A: I went round the world you know . . .

B: (*hurriedly*) Yes, yes, I know. How was it?

A: The world?

B: Yes.

A: Oh, highly enjoyable.

B: China must be very interesting.

A: Very big, China.

B: And Japan . . .

A: Very small.

B: Did you eat shark's fins, and take your shoes off, and use chopsticks and everything?

A: Practically everything.

B: And India, the burning Ghars, or Ghats, or whatever they are, and the Taj Mahal. How was the Taj Mahal?

A: Unbelievable, a sort of dream.

B: That was the moonlight I expect, you must have seen it in the moonlight.

A: Yes, moonlight can be cruelly deceptive.

B: And it did not look like a biscuit box, did it? I have always felt that it might.

OPPOSITE: The Parthenon and the Acropolis standing for regional identity in a global culture; FROM ABOVE: The beauty and exoticism of the Taj Mahal. Agra, India, 1631-48; Sydney Opera House on completion c1973

That, of course, is from Act I of Noël Coward's *Private Lives*.[1] It shows an extreme globalist view: regions indicated by a few brief clichés. Japan is synecdochically reduced to shark's fin soup, India to the Taj Mahal.

An example of the converse, of tokens of global culture being assimilated in a local context, would be the air-conditioned office spaces in which multinational companies work. The globalist image might be expressive of a matter of fact (that the company operating from the building actually does operate internationally) or it might be expressive of aspiration (that the company would like it to be thought that it operates internationally). There is a fast-food restaurant in Istanbul, where the presentation of the food, but actually not the food itself, is closely modelled on, or 'inspired by', McDonald's. In doing this the proprietors are showing that they have a further horizon than that of the immediate region, even if they have only a single restaurant to manage.

Now these are examples of the global and the regional fusing together in a single building, not working to produce different kinds of buildings, in some sense opposed to one another; but being combined. There are regional ideas of global architecture and globalist ideas of regional architecture: the relationship is one, not of versus, but of *vice versa*. The issue here is emphatically *not* architecture as built, but rather the culture in which architecture is assimilated: which is to say architecture as 'built form assimilated in the imagination'.

Taking the Taj Mahal as an example, we can see that when it is seen in a global culture it is consumed as an image of spectacular beauty and exoticism, as an object which completely escapes the dictates of 'common sense' as *we* know it. It makes an image of such instant recognisability and clarity that it reminds us (or at least it reminded Noël Coward) of the images which decorate biscuit boxes. In that frame of reference it is easily assimilated, and it belongs in association with the Pyramids, the Empire State Building and the others listed above. On the other hand, by contrast, in its regional culture, although it would remain apart from the commonplace, it would be a construct in a different reality. It would be understood as an extraordinary impressive funeral monument, expressive not in the least of exoticism but, on the contrary, of a well established cultural tradition, specifically Islamic tradition, and it would be seen as splendidly, and *naturally*, expressive of religious awe and devotion. In this frame of reference it would belong with a long tradition of mosques and funeral monuments.

Now the dialogue given above, or the example of the pseudo-McDonald's, shows very clearly that an aspiration to a global culture is an *aspiration* to be part of an elite, in fact to subscribe to the values of the developed world. That is inevitable, because the elites of the developed world are the only people who really have the mobility to shape a global culture, and they would not choose to operate in 'third world' conditions. Which is to say, that 'globalism' in this sense is no more than a polite and relatively innocuous name for cultural imperialism. And this problematises the relationship of *vice versa* mentioned above, because the reciprocity is unequal. In isolation, the ideas might be able to move in either direction, but once they are considered in connection with their power relations we can see that the view of a global elite will have more prestige than a local view and will be seen as a more important kind of view, which is to say that in practice it will become more true.

If we suspect that this is not how things should be then we might react by taking up the cause of 'Regionalism'. In fact this is what makes 'Regionalism' happen: there simply is no need to assert a regional identity until *after* that identity has been threatened. The assertion of *difference* is made only after the idea of being subsumed into *the same* has taken a hold. So we do not really escape the influence of cultural imperialism, because 'Regionalism' actually develops out of cultural imperialism and is just an inversion of it: a redescription from the point of view of the oppressed. In fact it does not free us, just makes us feel embattled. This is a genuinely regionalist stance (with the stress on the *ist* in 'regionalist') a view which is quite distinct from the unselfconscious local view.

In the case of Coward's jaded tourist, these very assertions of *difference*, represented by the Taj Mahal, the exotic customs and so on, are completely subsumed into the *same*, so that the different cultures being represented as exotically 'other' actually become completely equivalent and interchangeable 'attractions' (as the Walt Disney Organisation would call them).

We like to think of ourselves as serious people who visit foreign parts as travellers rather than as tourists, and of course we would deplore the facile 'biscuit box'

Cultures can now be far more spatially fragmented than they could in the past, and we can all call to mind isolated buildings in various cities around the globe which belong to an elite global culture, whether they are iconic clichés like the Taj Mahal or they belong to a current active global avant-garde. There will also be a local view of all these buildings, about which we usually hear nothing. In some cases this is understandable, appreciation of the Taj Mahal, which assimilates the building into our own culture without really changing what we know. We would certainly insist that it would be better to try to understand and appreciate the building from a more local perspective, to try to recognise the 'otherness' of the culture which is bound up with it and to see the way the building fits into that culture.

At first, this sounds to be uncomplicatedly a good idea, but in fact it is not without its problems. We can see that, with all the best intentions, a collusion could develop between the locals and visitors, both groups resisting change to the local identity and tradition. The locals could be trapped into their quaint rustic way, as does happen in places where these two cultures meet; for example, where the holiday farmhouse-owning classes meet the surviving vestiges of peasant culture in Provence and Tuscany. In such circumstances a regionalist stance can begin to look deeply reactionary.

A process of reinterpretation is very clearly in operation when we consider foreign cultures, which we feel we ought to make and effort to understand. But it can happen closer to home. For example, there is a house on the outskirts of Wigan, UK, which was built around 1968 and clearly evokes the form of the Villa Savoye, but with enough creative obliquity to save it from being a copy: a white flattish cuboid form poised a storey above the ground. To anyone conventionally versed in the history of twentieth-century architecture it would seem to be clearly and straightforwardly a respectable building and would be recognised without any hesitation as a house designed by an architect. But it happens that there is a bus stop outside the house, and the architect was mortified to learn that people who wanted to alight from the bus there would ask for the 'crematorium' stop. This was not a problem: it is not particularly worrying if an individual house does not conform to mainstream tastes, so long as one's friends are not frightened away by it; but in a building with a more public role, such a mismatch could be much more worrying.

The building here would be understood and valued very differently by those two cultures: the culture of the person on the Wigan omnibus and the culture of the architect and client. The architect's culture here was international, the omnibus culture regional. The built form and its location remain the same, but the building as experienced, as phenomenon, is radically altered. Each culture creates its own reality, even if most people believe that they simply and directly perceive the self-evident truth. From the point of view of the consideration of Globalism and Regionalism the point worth stressing in this particular case is that we *really would be short-changed* if we were offered the local view as the

only view that mattered. We should not jump to this because the view may well be of no more than local interest; but in others the local view may make the global view seem shallow and insensitive.

A unified global culture can give a bearing on the appreciation of buildings in widely separated locations; conversely, different cultures can have a bearing on the appreciation of a building in a single place. Where built form is concerned, there simply is not a clear-cut relationship of opposition between the global and the regional, not in the sense of it *being* either one thing or the other. Even buildings which have a strongly regional character can be assimilated into global culture. Such buildings are both global and regional *at the same time*. To suggest that the Globalism or the Regionalism is in any straightforward way in the architecture is a mistake. The Globalism and the Regionalism are ways of understanding, and both have their uses, both can be damaging. Which way of understanding we make use of will depend both on our frame of reference, our own culture and crucially on what we are trying to do. The building's fabric is only ever a part of the story: to take hold of it with the ideas of another culture is to create another architecture.

Notes

1 Noël Coward, *Plays: Two*, Methuen, London, 1979. Dialogue from Act I, between Elyot (A) and Amanda (B), written in 1929.

Andrew Ballantyne is a lecturer in Architectural History and Theory at the University of Newcastle upon Tyne. He has taken a particular interest in the cognitive aspects of buildings and is a regular contributor to The Times Literary Supplement.

THE ARCHITECTURAL ASSOCIATION

ALAN BALFOUR

The Architectural Association was founded almost 150 years ago to radically reform the education of the architect. It was created to be wholly independent and private, free from the influence of government, and would have as its central concern the imagination of individuals. Underlying this concern was the realisation within progressive society for the preparation of individuals whose imagination belonged as much – if not more – to themselves than to the State. These concepts still form the character of the present school's programmes, where the most important task is the *cultivation within the individual imagination of what might be called landscapes of desire: visions of the future grounded in a clear strong sense of architecture as a noble embodiment of liberty, coupled with the competence and the will to build.* The AA has had since its foundation a direct relationship to changes in the culture; over the past 40 years that influence has been worldwide, for the School was at the architectural centre of the liberal revolution that swept through Europe in the 1960s. Warren Chalk, Dennis Crompton, David Greene, with their colleagues Cook and Herron, made the AA the focus of all the enthusiasms of Archigram. Equally influential, politically and professionally, were graduates of the previous generation – Michael Hopkins, Richard Rogers, Nicholas Grimshaw. In the aftermath of the worker/student revolt of 1968 Paris, many young architects throughout Europe and beyond were in search of a setting, a school in which all the promise of a radicalised reality could be developed and implemented. Thus, Tschumi, Koolhaas, Boyarsky and, later, Krier and Libeskind as well as many others, were drawn to the AA as the only institution capable of giving form to provocative dreams and post-revolutionary frustrations. The School has maintained this reflective and receptive relation to the ambitions of those who seek progressive change.

The AA's three major divisions – the Intermediate School, the Diploma School and the Graduate School – maintain in all aspects the radical liberal agenda established at its foundation. Apart from providing a broad grounding in history, theory and technology, the school has no set curriculum. Each student must make the critical choice of a design unit, within which he or she is free to shape an individual programme of study from the extensive offerings of lectures and seminars. Also, just as in the beginning, the School maintains no permanent academic staff – all teaching appointments are renewed annually, allowing for the continual readjustment and redirection of the programme's relationship to architecture. Academic staff are chosen not only for their commitment to progressive thought, but also to represent a broad range of concerns in architecture. The design units, although widely different in content, are linked at all levels by a common concern for individualism. Subjective originality and an empathy for the full performance of architecture, physically and poetically, shape their programmes. The culture of the School as a whole is characterised by its distance from prevailing issues of style, reflecting the wish to continually re-originate architecture.

Schools of architecture evolved in essence to ensure that the dominant authority – Church, King or State – was provided with agents capable of constructing buildings with form and content appropriate to their public responsibilities and aggrandisement. This has remained consistently true from the first establishment of formal schools in the 18th century, cultivated to represent the splendour and public performance of the French court, to those now instructed to be inventive around the more modest needs of Holland's social democracy or California's objects of ethical consumption.

The historical significance of London's Architectural Association is that its creation was explicitly in reaction to a system of education controlled by the state and by the establishment. In his book titled *The New Leaf Discourses* out of which the idea for the new school developed, Robert Kerr, co-founder and first President of the AA wrote in 1847:

Greek and Gothic – two giant powers divide a world itching for war. Between these two stools architecture may happily tumble to the ground. Then perhaps architects will at last determine to think for themselves.

The present uncertainties in evolving a form of architecture are but a distant echo of a 19th-century condition when the elite struggled to come to terms with the expanding dreams of liberalism, the enfranchisement of the masses. Much more than is realised today, these two opposing realities were invested with confused moral and political significance. Greek forms represented the rational and the democratic; Gothic, free wills united by common belief. Kerr reflecting on the state of architecture in mid-century Britain wrote:

> we have the greatest skill ever attained, we have the greatest demands ever made, we have the greatest command of materials ever had, and so might we not hope for great things?

Moulded by Scottish education and influenced by a brief stay in the United States, Kerr saw the need for a type of school that would respond to the uncertain demands of liberal democracy. The only two paths then available for the study of architecture were the Government School of Design and the apprenticeship system, which involved becoming an article pupil of a practitioner. In both, the student architect was absorbed, without question, into the architectural values of the establishment. Kerr, in reaction, created an organisation which aimed at promoting a free association of young architects coming together to learn. They engaged in critical discussion of their own work, inviting the participation of practitioners who interested them, and these exchanges allowed their idea of architecture to be renewed and diversified through a continual reappraisal of the conventions of then current practice. It was not conceived of as a school in the conventional sense, but as a community whose members, both students and practitioners, were committed to a continual readjustment of the project of architecture in response to changing needs in society. There would be no tenured teachers and no external authority.

Underlying this arrangement was the radical, political realisation that the imagination of the architect belonged as much, if not more, to the individual and his or her own experience than to any external authority he or she was obliged to serve. In Kerr's words: 'No manner of instruction is complete until the pupil becomes a self-teaching student, studies, thinks and reasons for himself.' The Architectural Association has maintained this agenda to the present day.

Unlike the AA, other schools of architecture throughout the world are agents of the state and in most countries the few that are private are nevertheless obliged to control their programmes under the guidance of the profession.

The emergence of a European economic union is coupled, in paradox, by aggressive assertions of nationalism. Consider for example what is already underway in those nations lately released from the grip of Russia – Hungary, Poland, Romania – where architecture is seen as the most potent means of restoring and representing the national identity. Students are being encouraged to resurrect ancient mysteries, that is, to imagine objects that may unwittingly reinforce racial and tribal differences. In spite of good intention, the monsters may return. This compulsion to construct future realities based on national identity is not only the product of conservative politics. The exuberant new architecture of Barcelona, the rationalism of Berne, the emotionalism of Graz, are all discussed much more in terms of regional character and desire than as the unbroken evolution of international modernism. *Critical Regionalism seemed at first a benign proposition but is now proving to have a sinister subtext.*

It has nothing to do with taste or of achieving social stability through the application of authority structures drawn from architectures past. Such forms may bring with them all the wrath of unresolved injustices, and the failure to find an authentic reinforcing architecture of the myriad nuances of emerging liberal order could prove catastrophic. Architecture must hold its place in this maelstrom of mediated reality that will increasingly try to dislocate the future. It cannot all be left to television, and to construct the present only from the past is to condone the death of the future.

Alan Balfour DA (Edin) MFA (Princeton) RIBA, is Chairman of the AA School of Architecture, London

GLOBALISM AND THE REGIONAL RESPONSE

EDUCATIONAL FOUNDATIONS

CHRIS ABEL

Methods of learning and teaching aimed at the production of a modern regional architecture for developing countries is an area of importance, where the problems generated by the importation of universal forms of architecture from the West are particularly acute. I shall attempt to explain more clearly what I mean by modern regionalism. But for the time being I shall assume that 'regional architecture' refers to forms of building which enhance the sense of place and cultural identity particular to a given area of human habitation.

BAUHAUS LEGACY

The importance of beginning design education in encouraging or discouraging student attitudes conducive to the appreciation of regional architecture cannot be exaggerated. In this respect, the Bauhaus has a lot to answer for in propagating, through the educational model set by Johannes Itten's Basic Course,[1] supposedly universal methods of teaching which make it difficult if not impossible for students to produce architecture which is sensitive to any kind of regional context. It is worth contemplating why this should be so, since, though many schools in the West have long since rejected the model of the Basic Course, it still dominates beginning design education in schools of architecture throughout the Third World, as I have found in countries as far apart as Malaysia, Saudi Arabia and Chile.

It should be acknowledged that Itten's teaching methods would not have been as influential as they have been if they did not possess some merit. The concept of 'learning by doing', in which passive learning – sitting at the desk listening to teacher – is replaced by activity or project based learning involving the full participation of the student, was inspired by progressive education theory at primary level,[2] and has since passed into all levels of education. Few teachers would quarrel with such an approach as one of the essential methodological building blocks of a liberal education.

But if 'learning by doing' is sound in principle, it must also be asked, 'doing what?' The now familiar exercises that Itten devised for the Basic Course were based on both his experiences as a school teacher and on his colour theories as an abstract painter, which emphasised the immutable 'essence' of primary colours and forms, best appreciated by first clearing the mind of all cultural preconceptions.[3] Itten also strongly believed that, in a materialistic world, it was the inner, spiritual life of the student that required most development. The emphasis in the exercises was accordingly on the manipulation of abstract form, shape and colour, with self-exploration and self-expression of the student being the main aim. Even the experience of different materials was mostly confined to their assemblage in abstract compositions. At no time was there any attempt to relate exercises in the Basic Course to any worldly purpose or activity.

Itten's exclusively inward-looking orientation, with its strongly mystical aspects, soon clashed with Walter Gropius' outward-looking aims of teaching students to master the new tools of production and to work directly with industry.[4] Itten was eventually ousted from his position at the Bauhaus, but in retrospect, it can be seen that it was his approach which has had the most influence on the course of architecture since. By contrast, Gropius promised a 'new kind of collaborator for industry and the crafts, who has an equal command of both technology and form',[5] only now finally emerging in the wake of Foster, Rogers and Piano. More commonly, orthodox modernists and post-modernists alike have been preoccupied with form, whether pure or impure, leaving technology to the engineers and industries who design and make the parts of the buildings they conceive.[6]

I do not pretend to judge the merits of Itten's approach as a foundation for art education, but I do emphatically protest the idea that such an education provides, or ever could provide, a sound foundation for learning to be an architect. Students cannot be expected to make the leap from such highly abstract and introverted exercises to dealing with the real world problems of architecture, which must necessarily involve considerations of social function, structure, climate control and site; in short, all those things which go to make architecture what it is as a culture-form, and which are deliberately excluded from the Basic Course.

This applies as much to Western as to non-Western students. The inevitable result of teaching architecture in this fashion was that students disregarded or downgraded all those qualities of architecture which relate a building to a particular place and culture; everything, in fact, to do with regional architecture. Peter Collins summed up the problem very well:

> the danger to architectural design of laying too much emphasis on abstract painting and sculpture as formative disciplines is that they lead to the idea of a building as simply an object in space, instead of as part of a space. They thus accentuate the evil . . . of considering architecture as something isolated from its environment, and from other buildings amongst which it must find its place.[7]

LEARNING BY EXAMPLE

For reasons such as these, we find ourselves today searching for ways to repair the damage. If 'learning by doing' is to be an effective method of teaching architecture that responds to place, culture and climate, then the 'doing' has to involve exercises which get students to grips with all those issues and problems which define regional architecture for what it is.

My own preferred approach is to locate the centre of learning in selected exemplars, devising exercises to enable students to assimilate their full value as learning models. I do not believe that architecture can be effectively taught by verbal explanation or by abstract principle or theory alone, though these are undoubtedly essential to a full and balanced education. In short, architecture is best learnt by example. If we want students to produce a regional architecture, or at least to avoid producing certain kinds of buildings that disregard regional context, then we need to connect them up with suitable models in an appropriate educational framework.

It needs to be stressed that learning by example is not only the best and most effective way to learn architecture, it is arguably the only effective way to learn any complex body of knowledge. This is the case even in the so-called 'rational' sciences, where the exemplary function of key scientific experiments, embodying specific models, techniques and criteria for the evaluation of results, is now recognised to play a crucial role in the formation and evolution of scientific paradigms and in the shared traditions that go to make up 'normal science'.[8] The reason is that a large part of learning involves tacit as well as conscious processes of cognition. The educational theorist PH Hirst explains:

All knowledge involves the use of symbols and the making of judgments in ways that cannot be expressed in words and can only be learnt in a tradition. The art of scientific investigation and the development of experimental tests, the forming of historical explanation and the assessment of its truth, the appreciation of a poem; all of these activities are high arts that are not in themselves communicable simply by words. Acquiring knowledge of any form is therefore to a greater or lesser extent something that cannot be done simply by solitary study of the symbolic expressions of knowledge, it must be learnt from a master on the job.[9]

TACIT KNOWING

The scientist and philosopher Michael Polanyi went even further in stressing the importance of what he called 'tacit knowing' in acquiring any complex form of knowledge or skill.[10] Polanyi cites the now familiar technique police use in helping a witness to identify a suspect from memory. Asked to specify from memory alone all those unique features which make up a human face, most of us would not be able to describe such features in any degree of accuracy or detail. But given a collection of noses, foreheads, jaws etc, to pick from and assemble, the witness can usually put together a fairly accurate portrait.

The example, Polanyi claims, demonstrates a fundamental principle of human knowledge: 'we know more than we can tell'.[11] Polanyi also stresses the importance of 'indwelling', or empathy, in the process of tacit knowing. In learning a language, for example, we do not acquire all the 'rules of the game' by having them explained to us as explicit rules of grammar. We learn to speak a language, as language teachers know well, by process of total immersion, or 'entering into' the given language, at best in the country of origin. In so doing, we empathise, as it were, with the native language speakers and their way of life.

In the same way, the complex forms of knowledge and skills involved in architectural design cannot be learnt by explicit means alone.[12] We teach separate classes in history, design theory, site planning, construction, environmental control and so on, because that is the only way specialist teachers know how to handle these subjects. Yet all of these factors have to be brought together somehow in the design process. That, of course, is where the project studio plays its part and where the student is supposed to synthesise all of his specialist teachers' different kinds of expertise. But how to teach the most important form of knowledge and skill of all, which is the synthesis itself? Here the exemplary work comes in. Only by intensive study of relevant models, or by following the example set, as Hirst put it, by a 'master on the job', can students hope to produce an integrated and convincing whole out of all the fragmented bits and pieces of knowledge acquired in different subject areas. Neither – to anticipate one possible objection – does the use of exemplars compromise the process of creativity. As Arthur Koestler and others[13] have taught us, creativity comes about not from starting with any blank sheet, as Itten and his followers assumed, but from making new connections between previously known but hitherto unrelated ideas. Far from being any hindrance, familiarity with known models is an essential springboard for creativity in architecture.[14]

HYBRIDISATION

If, therefore, learning by example is as important as I suppose it to be, then the choice of exemplars becomes absolutely crucial in directing students towards any specific educational or architectural goals, in this case a modern regional architecture.

True to my preferred method, I shall attempt to clarify what I mean by a modern regional architecture by reference to exemplary works, based on a liberal interpretation of Regionalism grounded in the realities of global cross-cultural exchange. It is not just that worldwide cultural exchange is an unavoidable fact of late twentieth-century life – it was always a vital fact of life. Whether by peaceful commerce, the spread of major religions, the migration of peoples, or by conquest and colonial domination, there has always been a constant global exchange of ideas and culture-forms throughout recorded history, affecting architecture as much as anything else.[15]

The built results of this massive and continual trade in culture varies greatly in terms of what was changed in the process of exchange and what was not. It frequently involved the wholesale export and import of building types and styles with little change, especially in the case of colonialism. That much might be expected. After all, a major purpose of colonial architecture was to recreate the home environment of colonists as far as was possible. What is more important to our concerns is that imported architecture of this kind, even in situations of apparent clear domination of one culture by another, also often undergoes significant changes in the process of being adapted to the new location, and, especially the new climate, taking on some essential features of the local architecture along the way (Fig. 1).[16]

Similar processes of hybridisation characterise modern Regionalism, some of the best of which is designed by knowledgeable and empathetic foreign architects. Among notable exemplars, the Ministry of Foreign Aff-

airs in Riyadh (Fig. 2) by Henning Larsen is shaped not only by the desert fortresses and inward-looking courtyard houses of the central Arabian peninsula in which it stands, but also by the more distant Taj Mahal in India, which inspired the plan form.[17] The Aga Khan University Hospital in Karachi (Fig. 3) by Payette Associates also draws on Pan-Islamic models and features a low level, asymmetrical space planning concept of linked courtyard buildings, akin to the palaces at Alhambra in Spain and Fatehpur Sikri in India. Here they serve similar purposes of climate control and provide tranquil open spaces for patients and visitors.[18] Moving to a very different region – and local designers – the master plan of Thammasat University near Bangkok by Sumet Jumsai is based on the temple city of Angkor Thom, in what is now Cambodia. Like the architect's model, the plan is organised around monumental axes, as well as a complex matrix of canals and storage lakes which siphon off the rain storms and ornament the buildings and site. Also clearly in evidence is the model of the traditional Thai house-on-stilts, similar to those in Malaysia and other parts of the Asian-Pacific region.[19] Much of the communal life of the University takes place, in traditional fashion, in the open air in the shaded spaces provided beneath the main structure. Even the international tower type is not immune to suitable treatment. Both in his Menara Mesiniaga office building in Kuala Lumpur (Fig. 4) and in his more recent MBf Tower in Penang, Ken Yeang has demonstrated that, given the right approach, the most standardised of building types may be successfully adapted to local cultural and climatic conditions.[20]

In all of these cases, whether the borrowed type or form is drawn from within a related cultural sphere, as in the wider Islamic world, or from various parts of southeast Asia, or from further afield in the West, what is clear is that the imported idea has been *localised* in some significant way to suit the new place and purpose. It is this kind of transformation of imported models and types which lies at the heart of a viable modern Regionalism, rather than any pursuit of myths of cultural purity.[21]

Cross-cultural exchange on a global scale then, yes, but with a local purpose. In this respect I should like to differentiate my position on globalisation from those who, following Kisho Kurokawa, propagate a Post-Modern, 'intercultural architecture',[22] based on an arbitrary collection of forms and ideas borrowed from anywhere in the world. To my mind, this can only devalue the meaning of any cultural exchange and leads, like most Post-Modern architecture, to nothing more than a mixed bag of superficial forms with no special relevance to time, place or purpose. The authentic works of our time, by contrast, are distinguished as the reciprocal product of local as well as global imperatives and are uniquely suited to their specific situation.[23]

NEW BEGINNINGS

But how to encourage students in developing countries, faced with the in-roads of a global and ruthless consumer culture, to produce architecture of this kind and quality? My own approach to teaching architectural design, especially in beginning design education, is that of a shameless propagandist for regional architecture of the sort I have been describing. The student projects that follow are therefore based on a clear set of values, rooted in the belief that an authentic modern Regionalism has of necessity to confront the lessons of the past with the realities of the present and may, at its best, draw on both local and global cultures.

My first group of projects is taken from the first year design studio at the Department of Architecture and Planning at King Saud University in Riyadh, where I taught from 1982 to 1985. The aims and contents of the course were conceived as an alternative to what students were getting at that time as a beginning design or foundation education, which was effectively a version of Itten's Basic Course, introduced some years previously, as is usually the case, by returning graduates educated in the West. The new course was divided into two distinctive parts, corresponding to one semester each. The first part was called 'Principles of Islamic Ornamental Design', and the second, 'Principles of Regional Architecture'.

Ornamental design is an integral feature of Islamic architecture,[24] and, though the principles of design involved are abstract, there are fundamental differences with the abstract qualities of Western Modern art. Where, for example, the compositions of Western artists are limited mostly to finite arrangements on a canvas or other restricted surface, Islamic ornamental designs have evolved out of the need to decorate a continuous building surface, their effects arising out of infinite repetition of the same basic pattern. Although students therefore begin by studying two-dimensional forms of design, the connection with architectural design is still retained in a direct and concrete way that is not achieved in the learning of purely abstract forms and compositions as espoused by Itten and his followers.

Historically, the abstract, geometrical nature of the motifs and patterns is due to the Muslim belief that the reproduction of human and animal forms would be an offence to the 'original Creator'. All patterns are based on segmenting the circle – a cosmic symbol of unity in the control of architectural form throughout the Islamic

FROM ABOVE FIGURES 1 & 2: Colonial-era villa in Penang, Malaysia, features a hybrid mix of European and local architectures; Ministry of Foreign Affairs, Riyadh, by Henning Larsen

world. These restrictions did not, however, limit the creativity of Moslem artists but rather stimulated the creation of highly complex, abstract forms of decoration of three main motifs: geometric; interlaced geometric; and plant and floral. Similarly, the sense of infinite continuity which has also been mentioned points to a fundamental religious inspiration and is expressive of the Muslim belief in the 'oneness of God'. In the same way, optical effects are carefully manipulated to produce an illusion of transparency or a dematerialisation of the wall surface and are intended to emphasise the primacy of the spiritual over the material world.[25]

Three general principles of design underly the most common forms of ornament and together help to create the desired visual effects: repetition, symmetry and reciprocity or reflection (positive and negative mirror images).[26] Based on these principles of design, students were given a series of seven projects of one to four weeks duration carefully structured to lead the beginning student from basic geometrical configurations through increasingly complex patterns, to the point where the student was able to create his own ornamental designs for a specific architectural space. In all of these exercises, the entire pattern is constructed in the traditional manner with only a compass and short straight edge in order that students fully appreciate the underlying geometric order based on the circle.

There was one particular moment during these exercises which confirmed our faith in our new approach. In the more advanced exercises, students were asked to construct complex patterns based on the double hexagon and then to create their own colour interpretation, groups of three or four students working on the same basic geometrical pattern. At the end of the exercise the studio walls were covered with these sets of different colour interpretations of more than a dozen geometrical designs. Placed side-by-side, the variety of interpretations quite astonished us all, students and teachers alike, such that in some cases it was difficult to believe that some students' work was really based on the same pattern. Subtle illusions of transparency or shifting patterns were also apparent, suggesting the sought after visual effects created by traditional craftsmen. Not least, a 'Gestalt switch' effect was also noticeable, resembling the famous vase/face illusion, where two interpretations vie with each other, neither one dominating but instead constantly switching between the two images. It is this illusion in particular which gives rise to the hypnotic, shimmering effects which, in turn, give the illusion of transparency and immateriality – how much better that students should acquire an understanding of Gestalt psychology

FROM ABOVE FIGURES 3 & 4: The Aga Khan University Hospital, Karachi, by Payette Associates; Menara Mesiniaga, Kuala Lumpur, by Hamzah and Yeang

through their own traditions, than through any imported exercises.

All this, it should be noted, was achieved by beginning students who had had minimal art education. Furthermore, though our source text books explained in detail the geometry of each pattern, they offered no guidance in the subtle arts of colour interpretation or the manipulation of colour patterns for different effects.

How then did these students acquire their new found skills? The answer lies in Polanyi's riddle, 'we know more than we can tell'. Even had they been available, explicit rules alone would not have sufficed to teach these students all that they achieved. What they learnt in these more advanced exercises they acquired by process of immersion in the art of Islamic ornamental design itself.

URBAN OASIS

The second half of the course was designed to introduce the beginning student to the full meaning of the subject of architecture, though still rooted in the historically well defined framework of traditional Muslim architecture, specifically, the mud-built courtyard dwellings of the central Nejd region.

As in the first half of the course, the aim of introducing students to architectural design via their own or closely related cultural traditions is twofold. In the first place, it teaches students to respect and value their own architectural traditions and so to view them as living traditions and a continuing source of inspiration. Second, the characteristics of Saudi traditional architecture are relatively easily comprehended by the beginning student, compared with the increased complexity of modern building types and methods of construction. Thus, it is possible for the beginning student to assimilate a synoptic view of architecture in his first year of study, in place of the usual fragmented introduction. In this course, the emphasis is on the study of the relationships between all the multifarious aspects of architecture, such as the relationships between building form and culture, technology, climate and landscape. It was intended that the first year student should achieve this understanding, to the point where he/she could apply the principles of design learnt to the design of a simple modern courtyard dwelling.

Projects were divided into two study exercises and a final design project. The subject of the study exercises was chosen to be the old town of Deraiyyah, situated just outside Riyadh. Deraiyyah was the original home of the Saud family and is therefore of major importance in recent local history. Aside from that, it affords a convenient and typical subject for the study of traditional settlement patterns. In the first exercise, called 'The

story of Deraiyyah', students were asked to describe the location, history and form of the settlement, its growth, eventual destruction by invaders and current rehabilitation as a historic site. All information was presented on a single sheet so that different aspects of the study could be viewed together as an interrelated totality. In the second exercise, students made measured drawings and analytic studies of a typical courtyard house in Deraiyyah, showing how it was built, how it was used and how it responded to the local climate, all again on a single sheet of paper.

Up to this point, then, students were simply assimilating the lessons of the past. The crucial creative step came next, in the final design project. In presenting the exercise it was suggested that many imported models of architecture, though popular with the ruling elite, might be actually unsuited to both the regional climate and Saudi cultural values – a point of view strongly supported by most of my Saudi colleagues. The first villas in Riyadh were built by government agencies according to plans drawn up by Western consultants, so it is understandable that other Saudis should want to follow their leaders' example and prove that they were being 'modern' by living in similar villas. Given the fact that courtyard houses are mostly identified with mud building and poverty, it is also not entirely surprising they should also choose to reject the past. However, Saudis also still value their privacy, traditionally protected by Islamic law,[27] so they try to correct the deficiencies of their detached and exposed villas by putting frosted glass and heavy curtains in all the windows and erecting tall barriers all around the perimeter to keep out prying eyes. Thus, deprived of the traditional private courtyard for open-air recreation, Saudi women and young children now spend their lives around the clock in an artificially lit and air-conditioned environment. In addition, compared with the sheltered courtyard dwelling, the exposed faces of the detached villa afford little protection from the intense sun and actually maximise the internal heat gain. It was further suggested that the design principles on which the courtyard house type was based were not necessarily restricted to traditional methods of construction – though these should not be rejected out of hand – but might be successfully adapted to modern conditions and building techniques. Based on their understanding of these principles, students were asked to translate their knowledge into the design of a modern courtyard house – not an isolated building but part of an appropriate new housing settlement with both modern and traditional features.

The context for the exercise was provided by a scheme for low-rise, high-density housing drawn up by a senior student in the same department. The scheme incorporated all of the modern trappings and infrastructure of a dispersed city such as Riyadh now is, but was organised around human-scaled clusters of courtyard dwellings with separate systems of vehicular and pedestrian movement – a relatively safe and intimate urban 'oasis' within an otherwise increasingly fragmented and hostile city. Relevant models of recent modern courtyard housing schemes in the Middle East were also discussed. The result was a series of house designs that are recognisably conventional in terms of layout and social use – the traditional emphasis on privacy and the division into male and female zones were major features, but incorporate all the modern amenities a middle class Saudi family now takes for granted. No less important, students also learnt that the sheltered courtyard house plan helps moderate the severe local climate as well today as it did in the past. Even where air-conditioning is preferred, as tends to be the case now (dust storms are a regular problem in the region), the sheltered courtyard form usefully reduces energy consumption.

TROPICAL TOWER

My last educational exercise takes us to a very different culture and climate and also brings us up to the present time. As part of an optional studio course on Tropical Architecture, fifth year students at Nottingham University School of Architecture were this year given the task of designing a mixed use tower block in a central area of Kuala Lumpur. The long-term aim of the new programme is to provide senior students at Nottingham, who include many overseas students from Southeast Asia, opportunities for dealing with the special environmental conditions pertaining in the Asian-Pacific region, in which many of them will find future employment (not only native students but many British students and graduates are already seeking, and finding, work in the region). The short-term objective was to choose a sufficiently challenging project which would engage students with the full range of issues involved in designing modern building types for the Tropics.

The final project and brief was formulated *in situ* on a recent visit of mine to Kuala Lumpur, in close consultation with local architects Ken Yeang and Jimmy Lim. A suitable high profile site was eventually selected in the 'Golden Triangle', Kuala Lumpur's Central Business District. Further specialist advice from Ken Yeang yielded a brief for a mixed-use tower composed of underground parking, a lower section of shops, restaurants and entrance foyers, a middle section of offices and a top section of service apartments and hotel. A primary requirement was that the building should be

designed as far as possible to take full advantage of natural ventilation and other passive techniques of climate control. Where appropriate, building users should also be able to enjoy the benefits of an open-air lifestyle made possible by the all-year round balmy climate. Yeang's own written and built works[28] provided the primary guidelines and exemplars for the project and the architect was able to offer his personal comments on students' work as visiting critic at the penultimate review.

Like most CBD's the world over, the Golden Triangle is largely composed of undistinguished high-rise offices and luxury hotels, which offer no sign whatever of their location in a tropical zone. Against this bland backdrop, the students' designs present a compelling vision of an alternative high-rise architecture, responsive to the tropical climate and lifestyle and uniquely suited to its location. The variety of formal and structural solutions belies any common approach. Nevertheless, a number of similar features can be detected in most of the schemes which point to a consistent set of design principles and distinguish the new building type from the standard international model.

Most apparent is the complex, serrated profile of all of the schemes, which is a direct result of the need for a permeable wall surface and building volume which maximises air flow through the building and interior spaces. Generous open terraces and 'skycourts' – usually double height or more – placed at varying intervals up the building, in a spiral or other formation, add to the impression of permeability. One of the most appealing features of the new type, these tropical 'hanging gardens', is that it offers open-air recreation for the inhabitants and a welcome contact with nature rarely experienced in high-rise building. Further detail and variation is added to the profile with different forms of sunscreen, arranged not in uniform fashion as is common with the international type but only where needed. Circulation cores and toilet spaces are placed outside the main building volume as separate elements in such a way as to provide additional shade, making it also easier to provide for natural ventilation in these spaces. Generally, most students sensibly plumped for a combination of passive and active climate control systems as needed, favouring active systems in the office working spaces or in the larger public rooms, and passive systems elsewhere, resulting in yet further differentiation between functional parts of the building (the handling of these climate control systems in themselves produced some of the project's most exciting innovations). All of these features, which complicate the building mass and create asymmetrical loadings, called, in turn, for novel structural approaches which enhance the unique character of the designs.

The combined effect of these measures has been the production of a complex and articulated regional architecture which breaks just about all the conventions of high-rise design. It has also produced a striking range of tall buildings, which, were any of them to be constructed, would undoubtedly transform the skyline of central Kuala Lumpur, which indeed was one of the main objectives of the project.

AMBIGUOUS CHALLENGE

What these projects demonstrate is that students can be taught to handle the most complex cross-cultural problems of design, provided they have access to relevant exemplars and understand the nature of the basic issues involved. Contrary to what is often thought, there is no hard and fast choice between the local and the global. The real and more ambiguous creative challenge lies in the interaction between the two.[29] What was most heartening for a teacher struggling to create bridges between different cultures has been the apparent readiness of students of diverse origins to make the empathetic leap involved, and to comprehend a non-threatening situation in which there is a place for both a familiar and an other world. That, in the present global environment, is something to be thankful for.

References

1 Johannes Itten, *Design and Form*, Thames and Hudson, London, 1975.
2 Anita Cross, 'The Educational Background to the Bauhaus', *Design Studies*, October, 1981.
3 Frank Whitford, *Bauhaus*, Thames and Hudson, London, 1984.
4 Frank Whitford, *ibid*.
5 Walter Gropius, 'Principles of Bauhaus Production', in Ulrich Conrads (ed), *Programs and Manifestos on Twentieth Century Architecture*, The MIT Press, Cambridge, 1964.
6 Chris Abel, 'From Hard to Soft Machines', in Ian Lambot (ed), *Norman Foster: Buildings and Projects, vol 3*, Watermark Publications, Hong Kong, 1989.
7 Peter Collins, *Changing Ideals in Modern Architecture*, Faber and Faber, London, 1965.
8 Thomas S Kuhn, *The Structure of Scientific Revolutions*, University of Chicago Press, 1962.
9 PH Hirst, 'Liberal Education and the Nature of Knowledge', in RS Peters (ed), *The Philosophy of Education*, Oxford University Press, 1973.
10 Michael Polanyi, *Tacit Knowing*, Doubleday, New York, 1966.
11 Michael Polanyi, *ibid*.
12 Chris Abel, 'Function of Tacit Knowing in Learning to Design', *Design Studies*, October, 1981.
13 Arthur Koestler, *The Act of Creation*, Macmillan, London, 1964; Donald Schon, *The Displacement of Concepts*, Tavistock, London, 1963.
14 Chris Abel, 'The Role of Metaphor in Changing Architectural Concepts', in B Evans *et al* (eds), *Changing Design*, John Wiley and Sons, New York, 1982.
15 Chris Abel, 'Regional Transformations', *The Architectural Review*, November, 1986.
16 Chris Abel, *ibid*.
17 Chris Abel, 'Henning Larsen's Hybrid Masterpiece', *The Architectural Review*, July, 1985.
18 Chris Abel, 'An Appraisal of the Aga Khan University and Hospital Buildings, Karachi, Pakistan', *Atrium*, no 6, 1989.
19 Chris Abel, 1986, *ibid*.
20 Ivor Richards, 'Tropic Tower', *The Architectural Review*, February, 1993; Chris Abel, 'Cool High-Rise', *The Architectural Review*, September, 1994 (a).
21 Chris Abel, 1986, *ibid*. For further examples from the Middle East, see Chris Abel, 'Model and Metaphor in the Design of New Building Types in Saudi Arabia', in Margaret Bentley Sevcenko (ed), *Theories and Principles of Design in the Architecture of Islamic Societies*, Proceedings of the International Symposium, MIT, Cambridge, November 6-8, 1987, The Aga Khan Program for Islamic Architecture, Cambridge, 1988.
22 Kisho Kurokawa, *Intercultural Architecture*, Academy Editions, London, 1992.
23 Chris Abel, 'Localization Versus Globalization', *The Architectural Review*, September, 1994 (b).
24 Issam El-Said and Ayse Parman, *Geometric Concepts in Islamic Art*, World of Islam Festival Publishing Co Ltd, London, 1976.
25 Issam El-Said and Ayse Parman, *ibid*.
26 Issam El-Said and Ayse Parman, *ibid*.
27 Saleh A Al-Hathloul, *Tradition, Continuity and Change in the Physical Environment: The Arab-Muslim City*, unpublished PhD thesis, Massachusetts Institute of Technology, 1981.
28 Ken Yeang, *Bioclimatic Skyscrapers*, Aedes, Berlin-Wein, February/March, 1994.
29 Chris Abel, 1994 (b), *ibid*.

Chris Abel has taught architecture in many parts of the world and specialises in the Theory and Criticism of Architecture in developing countries. He is currently senior lecturer at the University of Nottingham.

OBSERVATION ON EDUCATION OF ARCHITECTS

DANIEL LIBESKIND

Schools are not here just to produce the kind of people needed by a society. They are meant to educate people to the responsibility which is, of course, practical, ethical and political for the work in architecture and in planning. Students should be given the chance to question and to respond in contemporary ways to the changes in society. A school should mirror global transformations of technology, education and thinking and should not conserve a provincial attitude in treating only local issues. It should wake up out of its sleep. Most schools do not seem to be as alive as the people who are there. People are talking about issues that have already been discussed back in the fifties and sixties.

There is a fraction in all schools that would like to impose ideals of homogeneity, typology or style, a fraction which follows an idea of eternity in architecture. But eternity begins in bed and ends in bed. This kind of frozen theory, implying a blind acceptance of certain rules and regulations cannot run a school any longer. We know this from the totalitarian modern experience and all the 'isms' that are bygone now. This attitude is very regressive because it harps to a time when people were not allowed to question or to challenge a myth of power. Kim il Sung died some time ago. That generation is disappearing and I hope it will not be replaced by another generation of dogmas, but by one open to new ideas.

I should recommend that students of architecture become aware of what is happening in the world by travelling and seeing different societies in Asia, Africa and South America and not only in Europe and North America. It is important for students to express some more fundamental questions about the existence of architecture in the 21st century and to get out of this sleep in which the world of architecture seems to have fallen somewhere in the 18th century. Students have a tremendous role to play. They are not only the respondents but also the creators of awareness. They have always challenged the prevailing opinions and are the catalytic factor in transforming knowledge. It is time that students remembered that schools were set up to challenge the wisdom of the world and its corruption rather than to reinforce it.

Daniel Libeskind recently moved to Los angeles where he has been appointed a tenured Professor of Architecture at UCLA. His architectural office continues in Berlin with the building of the Berlin Museum with the Jewish Museum and other European based projects. He has opened up a second office in Los Angeles where he will centre his American and Asian architectural activities.

OPPOSITE AND ABOVE: Jewish Museum with the Berlin Museum, 1989. Construction sites and second floor plan

WHAT HAS ARCHITECTURE GOT TO DO WITH THE SIEGE OF SARAJEVO?

LEBBEUS WOODS

As I believe that education is more about asking questions than giving or receiving answers, I begin my comments with the question: *what has architecture got to do with the siege of Sarajevo?* If you believe the answer is 'nothing', then there is no need for you to listen further. If, on the other hand, you think it a question worth asking, then I invite you to think a bit about it.

What has architecture got to do with the siege of Sarajevo? I shall take the radical position of saying that the future not only of architectural education, but of the profession of architecture itself will turn to both the asking of this and other questions like it, and to the answers we are able to come up with over the next few years.

The most important answer to this question is an ethical one: *it is not possible for architecture to detach itself from the human crisis in Sarajevo.* When a civilised city is being destroyed for the most uncivilised of reasons, namely nationalism and racism, no activity that claims to be civilised can consider itself aloof from the struggle against them. More than simply acknowledging their abstract connection to the struggle, civilised institutions and individuals must organise themselves in some way to act. Good wishes and intentions are not enough. For the medical profession, this means finding ways to relieve the suffering of people, in whatever way, physically and psychologically, in the struggle. For the legal profession, this involves implementing the juridical means to help refugees and other persons deprived by war of a state to find legal status within the remaining civilised community. For the architectural profession, this means helping people to rebuild the physical tissue of their lives that has been destroyed by violence, even while the war – in this case, the siege – continues. There is no ethical way to side-step this responsibility – none whatsoever. And if this responsibility cannot be met at a government level, or even on a level on the professional community itself, then it must be undertaken on a personal level. This means not simply as a good citizen or samaritan, but as an architect, and by finding ways to bring to bear all the specialised knowledge one has, and by being willing to learn something new in the process.

What has architecture got to do with the siege of Sarajevo? Everything. As an activity which claims to be based on knowledge, architecture is challenged at its roots by the global phenomenon of which Sarajevo is not only a part, but, today, a critical, even pivotal point. Sarajevo is, according to the Sarajevan theatre director Haris Pasovic, 'the first city of the 21st century'. I believe this is a true statement, and not only because political changes, radical, and sometimes violent political changes are inevitable as our culture rounds the corner into its third millennium 'AD', but more so because what is happening to Sarajevo is happening to the rest of the world in a way that sets the course of its future. I should like to put this within the framework of architecture.

The world is changing at such a rate and at such a fundamental level that architecture is faced with questions that our forebears in this field – even the fabled modernists, who had to cope with a society revolutionised by industrialisation – never had to confront. If you do not believe this, then consider that industrialisation was the logical extrapolation – however abrupt and extreme – of long historical trends in the West. Steam engines, spinning machines, airplanes and mass-produced automobiles were the fulfilments of ancient dreams and goals, and could be fitted into a framework of logic and philosophy that had not only existed, but had been predominant in Western culture for hundreds of years.

When Le Corbusier held up the ocean liner and airplane as standards by which Modern architecture should be measured, he was confirming a world long ruled by principles of mechanics and Rational Determinism, the world described by Newton and Descartes. His celebrated 'machine for living' was a radical shift in standards of architecture, to be sure, but only in degree. Things were moving faster, farther, quicker, but they were still 'moving' in the historical sense of the word, still subject to laws and rules of thought as it had been codified in the Enlightenment, and rooted in thinking much older. Neither Corbusier, Mies, Gropius, Wright, nor even Kahn had the chance to consider the qualitative changes in culture that have come in the past 30 years; changes which go *against* all that was previously built up in the way of thought and work and that represent an entirely new set of conditions to which architecture – the art of everyday life – must somehow respond.

What has architecture got to do with the siege of Sarajevo? In many ways it is a Newtonian siege. The laws of mechanics still describe well enough the trajectory of mortar shells and the nationalist, racist ideologies which direct the shells that continue to kill the innocent. But Rational Determinism, the laws of cause and effect, collapse before the effects of this siege. Generated by instant television coverage and electronic communications sent at the speed of light through vast computer and satellite networks, these effects cannot be described in mechanical terms. The best we have at the moment are new epistemological devices such as chaos theory – the theory made possible by modern, solid-state, quantum technology – and these barely begin to describe the complex and multilayered, continuously evolving repercussions of a mortar shell that falls in Sarajevo, killing 68 people at a stroke, and wounding hundreds of others, which is told instantaneously around the world. Mechanics, simple cause and effect, simple action and reaction, collapse before the fact that knowledge is now simultaneous with the events its purports to explain. There is no time for reflection, for historical distance. Time has been collapsed by the instantaneity of human perception into an unrelenting present of experience. We can debate whether this is for the better or for the worse, but that will not alter the fact that civilisation at present is undergoing a profound qualitative change: knowledge, the certainty that we believe should precede our actions, is being compressed into smaller and smaller spaces of time. This has tremendous implications for the art and profession of shaping meaningful space. Architecture, once the domain of the most deliberately measured thought, the jewel in the crown of reason, now falls within the claustrophobic space of this experience – it cannot escape it. If it tries to, architecture will simply cease to be relevant. This is because the whole human world is slipping into the asymptomatic space of the present, the gutter that lies between the pages of history, the abyss of the existential. Architecture, if it is to remain as it has been – a quintessentially human act – must now find ways to inhabit this space along with the people architecture purports to serve.

There is no time to regret this fact. There is no time to wish that architecture could remain as it was, when the universe was ruled by predictable mechanics. Then it was a slow and gradual and well ordered and well designed, noble and clearly purposeful activity. In the compressed space of the present it is only one activity

PAGE 90: Scenes depicting physical and psychological destruction caused by war; FROM ABOVE: UNIS towers destroyed by fire in May 1992; ruins of the old tobacco factory in Marin Dvor, destroyed by artillery fire. Architects working for Sarajevo Reconstruction and Resistance believe Marin Dvor is an area ripe for development in the future

among many, no better and no worse, no higher and no lower than, say, the synthetic act of an earnest dialogue. There is a goal, or there is not a goal; there is a meaning, or no meaning – in a sense it no longer matters, because it is only important that there is any dialogue at all. Architecture must now get its hands dirty with the messiness, the *chaos* of dialogues. Design can no longer be founded on the dictatorship of the designer. In the dense, complex, confusing space of the present, the architect is not a dictator, standing at the apex of a pyramid of authority over building, but a participant, struggling to establish his or her own authority on a plane with others. And this holds true even though he or she designs for the elite of society, or for the most poor. Today – let it not be forgotten – the elite is by no means a stable, predictable group, as it once was. In the tight, intense space of the present, even the elite, the *aristoi*, the governments and corporations and the developers are struggling to establish their presence in the evanescent present. Sudden shifts in fashions of design are only one demonstration of this condition. A much more telling demonstration is the degree to which this elite caters to the shifting tides of public opinion, following the speed-of-light impulses of its instantaneous experience across the flickering landscape of television screens. The elite, who once enjoyed a certain luxury of time, will remain elite only to the extent that they can today ride the waves of quantum change – and they know it. As for the poor, who is asking them?

For the architects motivated by the idea of public service, how can they serve a public that only knows what it needs in the moment that it needs it? How can architects any longer base their architecture on prediction and control? When will they learn to be mobile, spontaneous, expansive in their engagement with the world? It will be increasingly difficult for architects who refuse to believe that this is becoming the only acceptable condition for making architecture, for architects who believe that architecture represents the eternal verities, something of the human that is more universal and timeless than the messy, ephemeral events of the present – the architects who believe that architecture has nothing to do with Sarajevo.

What exactly, then, does architecture have to do with the siege of Sarajevo? Can you old-line modernists, you 30-years-ago-liberals still speak of social housing as the answer to social conscience? What, today, is 'social'? Is it only that territory of responsibility defined by stable cultures, those with plenty of jobs for people, with assured incomes and medical care, with a surfeit of consumer goods? If so, then you must admit that yours is a narrowing world, one that excludes the growing number of human cultures struggling to

FROM ABOVE: Automobile wall against snipers; facade of buildings on Obala

emerge from desperate conditions. And you must ask, what, today, is 'housing'? Is it only blocks of flats woven into an urban fabric laid down in the 18th century, something now only to be in-filled, and thereby fulfilled? If so, then you must admit that a large part of the world's people is left out of your definition, people even in Europe, in Sarajevo, where the rich and poor alike are living in buildings blasted by the Enlightenment's mocking revenge on our modernity. Better that you ask, 'what does it mean to be housed', in a world where it is no longer possible to plan with certainty. Better to ask, 'what does it mean to be a member of society', in a world where the mechanical meets the electronic in the chaotic and sometimes violent collisions we have already seen, and are certain to see again and again the years to come. Instead of defending the old defini- tions, the exhausted verities, should you not ask: *what new forms are struggling to be born?* and *what new worlds are struggling to emerge from the ruins of the old?* On these questions we can begin to build our schools of architecture, and with them, an architecture of our new times.

Lebbeus Woods is co-founder of the Research Institute for Experimental Architecture (RIEA) and a Visiting Professor of Architecture at the Cooper Union in New York City. He has also been a Visiting Professor at the Southern California Institute of Architecture (SCI-ARC), Columbia and Harvard Universities. His latest monograph is War and Architecture/Rat I Arhitektura *(Princeton Architectural Press, 1993). He has travelled to Sarajevo three times during the siege and in March of this year made, in collaboration with Thom Mayne and Ekkehard Rehfeld, a series of workshops for architects and students in Sarajevo focusing on 'Reconstruction and Resistance'.*

OPPOSITE, FROM ABOVE: 'Elektroprivreda' building; red Cross building; FROM ABOVE: The National Library built at the turn of the century under Austro-Hungarian rule once blended elements of central European and Moorish styles in a uniquely Bosnian mix that would encourage Sarajevans to think of themselves as a people distinct from their neighbours in Serbia; an apartment block bears witness to a city under siege

A COLLECTION OF WRITINGS, 1985-94

KEVIN RHOWBOTHAM

ARCHITECTURE AND FREEDOM

That mendacious ideology of the 'natural', which in the late twentieth century has become equated with a certain wilful subjectivity, is the teleological subtext to current notions of existential freedom. The disengagement from culture *per se* which this notion of the 'natural' seems to connive at, belies its covert investment in ideas derived from the very context against which it strikes. Here, freedom is an instrumental objective: freedom for and not from the attainment of objects. It avoids the unfreedom of culture by exercising choice. It is itself commodified.

If there is any architectural freedom in the cultures of the late twentieth century it retains no volitional valency. The insidious institutional nature of the profession has accommodated the values of commodity fetishism without protest and without due regard to the consequences this might have for the scope of its own intellectual operation. The comical myth of the architect as hero genius is the sublimation of the idea of the freely creative architect. Its function is to marginalise the heroic possibilities of unfettered creativity by regarding such example (Le Corbusier *et al)* as of an unachievable standard, thereby proscribing the effective scope of 'lesser' architects and students. What remains is a freedom to choose among restricted alternative forms, alternative materials, alternative commodities; indifferently supplied by a surfeit of indistinguishable magazines.

ARCHITECT AS HERO

For architects, the term plagiarism is doubly loaded. Its overt, pejorative function connives at a fabricated notion of genius, as origin, by conferring disdain. Its covert, generic function provides a mechanism for the equivalent appropriation of tectonic forms.

The myth of the architect hero is teleological to the first of these readings. Its requisite and predicating support structure, the architect as acolyte/proselyte, is generated by the second. Genius, the fictitious quality of the architect hero, is preserved as singular, unitarian and originary, in order to accommodate the vested purposes of critics and historians, who in like manner to the objects of their discourses, prefer acclamation to truth.

THE ARCHITECTURAL AVANT-GARDE

The marginal affectations of the institution provide the means by which its incumbent elite can define and maintain the parameters of its operation.

Avant-gardes are fated to contrive only complicitous propositions since they aim at higher values, in order to procure constructive truths. This absurd purpose is a manifest delusion. There is and can never be any purpose in human culture other than the pursuit of truth: and this is a destructive act.

When the ideology of the figural object replaced its close ally, the ideology of figural space, the effective, political experience of the city failed to change at all. In the contemporary city, bourgeois values remain intact.

The professed purpose of the Modernist, neo-rationalist or pre-Modernist marginals – to expose the pressing truths of the immanent present – exerted little pressure on the issue of value, which was, and continues to be, assimilated as a natural adjunct to bourgeois experience.

The architectural debate continues to be engaged only at the level of the manifest form of architectural culture. It is thereby effective, insulated from the thorny political problem of active confrontation with vested interests. Little surprise therefore that these successive marginal positions remain more engaging for their pathological genuflections than for their achievements.

For any succeeding avant-garde to be effective the edifice of value must be destroyed, in order to undermine the hegemony of bourgeois venal interests. This cannot be achieved by offering simple minded reparations in tectonic form.

BEAUTY

The mendacious myth of beauty fits its vision to the object; its purpose being to secure a permanent, narcissistic relationship between human psychology and its products. The object is not and never has been intrinsic to its vision of beauty, as, likewise, this vision is not and has never been intrinsic to it.

ARCHITECTURAL HISTORIAN: ARCHITECTURAL CRITIC

This vacuous fart of contemporary history and criticism connives at few ends, none of which engages a truth. They aim to avoid all change; *plus c'est la même chose, plus ça change.*

THE RIBA: THE JANUS POSTURES

The RIBA maintains a posture of apolitical professionalism which obviates any commitment, on the part of its member architects, to political resistance through the architectural debate, by constraining it to innocuous issues of programme and process.

Questions concerning, for example, the nature source and margin of client profit, the appropriateness of buildings to context, the motive of the client to build, or even the pertinence of the client's brief to user requirements, are considered to be questions external to the profession.

Beneath this umbrella of apolitical indifference, the profession dispenses its unexamined values as if in a state of grace. Unaffected by the immanence of cultural transformations it has passively abdicated its will to act: replacing it with a teleological view of history in which the demands of a bourgeois society set the parameters of the mythical *Zeitgeist.*

The RIBA's posture of pragmatic expediency insidiously defers the architect's responsibility to arbitrate on environmental issues. Preferring moral duplicity, professional practice is too willing to pay lip service to the highest cultural values and the most optimistic civic ambitions, while at the same time accepting the demands of the money markets as natural, normal and unassailable. This deferment of responsibility is symptomatic of that paranoid condition in Western culture which has accepted the primacy of pragmatism over poetics and which has precipitated a general devaluation in the esteem of the visual arts.

The anti-intellectual posture of the profession, its most degenerate and totalising posture, defers its would-be-commitment to pursue the consequences of progressive theory. It is the definitive expedient, by means of which the venal professional establishment reduced the breadth of the architectural debate to those concerns which fit its own view of the world, which it promotes as natural, as intrinsic and as necessary, refusing to recognise what it cannot classify. It is a construct of the ideology of obedience and of quietism, grounded in an ethic of duplicity. Both conservative and reactionary, the profession maintains a liberal profile by offering its discontented a forum to air criticisms, having initially diffused any potential impact

which these criticisms may engender, by marginalising the authors as intellectual theorists concerned only with speculation and supposition.

ART, ARTIFICE, ARCHITECTURE

Clearly, what is science is not art and that which attributes to itself this name in architecture kills all passion and driving for the heroic. That which is the act of architecture fairs no better. It aims merely to make the sight of life more bearable as a mask might.

Those who believe themselves to be architects of the first kind (scientists) are silent in the face of politics. Their mindless pragmatics condone all acts of cultural violence. Those who are of the second kind (artists) impotently mime the terms of cultural change aiming only at reconciliation.

The second of these is surely worse since it condemns real improvement by deflating those very passions which coerce the disaffected to action.

NON-SPECIFIC URBANISM MANIFESTO

NSU was established to engage the current machinations of the architectural debate which, in predictable fashion, continues to avoid the political difficulties of an analysis of its own blinkered operation.

NSU argues that architecture survives by forcing its subjects to define their own interests as narrowly as possible.

NSU argues that all previous urban theories are bankrupt to the extent that they adopt, as natural and normal, the convivial values of the middle-class city.

NSU aims to expose the pseudo avant-garde's obsession for neurotic formalism and its debt to nostalgic representations of historicist and modernist sources.

NSU condemns all phenomenological babble and its vacuous references to GEIST, space, essence, rule, content and context as a proscriptive jargon which seeks to restrict all speculative operation.

NSU seeks to liberate architectural work from the choking dogmas of history and to engage the 'current' in all its forms at the quintessential moment of fashion.

PREAMBLE TO THE APPROPRIATION OF EVERYTHING

An eminent philosopher among my friends, who can dignify even your ugly furniture by lifting it into the serene light of science, has shown me this pregnant little fact. Your pie-glass or extensive surface of polished steel made to be rubbed by a house maid, will be minutely and multitudinously scratched in all directions; but place now against it a lighted candle at the centre of illumination, and lo! the scratches will seem to arrange themselves in a fine series of concentric circles round that little sun. It is demon-

strable that the scratches are going everywhere impartially, and it is only your candle which produces the flattering illusion of a concentric arrangement, its light falling with an exclusive optical selection. These things are a parable. The scratches are events and the candle is the egoism of any person now absent.
George Eliot, Middlemarch

HOUSE FOR A STANDARD GEORGIAN FRONTAGE

This house is a lipstick, a couture attachment, a waddle, a gyration, a manicure – a pedicure even; Mme Blavatski's mammiferous follicle; expectorated history; a cadaver leaking fluids; the cancerous decrepitude of the unreformed institutional body; Electra's prophylactic; the techno-haptic wing of the F-22; the joy of submission; aspects of ingestion; deformations of the mouth; rabid penetrations of chrome into flesh; that quintessential moment of the fashionable; flaccidity; a collection of confections; Kafka's excoriational machine; loaded die; the scapegoat; Breton's screen; excess; Felix Guattari; Diogenese; a thousand plateaus.

It pursues irreligiously, even Kinically, the elusive goal of DEEP SURFACE. That perfect, seemless, seductive, erotic, compelling, essentially fleeting and ephemeral affect (in the current American sense) of the commodity object, raised to the level of the impossibly exquisite. Beyond geometry, this is the body politic of architecture without undergarments, exposing its delicate genitalia in dandy colours – without programme and without morality. Its goal is inversion and unguarded titillation. The fleetingly superficial. That quintessential moment of the fashionable. The immanent present. Long may the regressive Moderns perish.

BARBIE-TECHTURE

Ordered, clean, uninterrupted by uncontrolled arrangements of objects or inhabitants, contemporary architecture projects its constructs as normative environments unaffected by disruptions, crises or specific everyday events. This is the aesthetic of the artificially 'spotless'; the sobriety of the clean, in which architectural praxis habitually re-presents the bathroom as a structural paradigm in order to counter a deep rooted anal paranoia. Architectural space is now a space of the excoriated, plucked body without excretions: a consequence of its retentive obsession for tidying away.

BARBIE is a body leaking fluids. The contaminated popular cultural body fetishised as the site of crypto-sexual precocity. The installation examined HER as an antithetical totem of architecture's anal retentivity. The site of the everyday and the innocuous, structurally opposed to the normative references of the traditional urban critique; laughing at the absurd omniscient pre-

tensions of a totalising heroic urbanism. Using the BARBIE fetish as a point of departure the exhibit examined the covert, essentially sexual possibilities of a projected space for the doll within the intimate territories and topographies of everyday life.

Of BARBIE as sexual object, of the voyeuristic BARBIE; of exhibitionistic BARBIE; of the violated BARBIE; of the lustful BARBIE; of BARBIE the selfless-lover; of BARBIE the giver; of sensuous BARBIE. It examined the territories of exclusion; of eccentric and marginal acts; of secretions and excretions; of projected acts of love invisible to mundane architectural praxis.

THE GILDED COLUMN

Environmental sculpture, Glasgow, for Television South-West Arts 1990 in collaboration with Janette Emery.

Fragmented, disembodied and burnt out, Alexander 'Greek' Thompson's former Presbyterian church has become dislocated from the social and spiritual culture of Glasgow. Its architecture remained powerful, although utterly familiar to the point of invisibility. Our project engaged the surface of the church as the site of intervention. By gilding a single column of the main portico we aimed to breath new life into it by employing a strict economy of means. References to the 'beautiful' and to the 'eternal', the iconography of the Classical column and of gold metal were combined in order to represent monumentality as surface. This act of gilding materialised the invisible column and momentarily provoked a memory of its forgotten stature.

CITY WISE

Paper to the RIBA Conference, 'City Wise', 1985.

Two kinds of statements have characterised this event so far. First, the proscriptive talk, which urges a reassessment of personal attitudes to the city, on the grounds of an 'ethic of good work', essentially an exercise in gratuitous wrist slapping, and second, the prescriptive talk, which exemplifies a 'pragmatics of good work' by means of demonstration, essentially the narrated slide show.

Both operate an ideology of naturalness, through which they claim to be equipped with that privileged currency, necessary to dismiss all that is excessive, extreme, or misinformed. This assertion of the so-called 'informed view' of the expert, or specialist, is of course the most blind ideology of all, since it leaves untouched those mechanisms which engender the institution of architecture itself, and which accept, as a matter of course, a myopic, essentially bourgeois view of the 'good life' as a universal point of departure.

Indeed, this 'ideology of naturalness' is openly hostile to all attempts to constitute what Roland Barthes has referred to as immanent analysis, by which he meant a sort of criticism from within, specifically a dissection of those mechanisms on which the production of knowledge is dependent. The current architectural debate avoids this problem by associating architectural knowledge with causal explanations, drawn from associated disciplines such as sociology, psychology, anthropology or history. This is done for it is easier to evaluate knowledge, so called, than it is to evaluate interpretations and criticisms of bourgeois perception and taste.

What has resulted, contingent on this demand for knowledge, is a division between the practice and theory of architecture. A division, by means of which practitioners position themselves before theorists, who they marginalise as visionaries and idealists, thereby constraining their criticisms to suppositions and speculations. This opposition between practice and theory gives rise to the impression that theory concerned with ideas at the cutting edge of the architectural debate informs practice at a distance, bringing about a slow transformation of architectural ideas, in a constant effort to maintain full contact with mass culture.

The partiality of both sides of the debate ensures that the criticism which emerges from it is circumscribed by bourgeois reality and by no other, to the extent that it provides a false unity on which to ground the ensuing discourse. Knowledge of the city is accepted without question as natural and normal and beyond examination.

Two questions emerge from this: why, for all its pretensions to do otherwise, has the post-modernist critique of urban modernity proved so ill equipped to tackle current cultural problems? and why, after almost a century of radical criticism of the modern city, does the profession still lack the necessary critical acumen and political will, with which to recognise and implement the productions of its theoretical arm?

I take the term post-modern to refer to those current urban theories, specifically rationalism and contextualism, which have adopted an aggressive antimodernist polemic. This is done to emphasise the immanence of this critique and to point out its would be relationship to arguments current to literary and fine-art criticism.

The post-modernists argue as follows: the humanist ideal of the rational city, they say, has already been achieved in the form of the imperial capitals of Europe. These cities, and records of these cities, retain fragments of an ideal vocabulary of spatial figures, the square, the loggia, the axial street, the terminated vista, the city gate, the colonnade etc, as a sort of absolute structure of forms which are assumed to retain intrinsic urban qualities, accessible to current practice as transformations determined by a theory of types.

This argument is a familiar one, but no less fallacious;

being predicated on the assumption that certain formal values are 'good to live with', that they exhibit intrinsic qualities of the good and the beautiful. It is a weaker version of those early twentieth-century arguments which proffered the liberating qualities of the modernist aesthetic. But in contradistinction to modernism, the post-modernist critique has introduced the notion of precedent as a proscriptive strategy. Without this strategy, the purely empirical nature of type theory would be freed to treat architectural artefacts arbitrarily and equivalently as beyond or outside values.

By proscribing typology with precedent, however, the post-modern critique establishes the site of value in a notion of tradition; but in an interpretation of that tradition which selectively privileges the urban figures of the Classical city. The concomitant unity which this arbitrary appeal to tradition provides, effectively centres the urban debate, but only at the expense of a disruption of its points of contact with cultural modernity.

Instigated by a polemical stance against urban modernism and its obsession with the figural object, the post-modern critique raised a theoretical barrier which prevented the assimilation of those aspects of modernist theory, specifically Bergson's spatialisation of time, which has since become rooted in mass cultural perception. Consequently, post-modernism can only offer a parody of a pre-modern culture of spectacle, in which the urban figure it favours was a meta-sign of state repression and enforced obedience. The resulting dislocation of post-modernism's radical and almost exclusively theoretical arm was the inevitable outcome, a position, incidentally, which modernism itself successfully avoided, but a dislocation which has, nevertheless, provoked nostalgia for a return to modernism proper as a sort of morbid parody of the original modernist initiative.

Ironically, however, neither post-modernism itself nor any new modernism which may displace it can hope to turn against the immanent present for long. That blind hope that sets up an ideology of tradition as the unifying ground of bourgeois urban theory, in an attempt to save the debate from the vortex of relativity, is bound to fail since an exchange of relativism for parody is no solution to this loss of centre.

Walter Benjamin has made the seminal case for the state of culture under commodity capitalism as one without 'Aura', without a universal model or permanent centre, at which cultural aspirations can be directed, such as the ideal of reason, the state, the people, democracy etc. Localised crises such as the space shuttle explosion, Boh Pahl, Chernobyl and Three Mile Island, and the general loss of faith they aggravate, is symptomatic of a crisis in modernity concerning technology, aesthetic experience, commodification, environmentalism and democratic control.

By maintaining its aesthetics of parody, the post-modernist critique cannot hope to confront this crisis or the crisis in urban culture which it has precipitated. Any post-modernism which attempts this, like modernism before it, must describe the structural changes which have brought about social consumerism and corporate capitalism and which continue to engender the arbitrary assimilation or rejection of tradition.

It is precisely because the post-modern critique of the city fails to do this that its definition of the post-modern *per se* differs so radically in content from those versions offered by other disciplines, which assert quite clearly this loss of cultural model or referent. And it is for the same reason that the products of post-modernist urbanism fail to mount any form of resistance to established perception and why they are so readily appropriated by the money markets as profitable commodities.

If you want to successfully challenge the evils of urban modernity, skating over the surface of the problem will never be sufficient. Architecture, the institution of making cities, must be brought into consciousness, where its autonomy can be broken.

As ever, what seems to be an issue of theory is in the end to do with praxis, the way each of us performs. Any urban criticism, therefore, must inevitably come to rest on the issue of the profession itself.

Notwithstanding, the remarks I have already made concern the contrived division between the profession and its theoretical margins. I shall now distinguish three postures, three beliefs if you will, which give some credence to this division, but which effectively insulate the profession from the effects of radical theory.

First, the posture of apolitical professionalism obviates any commitment, on the part of the architect to political resistance, by constraining the architectural debate to issues of programme or process. Hence, questions concerning issues such as the nature, source and margin of client profit, the appropriateness of building to context, the motive of the client to build, or even the pertinence of the client's brief to user requirements, are considered to be questions external to the concerns of the profession.

Under this apolitical indifference, the profession dispenses its unexamined values as if in a state of grace. Unaffected by the imminence of cultural transformations it has abdicated its will to act; replacing it with a teleological view of history. The demands of bourgeois society set the parameters of the mythical *Zeitgeist*.

Second, the posture of pragmatic expediency defers the architect's responsibility to arbitrate on environmental issues. Preferring moral duplicity, professional practice is too willing to pay lip service to the highest cul-

tural values and the most optimistic civic ambitions, while, at the same time, accepting the demands of the money markets as natural, normal and unassailable.

This deferment of responsibility is symptomatic of that paranoid condition in western culture which has accepted the primacy of pragmatism over poetics and which has precipitated a general devaluation of the esteem of the visual arts in general.

The anti-intellectual posture of the profession, its most insidious and mendacious posture, defers its would-be-commitment to pursue the consequences of progressive theory. It is the definitive expedient, by means of which the aggressive professional establishment reduces the breadth of the architectural debate to those concerns which fit its own particular view of the world, promoting it as natural and normal, refusing to recognise what it cannot classify. Both conservative and reactionary, the profession maintains a liberal profile by offering its discontented a forum to air criticisms, having initially diffused any potential impact which these criticisms may engender, by marginalising the authors as intellectual theorists concerned only with speculation and supposition.

To conclude with a neat aphorism is one way of making more acceptable the unproductive position of both the pragmatic and theoretical arms of the architectural debate. Indeed, it may even go some way to pacify those who have experienced a knee-jerk reaction to what I have just said. However, I make no apologies for the negativity of my position, neither will I attempt to offer any solutions, programmes or principles in an effort to seek converts or adherents.

My own position is clear and certain. The problem of the city, its effects of displacement and alienation, its infinite extension of lifestyles and roles, its perverse magnification of possibilities, its fascination with the themes of surveillance and voyeuristic sadism, are the only problems of the moment.

The contrivance of the institutions of the profession, whether practical or theoretical, to force some elementary formulation onto the structure of urban discourse, in the form of a universal notion of essence or centre, is merely a trick of assertion. Merely, the end-game of a discipline which is bent on reducing the human body to a technological object and which prefers deferral to revelation and acquiescence to resistance.

FASHION ARCHITECTURE TASTE

The anodyne eighties have left an overwhelming vacancy, lack of direction and crippling boredom in the arts. Everywhere, prevarication precedes adventure. Criticism is the main culprit. For all its post-modernist inversions it has achieved nothing, preferring rhetoric and declamatory pontification to provocation and direct action. It has, nevertheless, connived at the continued contraction of the visual arts, through its covert roles of anal retentive and chief cashier, seeking to tidy out the house of visual experimentation by recategorising anything saleable but marginal. Far from encouraging new and active directions it has, through its mail order catalogue (the review/magazine) and its grocery store (the gallery), pursued a restraining agenda.

Magazine criticisms, no less than visual art criticisms, adopt the form of the review, an *insouciant* instrument of vapid prejudice, in order to establish categories of difference and distinction – the categorical grounds for the erection of excluding taste regimes. Their purpose is to restrict the conferring of legitimacy to works which fall within arbitrarily determined limits. An act of suppression which connives at venial motives in the name of taste. This moral tourniquet stems the free flow of ideas creating a market of artificial scarcity.

The Gallery *ENERVATES*; volumes stupefy vision with a politics of repose, disinterestedness and somnambulance. All that it contains is asleep.

The magazine *INOCULATES*; the spectacle of the visual arts in perpetual retreat rest on the determination of the magazine to arrest *all tendencies to direct action* in the realm of the visual.

Fat farts at these miserable organs of the innocuous.

In defiance we offer you FAT, the first *GALAZINE*; the world's first *MAGAZERY*. A collection of multiplicities, cross-cuttings, re-readings, plagiarisms and samplings.

FAT's agenda: to cut deeply across the body creative of the visual arts, re-code its discrete categories: deforming their arrogant and jealous defended territories with intrusive relocations, re-inscriptions and re-inventions.

Fat's tactical procedures will forcefully dismember, re-aggregate and infect dominant taste cultures colonising them with their polar opponents to construct a nomadic, uncategorisable form – the lump, the sclerotic node, the swelling, the undifferentiated agglomeration, the interruption. An interdisciplinary thickening of the visual.

Its politics are the ecstatic politics of inclusiveness of dammings and gatherings of anti-individuations, of bursts, ruptures, breaches, currents and flows.

Its tastes are animal. Nomadic and wandering. Fat is a swarm: it gathers, acquires, fattens.

Its voice, the voice of declaration, unheard since the onset of the anodyne eighties.

Its productions, always multiple, simultaneous, coagulated, layered, superimposed, obese, FAT.

FAT is the machine of counterflows. Against interpretation it offers only SITES for the accumulation of connections, cross-codings, free associations. It is the communicating vessel. A machine of tastes.

THE INVAGINATION OF FORM

The metaphor which animates a common understanding of art production is that of inspirational invention. To such an extent, indeed, that it serves as the main qualification for all those things which come to be called art. From this perspective, art is that which retains, inherently, a trace or mark of the originating act.

To every artist worth his salt the MARK/trace is the vital component in the disposition of a declarative individuality, the purpose of which is to circumnavigate and ultimately represent the legitimate territories of authentic production. Its originary force implies artistic genius in the name of personal style or individual talent. In this role, it identies otherwise innocuous material as worthy of note and testifies to the presence of art.

The argument to inspirational invention relies on a central fallacy *vis* that objects retain, as part of some undisclosable and unfathomable 'nature', inherent qualities which disclose specific content. Art is a special category of such objects and is produced when specific qualities, beauty perhaps, but in a more contemporary vain, irony or even critique, are conferred on otherwise insignificant matter by the artist genius.

Circularity aside, this argument fails by dint of its emphasis on the implacability of content and its immediacy or transparency to successive readings. Contemporary criticism is infected by this absurdity.

It purposively displaces arguments which propose a transient, nomadic condition for the conferring of value and one which allows for no originary moments in the material history of art, only an exchange of 'sites' as the re-situation of the various materialities of art praxis in and beyond the intellectual preoccupations of the moment. This nomadic formalism dismisses:

AUTHENTIC PRODUCTION;
THE ORIGINAL WORK;
THE AUTHOR; and
THE MARK

as so much recalcitrant mouthwash, expectorated to establish arbitrary and fallacious categories of difference and distinction – the categorical grounds for the erection of excluding taste regimes. The purpose is to restrict the conferring of legitimacy to works which fall within arbitrarily determined limits. An act of suppression which connives at venal motives in the name of taste.

OUTPOST is a first nomadic shot across the bows of this grounded vessel. One hundred artists. One hundred works. 100 x 100. One hundred of anything emphasises the multiplicity and plurality of a practice which might produce such a number. Its scope is itself non-originary by dint of such a multiplicity. Without apology it is popular, nonspecific, drifting. Counter to a politics of exchange it offers a gallery of collectables without curation. A ready set, unsolicited and unsorted for recombination and re-reading. An exhibition beyond space, beyond fixity, occupying a city, Edinburgh, by acts of insidious appropriation.

POTSDAMER PLATZ

The Site

Precariously balanced on that point of commodification which converts dereliction to its very worst alternative, the wasteland beyond the absent Wall at Potsdamer Platz prepares for a new and more withering anonymity.

In the face of an altogether heroic, architectural opportunity to signify the establishment of the re-unified Republic on the Potsdamer site, the influence of international capital remains absolute. East has dissolved into West without trace and without protest; seamlessly, efficiently, anonymously, as the blurring remnants of socialism were exchanged for bananas and unemployment.

Architecture takes no position on this issue. Nor can it do so having opted out of any direct political critique of urban development in favour of the innocuous fripperies of history and style. In its present state, Potsdamer remains a most powerful epitaph, sporting the scars of recent history. Far too powerful indeed for a vehemently European Germany keen to obscure the recent past on both sides of the defunct wall, with the instrumentalities of venal democracy.

The Architectural Project

Architecture has been silenced by the soap opera. Overwhelmed by the visual power of more ephemeral commodities it has all but disappeared. Less significant than a TV advertisement it has been reduced to an adjunct of commodity lifestyles. A mere backdrop to everyday life, losing its role as the choreographer of the urban spectacle to advertising and to television.

The city is now truly flat. Its familiar geography disconnected by virtual electronic territories. It has ceased to exist as a figural experience. What was formerly three-dimensional and 'real' has been compressed into a snapshot, a postcard, a documentary, a phone-call, a photo-fax, and made to stand behind its simulation. The city is now made up of densely superimposed surfaces, manipulated in reproduction.

Architecture

The exchange of social values for land values makes real the progressive commodification of cultural life and related forms of cultural production as the 'Modern City', in the name of architecture. To this extent, architecture obscures the role of international capital interests, by diverting attention away from the political machinations of urban development, onto the innocuous issues of abstract form and style.

TERRITORIES, MAPS, COLONIES, SAPROPHITES

Having ceased to exist as a distinct geographical and phenomenological experience, the contemporary city is now exhausted of traditional significations. What remains of urban experience is prefigured by the form and force of the media message. The city per se has lost its signifying power to the media spectacle, becoming mute and inarticulate as its historical meanings are appropriated and re-cast.

To this extent, Modern City form is a hollow memory of historical and geographical distinctions: a simulation of relationships constituted by palpable regional differences which have since ceased to exist. Only the formal signifiers of territorial and geographical differences remain; and remain to be ultimately colonised. The Modern City signifies the location of global power-capital as spectacular figure. The totalising figures of the city, its signifying moments, are the nodes between which 'unlocated' institutions situate themselves. The points at which urban values are appropriated. Only the continued 'siting' of institutions within this net of significations maintains the value of the city per se. Without this colonisation and without the support of the media spectacle itself, the city as figure would fragment.

Geographical contiguity of urban functions in the city has been rendered unnecessary by the proliferation of media and communication technologies and by the continuing move towards a service-based economy. A free association and interchangeability of building uses is now possible and immanent within the existing city hulk.

Appropriating existing buildings, of note the unit, will examine the possibilities of operating within this degree zero urban context. Students will be invited to propose a comprehensive extension reuse of the general bulk of the appropriated building as an intrusive addition.

Proposals will take the form of an intervention which seeks to explore the possibilities for colonising both interior and exterior parts of the building, as well as existing services and structures. Disparate programmes will be grafted on to the host body in order to examine the possibilities of radically altering territorial values, enriching social mix and extending the disposition of contiguous uses.

Kevin Rhowbotham studied with Oswald Mathias Ungers and Colin Rowe at Cornell University. He started teaching in 1986 at the Bartlett and is currently preparing a book Form to Programme.

Ten suggestions for the budding

Avant-*Gardist*

1 Construct your own marginalities, micro-landscapes and trajectories. This is an easy task requiring one difficult step. You must forget the Oedipal imperative in every institutional connection. Become an orphan and a nomad.

2 In a world where the majority seek their own repression do not seek after instruction. All you can be taught is ignorance, inadequacy and deference.

3 Style is identity and signature. It is the antithesis of critical adventure. Celebrated architects are failures in this regard. If they were truly creative their first act would be to dispense with such redundancies and change their own work. Ignore them they are the dispossessed.

4 To become successful you must acquire the means of action. These are not talent, initiative, drive and ambition. They are influence and prestige. These are at your disposal through the manipulation of existing institutions. To begin you must become a self propagandist and adapt to what follows.

5 Do not fear the rejection of a critical elite. You can be certain that they will reject your work out of hand since they operate paranoically. Acquire the means of reproduction and proselytise your work. Its growing popularity will provide opportunities.

6 Laugh at all talk of authenticity. This is the language of the State and is fraudulent. Its goal is the suppression of all creative initiatives in the arts.

7 Cultivate a heated rhetoric and do not fear public rejection. This will establish your reputation more rapidly than liberal equanimity will.

8 Construct multiple initiatives for the publication of your work. One will never do since you will need one hundred possibilities to secure one certainty.

9 Avoid the authenticating drivel of critics, historians and other rag pickers of the miserable. Since distortion and idealism are their economy, they will transform your creative initiatives into banalities for the blind consumption of the State. Deal with them in their own terms. Invert their craving for certainties with false information.

10 Make no easy drawings. All demands for lucidity, clarity and transparency are acts of suppression. In the face of difficult work the reactionary squirms.

Kevin Rhowbotham ©1993

Projekt eines Portalbaues des Fischer von Erlach für das Palais des Grafen Dietrichstein Ano 1710

Grundriß Durchschnitt und Prospect

Michael Schmidt
8426316
1985

Tichelmann Martin   Karl-Marx-Hof   8426007

AUSGEFÜHRT IN : GRANIT & ALUMINIUM
LICHTE : 1·96 m × 3·20

ARCHITECTURE AND URBAN DESIGN

ROB KRIER

To have credibility in the eyes of young people, a teacher must be able to tie theory to practice. Some individuals are able to communicate an encyclopedic knowledge with passion and conviction, but in our field that is not enough. The art of architectural composition is illustrated by the example of models: its theories must take into account the laws of construction and the logic of internal planning. As an applied art, building needs a foundation that remains valid beyond individual displays of architectural bravura. My own work is an attempt to uncover the different facets of this architectural 'truth'.

My main area of concern has been urban development. The great hopes and promises of the pioneers of the Modern Movement were not fulfilled – as we well know. Holding to their arrogant, naive belief that each generation had to invent anew the themes of the city and architecture, the Modernists practically made it a crime to refer back to the experience of the past. My projects were quickly categorised by critics as old fashioned, reactionary and eclectic. I was told that they were 'not in keeping with the spirit of the age'.

During this century, the environment has been exploited on an unprecedented scale: we have seen more destruction, more power, than ever before. Our aggressive society and culture is reflected in the unbending form of the modern city – which I reject, sadly, and with bitterness.

My brother Leo has played a decisive role in my artistic development over the past 30 years. Possessing quite different talents and temperaments, we have found ourselves inexplicably on the same track, and have argued about how to realise our shared conception of architecture.

For a long time I found his unswerving, uncompromising attitude hard to understand, as I am personally not capable of such single-mindedness. Whereas Leo's whole, unblunted energy is directed towards architecture, I continue to waver – as indecisive as when I was 20 years of age – between architecture and sculpture. My vacillation means that my dreams of art always remain dreams.

However, if you chew on a piece of tough meat for long enough, with enough determination, you are bound to digest something in the end. The sheer physical effort will bring its reward. And so I continue to work with these divided desires, hoping at the critical moment to draw a strength from the poetic stalemate that would make the struggle worthwhile.

Rob Krier is currently Professor of Architecture at Technische Universität Wien. His projects and buildings are invariable informed by his views on the nature of urban space, which derive from the traditional city and the notion of a 'res publica' or civic realm

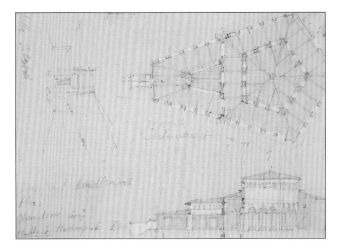

OPPOSITE, FROM ABOVE L TO R: The Palais des Grafen Dietrichstein by Fischer von Erlach, student: Michael Schmidt; Karl Marx Hof by Karl Ehn, 1926-30, student: Martin Tichelmann; Winarsky-Hof, Bauteil, by Peter Behrens, 1924-25; Aufgabe Postparkassenamt Portal by Otto Wagner, 1904-06; ABOVE: Project sketch by David Chamier

NOT ARTS AND CRAFTS

BRIAN HANSON

I shall address the relationship between the *idea* of building and its *reality*, and the relevance of this distinction for the teaching of architecture. I suppose firstly we should ask what is meant by the 'reality' of building. An advocate of a Platonic world-view – like my colleague at The Prince of Wales's Institute of Architecture, Keith Critchlow – would suppose that reality was something that exists beneath appearances, a reality of which any single building can only ever be a shadow. On the other hand, used loosely it could simply refer to the 'stuff' of building, that messy stuff – whether it be bricks and mortar or planning officers and estate agents – to which the architect's ideas need ultimately to be submitted if they are to be realised. I suspect the intention of most is to talk about the latter, rather than the former, 'reality', but I shall argue that building is a poor thing if it does not to some degree respect *both* these realities.

In his kind introduction Geoffrey Broadbent mentioned the work I have done recently on the architect Beresford Pite. I was led to take an interest in Pite by my fascination with John Ruskin. What fascinates me about Ruskin is the way in which he interpreted architecture as the unique meeting point between the reality of how things *are* and the reality of how things are *made*. He gained his insights into architecture from Nature, seeing the pattern made by the branches of a tree against the sky as a perfect diagram of the accommodation visible in all living things between external laws and contingent circumstances. In the order represented by these branches Ruskin believed he could see the hand of God. It may, perhaps, be difficult for us to follow him in this. The late Peter Fuller, who being both an atheist and a lover of Ruskin, felt this difficulty keenly and argued convincingly that even if we could not accept it as a mirror of the divine we could perhaps interpret this kind of order as a mirror of the self.

To address the issue of the relationship between ideas and reality in education I want to discuss a particular project currently being undertaken by students of The Prince of Wales's Institute of Architecture, of which I am Director of Studies. It is a design-and-build project for a Visitors' Centre for West Dean College in West Sussex, led by the architect Christopher Alexander. I have discovered in Christopher Alexander a sense of form replacing many of the qualities which I have admired in Ruskin. Like Ruskin he seems to be simultaneously aware of particular and universal realities. Form for Alexander is a mirror of the divine insofar as the divine is a mirror of common humanity, of our selves. In this Ruskinian/Alexandrian view of an architecture which emulates Nature in its balancing of the universal with the contingent, the contribution of *craft* assumes an importance denied it by those who approach the art chiefly from a conceptual standpoint – a standpoint which Alexander attacks in the introduction to his new book on very early Turkish carpets entitled *A Foreshadowing of 21st Century Art*. In this introduction he writes: 'I become more and more aware that the beauty of the building does not only depend on the beauty of its site, its plan, its rooms, but on the *fine structure*.' It is not the concept, but the intimate embodiment of that concept in actual materials, which for him produces 'life'.

Architects, he claims, have hardly dreamt of the way in which the order which arises from the microscopic organisation of matters affects us. In the 20th century we have become used to a conceptual approach to architecture, which gives rise to buildings with no soul, because they have no fine structure at all. Ruskin might have described such buildings as 'all Law and no Life'. For Alexander 'a carpet is a picture of God'. Like the tree which Ruskin observed, it points for him to a kind of order, containing elements of the conceptual and the practical, which mirrors our own Humanity.

This is the balance between the ideal and the real that architectural education no longer encourages, or perhaps even recognises. There is today a profound lack of understanding about how the parts and the whole relate in building, and it is not of as recent origin as we might think. It began in its modern form, in my view, with the Arts and Crafts architects of the late 19th century who, in addition to their buildings, bequeathed us a particularly English tradition of architectural education. But both in their buildings and in their educational system these architects let go by degrees the traditional balance Ruskin had recognised, dismembering in the process a particularly effective way of understanding and teaching architecture.

I can almost tell you the day on which this process began. It was the day in 1858 when Ruskin gave a lecture at the South Kensington Museum on 'Conventional Art', when to make a point he held up a picture of a naïvely stylised angel, which he claimed represented a 'barbarism which spelt the end of culture'. The young Philip Webb – soon to be William Morris' architect – was in the audience for Ruskin's lecture, and to him the angel brought different tidings. Webb thought rather that it was through 'barbarism' of precisely this sort that culture could be renewed. The rest of the Arts and Crafts movement, and the modernism which smoothly succeeded it, was a working out of this simple conviction, that abstraction is a cleansing force, that conceptualisation is more significant in architecture than fine structure. In this respect I see Richard MacCormac's design for the new Ruskin library at Lancaster University as only the latest – though particularly poignant – fruit of Webb's moment of revelation, the ultimate revenge on Ruskin of the Arts and Crafts tradition which is so often wrongly seen as indebted to Ruskin.

There are other, less obvious, examples one could point to to show how the tradition of conceptualisation has come down to us today. Nick Grimshaw's wonderful roof for the new Waterloo terminus is, like a great deal of so-called 'High Tech' building, a modern adaptation of an Arts and Crafts approach, where each significant element of the building is individually and lovingly crafted. However, the details of such a structure are crafted in absolute obedience to the order conceived for the *whole*, the whole is not any reflection of the part. And this formal hierarchy arises from what you might call a political prerogative – the architect determining the work of the craftsperson. You see how far we are from Ruskin's vision of a traditional architecture, akin to Nature, balancing an imposed order with an inherent one, where the whole *emerges from* the fine structure of the part, the product of God's providence or the craftsman's hand.

To get back to an architecture that lives in detail, rather than just looks good on the page, I feel we should get back to something closer in our education to pupilage and apprenticeship. The increasing fragmentation of the building world over the past century and a half has been mirrored by a fragmentation in the architectural curriculum. When I talk of pupilage and apprenticeship I am referring above all to three distinctive qualities: traditionally you learn something by doing

the same thing over and over again for years until you really understand how to do it; you learn by submitting yourself initially to *someone else's* idea of what is being aimed at; and you learn more about that whole not by resorting to concepts, but by putting all your energies into perfecting the part.

We have made a beginning in reintroducing something of this kind at The Prince of Wales's Institute of Architecture, in the project we have just commenced with Christopher Alexander who, on this side of the Atlantic, is best known for his works of theory, notably his *New Theory of Urban Design*, and *A Pattern Language*. It is not so well known here that for 20 years he has worked as a building contractor as well as an architect, and that this activity has enabled him to introduce a traditional form of apprenticeship into his teaching of architecture at Berkeley. The Visitors' Centre at West Dean will be Alexander's first British building. We are currently in the third week of a project which will be finished in just over a year from now.

The first thing our students did was to go to the site at the foot of the Downs, staking out on the ground an outline of a building of the appropriate size. These movements on the ground were matched on a 1:200 site model nearby. When the outline of the building was more or less fixed it was marked with brick dust. Up to this point, apart from a few guiding impressions, there were no drawings to speak of. The process is empirical, and drawings exist only as a *record* of something previously made. And so the client and the local planning officer become engaged at the outset not with drawings but with something much more tangible, and the effect on the client was that he felt far more of a participant in the process than usual.

Initially, the students' minds are on matters of *detail*. They are involved with the fine structure of the building even before they really apprehend what that structure will amount to in the whole building. By giving life to the details they contribute to the whole building having life, so in this first week there were experiments in brickwork, and in brick and flint, inspired by the vernacular of West Sussex and Chichester. Various colours of mortar were tried, using wood ash added from the West Dean boiler house, or different amounts of brick dust. This refusal to encourage conceptualisation, and utter concentration on the *making* of details, mark this out as quite unlike a conventional Arts and Crafts approach to design.

The students eventually grasp that their efforts are not some side-show to the main effort, but the essential effort itself. They are making a building, not a representation of a building. And the absence of the customary overriding concept means that the technology and the details are free to develop more directly in response to

S Michele, Lucca, by John Ruskin; part of the facade with details of columns and arches

human feeling. So as the concept ultimately evolves *from* the technology and the details it too bears the imprint of human feeling.

Unless the architect is a painter or sculptor, Ruskin averred, he is only 'a framemaker on a large scale'. Most of our efforts these days go into making frames. Ruskin's observation – much misunderstood, much maligned – implies that the sensibilities of the painter and the sculptor should determine the way we build. If we are to do this it demands an inversion of our usual way of making architecture. This is what we have attempted during these first weeks of work on West Dean.

If it is to succeed, the altered priorities this gives rise to have to be supported right through the process of building. However inspired the original vision, the building process of the late 20th century is designed to create conformity. Mostly this is done through economic means and, therefore, everyone associated with a project like West Dean needs to understand the economics of the project intimately. On the third day of the West Dean project detailed discussions were under way with the client about the distribution of money across all elements of the project. An unusual form of contract – which gives the architect control over the flow of money during the life of the project (and which, therefore, clients are often initially suspicious of) – means that the specification of the building can be modified if necessary during construction, enabling money to flow from those aspects of the building of lesser to those of greater importance. The architect deals in a traditional way with individual subcontractors. Often students themselves shoulder responsibility for features in the building they have designed, by themselves becoming subcontractors, or apprenticed to subcontractors.

The design process undertaken with this thrust is very different from the one beginning with the concept. There is a temptation with a conceptual approach to continually toss the cards in the air and start over. How is the validity of a concept measured, after all? How do you begin to feel certain about it? The practical approach, by contrast, is based on certainties and hard-won knowledge. Bound into this approach students become reluctant to let go of insights, which represent real practical steps forward. If the right 'feeling' (as Alexander puts it) is obtained in a trial piece of wall, or in the texture of a floor maquette, or the shapes in a scale model, that feeling must be cherished and literally built upon. Building upon such incremental gains in understanding creates a growing assurance in the student, quite unlike the often shallow attachment the student has to an abstract concept.

This is akin to the way buildings were conceived in

traditional societies, intuitive to Ruskin, but since his time we have become increasingly estranged from it. Philip Webb, in preferring a conceptualisation of design – a 'barbarism' from which nothing could emerge – drove a wedge between the practitioners of his art and the craftspeople who had nothing left but to seek the perfection of their crafts, often at the *expense* of architecture. It is now difficult to bring these two paths back together. Beresford Pite sixty years ago concluded that art and craft had become 'parasitical' to architecture. The approach we have begun to adopt at West Dean is hopeful, I think, in developing a different sensibility in student architects than 'design' education usually does, a sensibility which arises from them being bound to the whole process through a form of apprenticeship. And this sensibility ought, in time, to grow strong enough to embrace traditional materials and new materials together so as to weave them into a whole as richly satisfying as traditional forms we admire. Most architects today are in one way or another children of William Morris. Christopher Alexander is, in my view, one of the few that Ruskin might choose to own.

Postscript. October 1994
It is no use believing all of what I said above unless one is prepared to be radical in the application of the principles outlined in it. Such a distinctive programme cannot easily co-exist with a conventional style of architectural education, as the tendency is for this latter to dilute and diffuse the really very direct and simple aims of an apprenticeship approach. To take a small, but vital, example of how this can be done under the system outlined above, a successful model, being a template of reality, is of immense value and must be preserved at all costs. In a regular design studio a model is only a way of exploring an intellectual notion, and when the intellect moves on from this the model ceases to be of value. Even at The Prince of Wales's Institute, which is radical in a great many respects, the implications of an apprenticeship approach to design education are initially proving extremely difficult to absorb within a curriculum which in its structure (though not in its content) retains many aspects of conventional studio-based design teaching supported by lectures.

The conclusion in the short term for the Institute seems to be that project work should define an autonomous sphere of activity, into which students contract for a time, and where priorities can be reshaped, to serve this vision of building beginning with the perfection of fine structure. Customary expectations should not apply, nor must the 'strangeness' of the approach to our modern sensibilities –

our relativistic, self-determining, conceptual, impractical sensibilities – dissuade us from making the attempt.

Dr Brian Hanson has worked closely with The Prince of Wales since 1988 on all aspects of his architectural activities. In 1991 he was asked to set up The Prince of Wales's Institute of Architecture, which is already becoming a recognised force on the architectural scene. He has played an important part over the years in realising The Prince's vision for Poundbury, Dorchester, and has come to believe that it is mainly through such practical demonstrations that a new outlook on architecture and building will emerge. In April, two months after delivering this paper, the author redefined his role at the Institute to become 'Director of Projects', responsible for creating a practical framework for teaching and research of the kind outlined above.

The emulation of Nature by balancing the universal and the contingent as depicted in West Dean Gardens Visitors' Centre, north elevation

DESIGN IN A WORLD OF PERMISSIVENESS AND SPEED

PIERRE VON MEISS

LEARNING TO DESIGN
MASTER SCHOOL VERSUS UNIVERSITY?

There is little doubt that in schools of architecture on both sides ot the Atlantic, *architectural and urban design studios* constitute the central core of a curriculum that also consists of a multitude of technical and human sciences being taught.

The mere existence of these schools is based on the assumption that design can be taught at a university level. As self-evident as this statement may sound at first glance, it nevertheless remains open to question. Just remember that learning architectural design has been based for thousands of years on a master-to-pupil relationship. Since Durand we have barely 200 years of experience with institutionalised education which cites our discipline somewhere between the arts and sciences.

There exists so far no proof of the superiority of relatively de-personalised methodology – and research-oriented design teaching in universities as opposed to the master-to-pupil principle.

Even within today's universities, some of the strongest and most appreciated settings for design teaching and learning remain based on the idea of the traditional master sitting in the shade of a tree and talking to his followers on the wonders of architecture.[1]

In fact, cases of architecture schools having gained international recognition because of the exceptional quality of their teachers rather than because of the notoriety of their professing architects, remain valuable exceptions. (ie Bernard Hoesli at the ETH, Colin Rowe at Cornell, Vincent Scully at Yale, and Geoffrey Broadbent in Portsmouth. Harvard would be a caricature of the other extreme: it mainly *buys* names.)

This having been said, I still suspect that the university is for today's society a more adequate place for learning to design than what we might call the 'master-school'. I shall try to sustain the argument:

(a) The *master-school* suffers from some inherent flaws. The master's own production, or his projects and buildings, represents a physical example all too ready for imitation. Whether he wants it or not, he tends to convey his *style*, or in other words, his specific standard of ethics and beauty. Thus the 'master-school' tends to *foster certainties*. This may explain its short-term efficiency and the convincing performance of its design students (within the limits of 'the style').

On the other hand, one might question whether the notion of style still has any meaning other than fashion in an era where almost anything is buildable and where the media grant immediate publicity for all sorts of new forms and ideas to seduce students, teachers, architects, builders and clients alike.

Style in its positive connotation requires a sort of general acceptance of principles and reasonable laps of time duration which our present culture can no longer guarantee.

(b) The *university*, on the contrary, offers an immense reservoir of knowledge, research and experience: supra-personal, diachronical, interdisciplinary, pluralistic and challenging (just take a glance at their libraries!).

In our times of change, innovation and cultural uncertainty, the university is, ideally, a place where fundamental and more permanant principles of architecture might be discovered and taught beyond those of style and fashion. The prerequisite of this premise is critical thought and investigation. The question of ethics is shared by students and faculty alike. Uncertainties prevail on certainties; this is slightly uncomfortable and to some extent an unpopular environment for learning . . . but is it not a path towards learning how to learn?

The suggested opposition of 'master-school' to 'university' has to be taken as a ludicrous exaggeration to make the point. There is little doubt that under all sorts of pressures, competition and the necessity of fund-raising, the most prominent schools of architecture will continue to adhere to the 'master-principle' rather than to that of university (in the near future). One also has to consider that, surrounded by other faculties with more severe scientific standards for appointing faculty, architecture schools tend to compensate respectability by nominating famous architects.

This might, in the long run, turn out to be a convenient

but not necessarily progressive policy. In any case the question of 'master-school' versus 'university' awaits to be discussed seriously.

At the EPFL there coexist today all three: excellent design studios of the master-type (ie Luigi Snozzi, visiting critics, etc), there are part-time practitioners acting like smaller masters and there are those who, like myself, attempt a more university-like approach. I have to admit that this appears to be a wise compromise and the right 'mixture' for present times. Students' preference seems to rate from masters (1st) to teachers and last to practitioners. Nevertheless there exists no political cleavage among faculty along these lines.

TEACHING DESIGN IN AN ERA OF CONFUSED STANDARDS OF ELEGANCE
It is easier to talk about one's own concerns to improve the teaching of design. I shall mention two of my most enthusiastic commitments.

(1) I contend that learning to design structure, space and light is our most crucial task. It may be the only field where no neighbouring discipline can do the job. But designing space and light in plan and section remains an abstract undertaking for beginning students.

We therefore built a laboratory where students can build full size with a type of 'lego' we developed (LEA). Instead of merely theorising or drawing (uncertain) spatial configurations. The students actually experience space and light with their own design and its transformations. They work on spatial definition, structure, walls, openings and light at the 1:1 scale.

All our second year students pass in sequential groups, 4 weeks of studio in the LEA (Laboratory of Architectural Experimentation) with an experienced team of design teachers led by Jean-Pierre Stöckli.

Experience has shown that we can be far more efficient when we use the 'lego' blocks for what they are (a particular building system), rather than as a material for simulation.

The experiments are related to previous or forthcoming work in the studio. Students are asked to explore for example three basic spatial concepts of the 20th century: (a) *coincidence of space and structure* such as the Gothic, Perret, Kahn, etc; (b) *plan libre* such as Le Corbusier, Chareau, Mies, etc; (c) *Raumplan* such as Loos, Frank, some of Wright, etc. The students have to understand the basic principles of each. Then they build (or experience) each type by translating it in accordance with LEA building material.

As a result of this exercise, most of the students confessed that they really only understood the meaning of the preceding lectures after the LEA experience.

This relates to just one of many design-experiments having been carried out during the year. Depending on the studio they have to serve, the experiments may deal with housing, degrees of privacy or merely the window and its space, etc.

LEA has been in operation since 1977. It took several years to develop its most efficient pedagogical application. It is now part of what one might call a specific didactic trump of the EPFL. It is also occasionally used by other European schools of architecture.

(2) I contend that there should be no design teaching at a university level without design theory. Every studio teacher ought to be in a position to express his approach in terms of general principles offered to explain the phenomena of architecture.

Yet, we are suffering a terrible lack of text books in architectural theory concerning basic design. In the field of architectural history, Frampton and Benevolo have done a significant job after Giedion's previous effort. But what about theory of design?

Not much has happened since Zevi's *Learning How to See Architecture*, soon to be 50 years old without losing much of its pertinence. F Ching's book is seductive for students and pretty, but not very profound.

We also have to admit that the body of theoretical work on architecture has in most cases reached a very high level of specialised expertise and thus publication. Some are skeptical of the naiveness underlying any synthesis which attempts to give to the beginning student a convenient access to architectural design theory.

Convinced that it is nevertheless a pedagogical necessity, I took the risk to write and publish such an introduction to architecture.[2] It helps *me* to make my own lectures more profound and interesting.

In an era of confused standards of elegance I believe that we have to insist on the research publication and teaching of that which has proven through history to be of relatively permanent validity and to a certain extent beyond idiosyncracies. I do not think that my contribution is of capital importance because I still believe that it might be difficult to find a more relevant book on architecture for freshmen students than Alberti's 10 books written almost 500 years ago.

FROM BASEMENT TO ROOF: TEACHING SECOND YEAR DESIGN
In a time where architectural movements sustained by all kinds of medias are advertised and dispersed in such profusion, as to disorient the apprentice, it is necessary to question our ways of teaching this art.

I shall present my own pedagogical approach, refined over the years, anxious to favour *fundamental and lasting values in architecture.* The paradox being that if I want my students' design capabilities not to be obsolete a few years after leaving the university, the architecture which is 'in' and even present can no longer constitute the core of design teaching.

For didactic efficiency we have chosen to approach a variety of design issues through *successive identification* rather than simultaneously as done in a traditional design task. A series of accumulative exercises and specific issues build up an initiating path towards design. We attempt to leave aside, at least temporarily, a number of the usual reflexes and alibis justifying design decisions in order to concentrate on a single set of concerns at the time.

Starting with a relatively free underground composition (only one facade, the roof), the design evolves through the series towards a more complex and emerging pavilion establishing clear relationships between space, structure and light. Use is introduced afterwards by asking the pavilion 'what it wants to be'. The importance and poetry of materials, texture and construction are gradually increasing their role through the series. The scale 1:50 and extensive work on models are unavoidable.

One peculiarity of the approach is the predominance conceded to the design of space. Thus, in order to know what he is exploring the student has to choose one of three different approaches to space: the *space of structure* (ie the Ancients, Perret, Kahn, Botta); the *plan libre* (ie Le Corbusier, Chareau, early Mies); and the *'Raumplan'* (ie Loos, Frank and various English architects).

Such a programme cannot be conducted with the mere release of exercise handouts. It requires thorough theoretical attendance and transhistorical criticism of architectural works of today and yesterday. (The programme of exploring the design of near space represents half of our second year programme.)

The other half starts from territory, leading through the understanding of a specific city and site towards a work of architecture which is nothing more than a fragment, a humble contribution to the modification of the city.

THREE APPROACHES TO THE DESIGN OF ARCHITECTURAL SPACE

It might be that space has not in all times been a major subject of debate, but it nevertheless has always been and still is a central issue for design. Even if one most often and easily talks about *objects* which can be recognised and designated as appearances and things to be named, we nevertheless spend most of our lives and design effort within these things. Designing the implicit

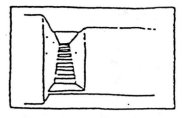

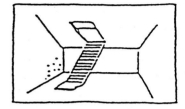

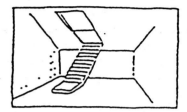

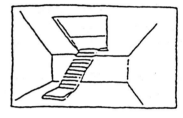

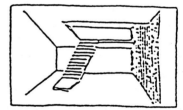

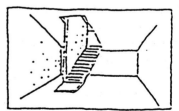

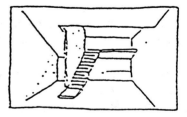

Seven the same stair and yet seven times a different spatial setting

which is space, therefore, is the central issue for
learning architectural design.

THE 'STRUCTURE-SPACE'

By structure-space we mean the rigorous match between the order of bearing structure and the figure of
space. It is structure which will define space.

From Antiquity to the nineteenth century this principle
has been confirmed as the way to create interior space.
It is the fundamental constancy through times and
styles, with the exception of Baroque. Thus, the heavy
constructional constraints of the past have granted a
certain visual and typological coherence to our cities,
streets and buildings, independent of time and style.
Even though today's construction capabilities have
done away with this rationale, there are significant
nineteenth- and twentieth-century architects, such as
Viollet-le-Duc, Perret, Kahn and to some extent Van
Eyck who continue to adhere to the principle of space
coinciding with structure. It is for them a design method
and even an ethics issue.

This attitude adopted with sincerity and vigour leads
to clear compositions stripped of ambiguity. Based on
precedents we may discover the following underlying
principles:
– The order and scope of structure is inspired not
only by materials but also by programme and spatial
intention;
– The bearing structure is the principal element to generate space. Following Kahn's logic, it would be a mistake to divide a structural field by a partition. The space
of a room is to be the one of structure;
– Structure-space favours spatial juxtaposition or a
sequence of distinct and articulated rooms. Whether
the design strategy be additive or divisive, the groupings and the whole remain subdued to the order of
bearing structure;
– Structure-space cannot get around geometric precision as it is loaded with the rationality of dimension and
repetition. It favours geometrical order and spatial
symmetry, for the basic desire of statical systems is
one of balancing the flow of loads;
– The positioning and dimensioning of openings stand
in a direct relationship to the order of structure. The
same is true for infill between a skeleton structure (see
Perret, Mies, Kahn);
– The concern with an organisational idea generated by
structure implies a particular attention to the ground
datum (foundations, base), the angles and the conclusion towards the sky (crowning, cornice, root); and
– In most historic settings it offers a favourable approach to urban continuity.
When structure-space is associated with elementary

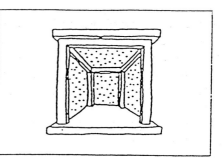

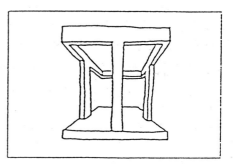

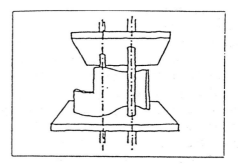

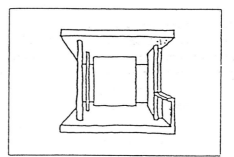

*FROM ABOVE: Two approaches to the
design of architectural space; structure-
space; plan libre*

geometric figures, such as a cube, prism or cylinder, it tends to generate institutional representation, solemnity and dignity.

As an approach to design it is in many ways reassuring. The structural choice will help most further design decisions. One of its difficulties resides in the resolution of unavoidable conflicts between the coarse and mechanical order of structure and the more variable needs and desires for programme and its spaces.

THE 'PLAN LIBRE'

To form space, contemporary technology allows the bypassing of the requirements of structure.

The destruction of the box, introduced intuitively by Frank Lloyd Wright and theorised by Le Corbusier's 'Maison Dom-ino' and his pledge for free plan and free facades are the antithesis of the space of structure. Our conventions are questioned to introduce a new spatial and constructive dimension: that of an order of structure which is not complying with the one of space.
At best, structure and elements of spatial definition are talking to each other by opposition or contrast (Le Corbusier, De Stijl, Chareau, Mies van der Rohe at Tugendhat). At worst, the two are not even conflicting but ignoring each other to form a random inaccessible whole. This is what might occur when an architect inflects partitions under the only pressure of programme and function without regard to the spatial complement of walls and structural framework.

Historical precedents allow us to uncover some inherent characteristics for designing space and structure in a way that each one claims its own rights without ignoring the other:
– Structure then is most often a skeleton system with slabs sometimes interrupting. It follows its own constructive and imperturbable regularity like rhythm in music. It accommodates more or less neutral voids which wait for spatial (melodic) articulation in accordance with a programme. This neutrality is nevertheless compromised as soon as slabs are supported by a grid of visible beams which tend to claim implicitly their own space.

– Structure concedes all or part of its role in defining space (the spatial limits) to nonbearing elements which may be partitions or boxes. The structure is shown, it may even show a dominating presence, but it will never be the only master of spatial composition.
– Space tends to be fluid. The notion of juxtaposed rooms is abandoned in favour of more ambiguous spatial interpretations. Measure and form are open to interpretation. The 'plan libre' and consequently the 'coupe libre' (free section such as produced by canti-

lever), open the path towards desired and even imaginary space.
– There is a great potential for 'plafond libre' or free ceilings. Even more so that partitioning the ceilings' new requirements for heating, ventilating and artificial lighting frequently does not want to follow the order of structure. Alvar Aalto is quite singular in coming to terms with the design of ceilings, the most forgotten element of the Modern Movement.
– Position, form and dimension of openings may follow the requirements of programme, as well as the designers' idiosyncrasies.
– Architecture based on free plan, section and facade may become problematic when located in an urban fabric mainly composed of buildings following the structure-space principle. The reason being that it tends to adopt an object-character which stands out from the fabric, even when this is not desirable.

For a student the free plan and free facade are at first rather seductive. The idea of *free* space holds out bright prospects like freedom of thought, freedom of expression and form. It would allow us to escape the dictate of structure in favour of *desired* space and place. The designers' redoubtable opponent is nevertheless arbitrariness. The designer may be incapable in justifying his decisions and it is indeed far more difficult to *invent* a set of rules than to follow the one suggested by structure.

THE 'RAUMPLAN'

This approach is more difficult to characterise and perhaps somewhat too 'frivolous' to be turned over to students. Where goes 'honesty' in architecture when structure is no longer an issue? Here, the structures' role is limited to accommodating a spatial atmosphere. It is hardly more than the utilitarian scaffolding to hold up the elements necessary for this atmosphere.

Raumplan concedes absolute priority to the quality of interior space. In this sense it offers enormous potential to domestic architecture. Its most significant parameters are spatial hierarchy, well balanced ceiling heights, a chain of linking spaces, which look at each other, and particular attention for materials and surface structure of facings.

Raumplan is a space design principle for which the most pertinent references are Adolf Loos and Josef Frank but it has its predecessors in Victorian as well as in Frank Lloyd Wright's early buildings. It is a living tradition for many contemporary Viennese architects.

Based on the works of Loos and Frank, we can extract some of the basic characteristics of this space-design approach:
– The heights of spaces are to be defined according to

the nature and the destination of places to be created: ie places of entry and welcome are not bedrooms; a children's playroom is not a dining room; the entrance stair is not the same as the one leading to the basement; a reading nook with a window is not a dining corner . . . The prerequisite to Raumplan is therefore to find out what each of these want to be.

– Spaces are clearly defined but, rather than being juxtaposed, they are linked and interwoven on their edges. Each space looks at others, and this occurs not only horizontally but on an oblique due to various floor levels and ceiling heights. The nook looks at the major space and vice-versa.

– Openings are designed for light and view; they are to command the atmosphere of the interior rather than facade appearance. In Loos' houses we are most often dealing with an interior design rather than that of exterior.

– Last but not least, materials, textures, colours and their structuring add precision to spatial definition and the sense of place. Indeed, the need for structural resistance requires materials which often cope poorly with the destination of interior space. Adequate facing ends up giving the space a welcoming envelope.

Raumplan does not presume any specific formal code just as structure-space and plan-libre do not. But Raumplan might be more adequate for what is meant to be a 'home' even beyond literal housing.

It is an approach where it is not so easy to grasp the compositional principles other than through experience and observation. Never forget that Raumplan is basically governed by *interior* space design. If this sum is to add up in a rather simple and coherent volume (ie a cube), we need to adopt a mixed strategy of addition and division analogue to a Japanese cube puzzle.

A design student who wants to work with Raumplan favours, most often without noticing it, certain ambiguity between structure and spatial organisation. He is seduced by an approach he most likely never experimented with. Sometimes carried by the fear of 'déjà vu' he may be motivated by investigating the possibilities of interweaving the spaces which privilege intimacy.

Notes

1 You may agree that real masters are hard to find and that not all great masters are good teachers, which makes them even fewer . . . In most cases, we find the country's better architects teaching part time along the master-principle approach.

2 Pierre von Meiss, 'Elements of Architecture', from *Form to Place*, Van Nostrand Reinhold (International), London, 1990.

Pierre von Meiss is Professor of Architectural Theory and Design at the École Polytechnique Fédérale de Lausanne (EPFL). His most recent book is Elements of Architecture.

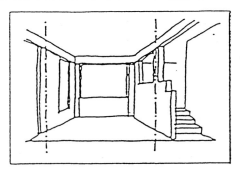

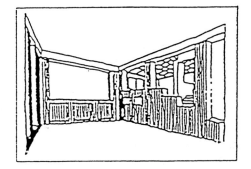

The last approach to the design of architectural space, raumplan

GLOBALISM AND REGIONALISM

EDWARD JONES

As I do not find the distinction between Globalism and Regionalism in itself immediately productive, I thought that I might reflect on my own preoccupations in architectural education. This experience could be said to be equally divided between England and North America. My observations are therefore mildly 'mid-Atlantic' and moderate between either a strictly English or American position, in any event a position of oscillation. Hopefully this will provide a personal context into globalism and regionalism.

During these architectural journeys two protagonists have presented themselves often in opposition and occasionally one as the sponsor for the other – one I shall call the architectural broker, the other the European city. The former, the prophet and mouthpiece of universal culture, the latter the repository of regional culture and its values.

On the one hand, I have become increasingly aware of the air traffic controllers or brokers on both sides of the Atlantic. Boyarski and Cook in London, Eisenman/Frampton in New York, and if one really wants to go global Isozaki/Futagawa in Tokyo. It might not go unnoticed how these metaphorical brokers reflect centres of world finance. They maintain the conversations and the flow of information in this global commodities market. Reputations are made locally and then, as a result, gifted architects are pulled out of their native soil, the soil that has sustained and nourished their production, and they are then invited to perform in less familiar territory, the territory of the critical present, the territory of critical regionalism. Alvaro Siza and Mario Botta come to mind in this category.

On the other hand, we have the European city and it remains a regret to me that English architectural culture and education can be so easily detached from the European experience. (This is less of a problem in Scotland.) Up to the late 1960s in Europe, generally speaking, the city was intact and exerted a profound influence on an understanding of architecture. Rossi's canonical *Architecture of the City* of 1967 acts as a useful testament to this. It is significant that this text was translated into Portuguese and Spanish over a decade before it received its first translation into English, ironically in America, in 1982 through the initiative of the broker *par excellence* Peter Eisenman. It was widely read by those who lived in cities and knew what cities were about. It spoke to a collective memory in its readership, a readership who intuitively understood that 'the nature of a building is born from the nature of its city'. That the two are somehow inseparable – this is not to suggest the dead hand of history as promoted by our future monarch or the rip-off of Post-Modernism but rather to understand the typological nature of cities and the role of architecture in this continuum. The steady and urbane development of contemporary Spanish architecture might be attributed to this theoretical underpinning.

By way of contrast, the teaching in British schools during the 1960s was given impetus by acts of radical transformation on the city, transformations indifferent to this nature, that were to find the entire enterprise wanting. When I was a student at the AA during the period 1958-63 we could not see beyond the horizon of the modern city. The devastation of World War Two followed by the massive rebuilding programme and its uneasy celebration of 1951 at the Festival of Britain produced the early polemics of Team X that would act as the architectural composte for my generation – a total rejection of the values of the Festival of Britain – with all its nationalism and sentimentality, dare one say regional impulses, coupled with a wish to get into better company. 'Mies is great; Corb communicates' was Peter Smithson's aphorism at the time. The post-war building enterprise had a momentum that carried all before it – under Attlee's post-war Labour government – new towns and the large scale reconstruction of existing cities were mostly carried out by local authority architects departments. Whatever the successes and failures of this post-war regime an agenda was given to schools of architecture – the national effort in public housing, schools and university building gave students during these two decades the raw material on which to base their architectural studies. James Gowan and Peter Smithson were responsible for the curriculum at the AA at this time. A simple but memorable structure that, after an introductory year, based the second year on the village, the third year on a provincial town, the fourth year on a district in the city (always London) and the fifth year was devoted to thesis. Building problems were then situated in or derived from exploratory plans for the renewal of these settlements.

Although the models were approximate and the architectural discussion at times rather primitive compared with the discourse of contemporary schools, there was a comprehensibility to the course and a very clear relationship established between towns and buildings. A momentary axis was coincidentally established between Rossi's Milan and London. By the mid-1960s the steam had run out of this post-war initiative and reconstruction. As the built production of this era came into general public consumption a certain fallibility began to emerge.

It could be said that we are still living through the disillusionment of this rude awakening:

The social divisiveness of large public housing estates with site plans requiring guide books for navigation through their unnecessary complicated and unique labyrinths.

High-rise apartment buildings built for families, once familiar with life in the bylaw street.

Buildings that negate the all time hallowed relationship and convention between street and block, front and back.

Buildings that later became subject to the researches of the likes of Oscar Newman and his book *Defensible Space* with its painfully obvious conclusions and so on.

From the mid-1960s onwards it became apparent that a position of critical resistance and reassessment was necessary and that alterations of a rather blunt and direct kind had to be found. It no longer seemed reasonable to destroy perfectly sound nineteenth-century urban terraces and to substitute them with something that resembled the aftermath of a train crash. Each time we saw a demolition team at work we knew that something inferior was to take its place. This was not a comfortable time to be an architect – the schools by the late sixties offered instruction in anything but architecture – Brian Anson had converted his studio in Bedford Square into a rifle range, the street farmers had plans for ploughing up Tottenham Court Road and the architecture of diversion and entertainment had arrived through the example of Archigram.

The socially responsible era or the period of the architecture of good intentions had finally come to a close. This was never more ironically expressed than by the blowing up of the Pruet Igo Housing Development in St

FROM ABOVE: Golden Lane project, Alison and Peter Smithson; Sea and ships pavilion at the Festival of Britain; Walking City: at sea, Archigram, drawn 1964 by Ron Herron

Louis in 1972 and in 1968 in England with the failure of Ronan Point.

And so to this position of critical resistance.

If a previous generation had become obsessed with the architecture and society of the modern city, we came to the not altogether unpredictable conclusion that modern architecture while producing some very remarkable freestanding buildings had been notably less successful in its relationship to the traditional city.

It might be said that this observation has underwritten my teaching and practice from the beginning of the 1970s to the present.

The exploratory housing projects from 1965 onwards entitled by critics at the time to be 'low-rise high-density' were attempts to revalue the urban house to avoid nationalist sentiment in proposals for mass housing in the form of Welsh fishing villages. We were given the unlikely title by Peter Cook at the time of the Grunt Group. Coincidentally, the first public grunt of disapproval was in the Portsdown Housing competition of 1965 (the year of Le Corbusier's death). Here, the good intentions of 'townscape' encouraged by the *Architectural Review* editorial of the day called for a 'mixed development' of tower block and terrace.

Our development of rational and elemental housing layouts found kindred spirits in Lionel March, Cambridge University, at the time where developments in the Fresnel Square applied to housing layouts – in a rather long winded way to post rationalise the practicability and desirability of perimeter development as found in the eighteenth-century garden square.

By this time, 1973, I found myself teaching a visiting studio in Cornell next door to Colin Rowe's urban design studio. For the half semester I spent in Ithaca we never spoke – you see I was invited by Mathias Ungers – apart from one exchange when Rowe walked into the middle of one of my seminars and pronounced: 'I see, here we have the architecture of the jolly old welfare state.' Colin Rowe, I think, has been very influential in this oscillation between regional observations and a global culture. It was therefore not surprising that by going to America I should acquire a greater understanding of the European city.

My most concentrated period of teaching was at the Royal College of Art, 1973-83. A School of Architecture *manque*, London's equivalent of Cooper Union was Peter Cook's assessment. It was a very small elite school of 36 students from a mixture of backgrounds; art school refugees with an inquisitiveness about architecture, world travellers from Peru, some Londoners and a constant Irish presence. A passion for drawing acted as a common denominator – opinions varied and criticism was frequently abrasive. The studio topics

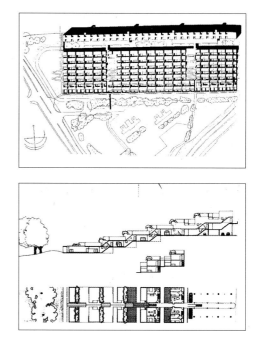

FROM ABOVE: Portsdown Housing, plan and section, Michael Gold and Edward Jones

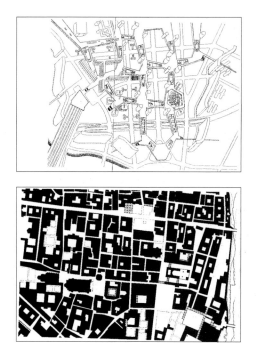

and themes were quite prescriptive as follows:

A case for the reconstruction of the European city being made by messrs. Krier, Porphyrios and Montés.

A grounding in architectural theory (and the history of the modern movement) related to studio and seminar topics by Ken Frampton.

Typological studies into existing urban buildings' arcades etc.

The tactile and physical aspects of design applied to quite modest building types – John Miller, Su Rogers and Birkin Harvard.

A reawakening of a relationship between landscape, the garden and urban design – Chris Cross, Elia Zenghelis and myself.

These various speculations were based on the intuitive proposition, at the time, that an enthusiasm for Modern architecture need not necessarily be inconsistent with an appreciation of the nineteenth-century city.

It could be said that we are in the process of coming out of a period in which there has developed an ever-increasing gap between the profession and the school. As architects became increasingly agents or mid-wives to a process they either did not understand or are not able to condone, so the schools were to stress theoretical discourse at the expense of design en-quiry. Indeed, in American schools the artistic activi-ties of the studio have become marginalised by the increasing interest in theoretical matters.

In Britain, on the other hand, there is much neglect in the area of architectural theory and history with almost total emphasis on the studio. There appears to be con-siderable confusion/ambiguity as to how studio teach-ing should be conducted. The boffin principle of allow-ing the private will to form to emerge from the student has always suited the English liberal tradition and much lazy, mediocre and occasionally magical work results.

In conclusion, one should always be critically respon-sive to the brokers of the day, to be on guard against their sophistry and to give a place to their occasional prophecies. If by regional we mean works that result from direct observation of a place with the capacity to extend and transform, then OK. The city should be the school's laboratory in its capacity to act as a con-science to the city fathers, to offer directions for the future and above all to raise the debate.

Edward Jones won first prize for the Mississauga City Hall in Canada in 1987, and in partnership with Jeremy Dixon is work-ing on commissions for the Royal Opera House and various University projects. In 1991 the practice won first prize in the Venice Biennale Gateway for Venice competition. Since the mid-1980s he has been visiting professor at various universi-ties in North America.

FROM ABOVE: Hapstadt, Berlin, Alison and Peter Smithson; plan of Parma

EDUCATION IN ARCHITECTURE

FRANCIS DUFFY

What is professionalism? If you were a sociologist you would remark on the enormous success of professionalism in the 20th century. The huge growth in the modern space judgmental professions has been tremendous due to the growth of formal architectural education from 1900 to the present day. There is a considerable amount of places in schools of architecture giving access to education and thus to the profession of architecture. But it is obvious that there is something curious about this when the evidence, certainly during 1993-94, indicates that the profession is under recession. Nevertheless, I think the students are wiser than we know for they believe in the importance of design and knowledge.

My definition of the profession is entirely in terms of its knowledge base and its ownership and extension in various ways, not least by an educational programme which transmits it from one generation to another. In architecture we have a particular kind of knowledge which is extremely interesting because it withers outside the context of action. Design, which means inventing the future not just for ourselves but for the people for whom we work, is the essence of the kind of knowledge that architecture represents. This can only be developed not in the world of commerce or just in the universities but through action in practices in the way architecture is delivered. Because the kind of knowledge that we are talking about is professional, is knowledge in action, it conjures up the question of what the right thing to do is. So the function of a profession is to develop and to transmit such knowledge in a way that can be undertaken by no other form of institution.

So, if you look at a professional institute, a simple question can be asked: what is it? Is it a building, is it a library, is it lectures and exhibitions, is it apparatus and schools, is it the members? No, these are simply the consequences of that collective voluntary desire to take a certain body of knowledge and advance it. It is easy to be cynical about professional bodies and there are, I have to admit, vices that are inherent in this system which have so many virtues. One of these vices is exclusivism, another is a tendency to conservatism. Nevertheless, the professional body that represents architecture

in the UK is robust, which is measured by the degree of its concern for education.

It is no accident that the RIBA won the battle over the funding of the five-year architectural course. This was an extremely important political act which was only achieved by a collective desire to assert certain educational values which were important to those who operated in that particular sphere of action. It is also possible through this voluntary association to protect the title of 'architect'; the symbolic consequences of the loss of which would have been devastating with the recession in Britain this decade. What you do not see is the energetic programme of restructuring the profession. In fact, the invention of new forms of professionalism which are inherently consumerist acts as an antidote to the vices of exclusivism, conservatism and protectionism, which were characteristic of past professions.

The Institute represents an enormously powerful cultural programme, finding ways of representing the nature of architecture and its values to a wider public. I took part in the debate, when I was in charge of education at the RIBA, insisting that it was an ethical obligation of architects to continue to educate themselves throughout their professional lives. This single change in the 'Bible' of the Institute that made CPD (continuing professional development) compulsory for all members of the Institute is the most important single act I have been involved with in the RIBA during my time there. I have to say though that I am far from satisfied with the situation in which we find ourselves. In fact, despite these general successes and despite individual initiatives, which have been marvellous among members, student members, practitioners, and intellectuals in the Institute, I am angry about the situation in which we find ourselves, anxious that we should push ourselves much harder than we are doing.

I do not think the present climate is particularly easy, but I think most of the challenges that we face are to do with our unwillingness to come to terms with the particular responsibilities of being architects. I think it is our own collective faults that we are not improving. I think we have failed, compared with Isi Metzstein for example, to advance the knowledge base of architecture fast enough. We have neglected research, we have known nothing in architecture except a few hints; nothing as powerful as the use of statistics to advance medical knowledge which is represented by epidemiology, for example, studying the pattern of disease in a systematic way and realising that understanding the relationship of disease to the way people live can lead to enormous advances in medical science. I do not find much evidence of that hunger for knowledge among architects. I think we have failed to push hard enough.

I think we have not come to terms with the enormous consequences of the use of information technology in architecture, which enables us to rethink the process by which buildings are designed and erected.

Also, we have failed collectively to understand systematically what the clients want from us. It is extremely hard to simulate client politics in the studio/educational realm. It has been easy to push out such politics, such issues about changing patterns of demand into an area which is not considered to be too chic and not considered to be possible. I think that neglect is very evident in the way in which architecture is taught in the 90s.

It has been too easy to confuse the Diploma Show in New York with success. That means (which I think is a fantastic aggregation of our responsibility) that students, teachers and practitioners accept more readily some of the best talents in the country, and some of the best international talents into our schools, and become accustomed to the idea that only 1 in 20 is going to be successful by these terms, in an architectural career measured in a very specialised way. I think that is an absolute scandal and is something that should weigh heavily on the conscience of all those involved in our educational programme.

I mentioned at the beginning that professionalism and education are the same – coterminous. That is the significance of the symbol of CPD and of my emphasis on research (that architecture represents action, but also reflection on that action). We need both the academy and practice, it is a coalition. The profession is as good as a school and the schools as good as the profession.

We need to understand this particular society which is said to value tertiary education. I think we have to maintain our position which we have done and which, I think, is one of the glories of architectural education, despite my criticism that we have never betrayed the importance of design as the basis of our education. The project-based design study which must be the essence of architectural training distinguishes what we do from that which is carried out in so many other studies.

We should allow people to succeed in our courses in a variety of ways. It should be easy to exit architecture with honour after Part 1. We have not forced our education programme into contact with the reality of the procurement of buildings, with the planning of sites or the construction of buildings that is understood by our colleagues in the construction industry. We have not in the latter part of our course realised the significance of knowledge, of the necessity of research and of the inevitable differentiation in skills that will be the consequence of giving honour to this knowledge. There are lots of different ways of succeeding, many different kinds of skills which will lead students to develop a variety of architectural careers. We have neglected the pedagogy of architecture and the way in which the architectural imagination has to be toned, refined, developed through working lives. All these neglects, all these criticisms were understood by Richard Burton and reversed in his programme, which was the basis by which the five-year funding was protected. This is, I think, an excellent programme for the development of architectural education as part of the professional programme. I think there is an urgent need for giving architectural teaching much more honour in our programme, not by separating it from the rest of the profession but by weaving it into the rest of the professional activities, by increasing the discourse, making the discourse more alert, more available, more challenging to more architects, all of whom are part of this educational programme in one way or another.

The steps forward for the institute are to make sure that the development of teaching skills is taken seriously; that the students who see themselves all to often as separate from the profession are taught to realise that they are part of it, part of its intellect, part of its knowledge base; that the research that will be the basis of practice in the future is seen to be a partnership between schools and practice; and that, in short, we live out every aspect of our professional lives – action, relating design to the world around us, inventing the future, honouring the past, but, all the time, relating the concept of professionalism to the ideal of education.

Such a theory should lead to the development of a form of education closely related, part of, integrated with, folded into the profession that will be by far the best in the world.

Dr Francis Duffy is President of the Royal Institute of British Architects (RIBA) and Chairman of DEGW, the leading European designers of the working environment, with offices in Amersfoort, Berlin, Glasgow, London, Madrid, Milan and Paris. His architectural education was in London at the AA and the USA at Berkeley and Princeton.

Summary of the Burton Report

Architecture bridges between science and the arts, between the client/consumer and built form, between resources/technology and ability to pay, between uncertainty and certainty. The resolution of these in harmony is vested in the architect through design, design management with the other design professions (see the *RIBA Strategic Study of the Profession*, 1992). The role of education is to prepare the architectural student for this highly complex activity.

The Steering Group wishes to reaffirm the central role that architecture plays in defining and raising the quality of life for the community, in serving the public interest and in contributing to the nation's heritage. The relationship between the architect and the clients and users of buildings is at the core of the process by which quality, good design, appropriateness and value for money are achieved, especially with the greater awareness of interdependent environmental issues.

In pursuing this role, it is essential that architects continue to benefit from advanced education and training, increasingly with a research awareness. It is for this reason that the profession has committed itself to lifelong learning, Continuing Professional Development (CPD) – shared wherever possible with other disciplines and designing professions.

The profession – and hence its education and training – must continue to change; failure to do so will risk its eventual marginalisation and the diminution of the qualities and values identified above. In taking up the opportunity offered by the Secretary of State, the Steering Group sees the recommendations in this Report as providing the basis for the further improvements, which will ensure that the profession continues to be properly prepared.

The overall curriculum needed review and this we have done. The syllabus has also been reviewed and will continue to be so. Both these reviews will lead to greater relevance of the courses to the contemporary requirements of clients, users and industry. They will be monitored by the professional validation system.

Our project-based learning system is a jewel which accepts and encourages response to change and development of judgement. It is an iterative system facilitating cross-disciplinary work. We agree it must be supplemented by further specialisms. We cannot risk not having the time for it.

In view of the profession's considerable financial contribution and society's increasing realisation of the centrality of and demand for good architectural design and landscape and the potential risks which would flow from inadequacy in education, government funding should continue for the full period of five years and the profession must be prepared also to continue its funding at or above current levels.

Value for society's money is clearly being achieved with substantial financial help from the profession. Funding is not expensive at less than half the cost of other five-year courses. Some more investment is needed for equipment and research because of the increased demands of an advancing profession requiring a well prepared student entering it.

The added value of the specialisms and alliances with schools in Europe and beyond is now very evident in our schools and they are responding to previous encouragement and demands from the profession; more is required. We need an even better-educated profession. The ability to speak and work in a foreign language has become highly desirable.

More thought is required in the institutions about cross-disciplinary working particularly with the construction-related departments, but also exploiting the wide range of connections available with such disciplines as social science, design, business and art. The industry and profession should better structure the student's year out by introducing more cross-disciplinary experience opportunities. In this way, the mutual respect of each team member's contribution, the creative talents of others and a common understanding of the design process will be fostered. The year in practice should also be better structured and controlled with a better rapport between practices and schools.

A critical burden now falls on full- and part-time staff. They must have time to carry out CPD, and HEIs should have a policy for this and implement it rigorously. A staff college concept is recommended.

The teachers are in many cases practitioners which is to be encouraged. It is disappointing that more women are not employed as teachers.

The talent and quality of our students is encouraging, they work hard. The entry numbers are increasing. This is welcomed. They should, however, be counselled that continuation to RIBA Part 2 will be based on high quality and suitability to the profession and that after a degree there are high quality, useful and honourable directions for those who do not proceed further. We are interested by the proposal that the intermediate RIBA exemption (Part 1) might be given only after the requisite period of practical training to complement this process.

We have recommended that the Institute review its policy regarding membership.

Student hardship is an issue which must be faced and a survey of it is necessary.

Other professions are realising the intrinsic value of our project-based, student-centred learning system with peer-group review of results. In addition, imagination is being used to look at new ways of teaching more efficiently using the potential of Information Technology and Distance Learning.

Research into architecture is essential to avoid problems and to innovate. It is at an unacceptably low level at present and it has an important future role in the teaching of students and in CPD. Further, in view of the centrality of the user and the complexity of the process and the risks, comprehensive feedback of information must be achieved.

Our system of education and training and supervision of it is lauded internationally, with RIBA recognition of 39 schools abroad and the RIBA being consulted on education and training and validation in Chile, China, Columbia, Czechoslovakia, Hungary, Russia and Saudi Arabia, supported by the British Council. All these countries accept that a minimum of five years' academic work is essential; some have six years. The system is a precious asset not to be wasted and now needs encouragement to evolve.

With the RIBA committed to CPD, we see our initial educational system of a minimum of seven years' education and training as the start of a lifetime of further study and personal development.

We appreciate that our recommendations together with CPD will place a considerable administrative burden on the RIBA education department, which will require resources to be able to respond to them, as will the British Architectural Library to support education and research.

This is a dense and complex subject meriting a serious approach. In our report there are aspects which should be taken into consideration by government, the profession, the industry and the institutions and their schools of architecture with their staff and student bodies. I hope then it will form a solid base for the education of a profession which will pay an essential part in the future fabric of our nation and beyond.

ARCHITECTS ON EDUCATION

The notion of a universality of human experience is a confidence trick and the notion of a universality of female experience is a clever confidence trick.

Angela Carter, UK

Leonardo da Vinci and Schlemmer constructed two fundamentally different models for the relationship between man and this world. As we slip further away from the model of Leonardo and past that of Schlemmer, into a time of revered artifice and spatial implosion, the relationship of man to this world has become a subject of renewed interest. What could a new model of this relationship be? Could there be one?

Elizabeth Diller and Ricardo Scofidio, USA

I was very annoyed with Post-Modernism. In the early beginnings I felt that we were just starting to find a way to deal with the present so why did we have to go backwards? I got very angry and I said: 'Well, if we're gonna go backwards, we can go to fish which are 500 million years before man'. And I drew many pictures in my sketchbook of fish and pretty soon I started to become interested in the fish itself. Inevitably you start becoming interested in what you are drawing.

Frank Gehry, USA

I believe that the world of architecture comes alive in seeing and experiencing its naked phenomenal mysteries. In the palpitation of space, or in physically inhabiting transparencies, all educational rhetoric is abolished. I believe teaching is a joyous exercise between the hope of an architecture and silence.

Steven Holl, USA

I had a unique experience while studying architecture to come into contact with three greats, Louis Kahn at Pennsylvania, Robert Venturi at Yale and Romaldo Guirgola at Columbia. In each situation I was able to form relationships with these men which have continued beyond my education. I think the dialogue set up in school with your professors and fellow students is invaluable. It has proven to be the case in my career and I am truly grateful.

Franklin Israel, USA

In traditional cultures, fundamental aesthetic and ethical principles are considered to be of universal value and this is where the controversy lies; namely in the question of a universal value transcending time and space, climates and civilisation. In traditional cultures, industrial rationale and methods are subordinate to larger themes, to larger concerns. In Modernist cultures, by contrast, invention, innovation and discovery are ends in themselves.

Leon Krier, UK

What is the implication of positioning a school of architecture in any particular institution and specifically in a university? Is it good for architecture and will it produce better architecture? I have no answer to that. I am of course sceptical . . . The point is that schools of architecture have obviously different provisions for different possibilities . . . With the increasing number of universities, those schools of architecture which have turned to universities find that their relationship to their institutions is greatly diminished . . . putting a school of architecture in a university and examining that relationship allows us to examine its architectural education . . . We are therefore subject to a new regime in regard to teaching which is based on a university ethos not derived from the nature of the teaching processes that the schools of architecture have generally been associated with; that is a project-based tutorial and a critical review activity with an extended face-to-face contact with individual students. This, I believe, is the most important component of the school of architecture's teaching base . . . I do not think [however] that the university is an unsatisfactory environment, but what I am worried about is that the general breadth of the architectural educational ethic is being accelerated by the effect of the autonomy of the university. I should therefore like to see this particular unification or solidification of architectural education questioned and that other means or other ways of setting up schools of architecture, or maintaining schools of architecture, should be kept in place.

Isi Metzstein, UK

I see architecture as always addressing the same questions throughout history. Each generation will try to answer the question of meaning in the work of architecture in its own way. For some, this reality will be found in the interpretation of programme or in the investigation of typology. For others still, the reality of the building will be sought in its lasting tangible presence, which speaks about the architectural principles behind its construction. That is where I would like to be.

Rafael Moneo, Spain

In spite of Gropius' efforts to emphasise the plurality and continued relevance of approaches represented by the individuals teaching at the Bauhaus, the school's achievements must be related to the social and political context that created it. It marked the culmination in the industrialising nations of Western Europe of more than half a century's attempts at social engineering through design reform. Its strengths, as well as its weakness, lay in the fact that it aimed to change the world through the discovery and application of 'universal' laws in art, architecture and design. Such Utopian concepts were, of course, not confined to the Bauhaus in the 1920s and 30s; they are also found in Dutch, Russian, Scandinavian and British theory. The pathos of such idealism has been revealed by subsequent events.

The fact that the school was destroyed by Fascism may have enhanced its credibility in post-War Europe and the United States, but its ideal of universality was a myth and a mirage, shattered by war, politics and the demands of a consumer society. Today no designer or design organisation could or would contemplate universal solutions to the problems of design for the real world. We are still in search of a theory, social commitment is still elusive, so we indulge in our fantasies, ironies and pastiche, which are more comforting (and more profitable) than that 'respect for stern realities' that Gropius demanded from architecture and design.

Gillian Naylor, UK

The number of different published magazines and books on or related to architecture has increased dramatically in the UK and Europe over the past decade . . . this saturation . . . creates an 'appreciation environment' which preempts discovery and experience of the real thing. This is most apparent among architectural students, who prone to strong opinions have often formed these based solely on media information. This blurring of real and artificial is very worrying. I do not want to appear elitist, recognising that the cost involved in visiting far away buildings is real, but it is leading to a dangerous situation where real experience is becoming less important, where important issues no longer appear at all in the theoretical constructs of architecture as a direct result of the media not mediatising them or deciding to filter them out . . . Since most of our education and learning has come through words, written and spoken, there is a need to unravel much which is camouflaging our ability to access the essence of situations. The amount of information which enters our brains is roughly 90/10, eyes/ears . . . Our architectural concepts should emerge from the preconcept, informing and providing the framework for developing the architectural design . . . Our ability to imagine and construct concepts is at the very root of architecture, and without them there can be no architecture, only building.

Ian Ritchie, UK

In the past we had Vitruvius and the position that a building could attain perfection through a complete control of its proportions and composition. The exercise of architecture was the exercise of creating a perfect and unchangeable object. This concept of built form related to the philosophy of a society wishing to define and fix relationships. The twentieth century has seen the transformation of philosophy away from static and hierarchical relationships (within society and between Man and God) to our present post-Einsteinian position where the philosophy of change now dominates thinking. This philosophical change has also motivated architecture and this shift in thinking has been accompanied by a complete transformation of the technology of building which has further undermined the principles of traditional architecture.

Richard Rogers, UK

For all architects a broadening of the terms of reference to include more than their own personal tastes can be a means of sharpening and refining their aesthetic sensibilities. Ranging beyond the confines of one's own taste, culture and conditioning provide an aesthetic jolt, opening the eye to new possibilities of beauty and reviving the creative energies. At least, it can help architects to understand the context in which they build.

Denise Scott Brown, USA

The purpose of education is to form a new mind – a mind that combines the scientific and the visual spirit. This is because the true scientific spirit and the true visual spirit are the only two attitudes in the world with a positive, creative energy. Every other activity is fragmented, instigating conflict and sorrow, therefore destructive . . . Intelligence is not cleverness . . . If you have a talent they teach you to become ambitious, to become the best, to have more. Specialised training will make you clever not intelligent . . . I am afraid intelligence does not come from books, teachers or gurus: it comes by being an individual who is honest, passionate, enthusiastic and open to learn, to question, to observe during the process of the 'making of something'.

Claudio Silvestrin, UK

A competition is only as good as the assessors. If the assessors are chosen by vested interests, you get Modernist architecture; so they make sure that Modernism continues and you will never break that influence. It's time to escape from that system. The architectural establishment is similar to the former communist establishment in Russia: it looks after itself. In the seventeenth and eighteenth centuries, cities were built without having qualified architects . . . [no one started] by winning a competition . . . Nowadays the system is so doctrinaire that it's very hard for anyone with talent to survive. By the time students have been brainwashed for five years in an architectural school, by the time they have gone in for various awards and found that the gold medals are only given to the good boys, they will have given up the pursuit of excellence. Anyone who dares to criticise the system is persecuted. But their absolute control since the war is beginning to crack, in places . . .

Quinlan Terry, UK

The architect in the Renaissance, like Alberti or Palladio, was un homme de lettres, *a humanist, a very educated man, who was able to communicate through writing. There is a difference between communicating orally and ordering your thoughts and writing them down in correct grammar; this requires education, exercise and experience. To be an architect was not only to be a craftsman, but also to be a man who was cultivated and who longed for education; not only an education in technology, but also an education in the cultural development of mankind, of human thought . . . You find very few people today who have this concept of themselves and the will to become* un homme de lettres. *Usually the architect today is a* doer.

Oswald Mathias Ungers, Germany

Why have practical men not acquired credit? For the reason that architecture is born of discourse. Why not the Men of Letters? For the reason that architecture is born of construction. To be an architect, one must seek discourse and construction together.

Vitruvius

Number of Architects and Students in the World

Statistics compiled by the Union Internationale des Architectes (UIA) from a survey sent to UIA
sections in 1992. Published with permission from ACSA News, Vol 24, No 2, October 1994.*

Country	Number of Architects	Number of Students	Country	Number of Architects	Number of Students
Albania	468	n/a	Korea	6,500	37,000
Argentina	35,000	n/a	Latvia	1,210	180
Australia	8,248	4,176	Lithuania	1,980	980
Austria	2,500	5,000	Luxembourg	373**	76
Azerbaijan	2,800	351	Macau	69**	n/a
Bangladesh	386	300	Malaysia	1,159	156**
Bolivia	1,850	3,568	Morocco	2,011	500
Botswana	40	n/a	Mongolia	416	45
Bulgaria	4,160	710	Namibia	99	n/a
Canada	7,000	2,000	Netherlands	5,187	3,250
Cameroon	125	n/a	Norway	2,835**	768
Chile	5,700	4,000	Pakistan	1,700	600
China	30,000	9,000	Philippines	11,060	10,747
Denmark	6,000	1,630	Poland	7,310**	4,234
Egypt	21,000	1,700	Portugal	5,020	n/a
Equador	8,886	5,575	Puerto Rico	514	99
Estonia	600	350	Russia	24,000	1,400
Finland	2,500	1,500	Singapore	933	370
France	26,246**	15,614	Slovakia	2,500	n/a
Germany	83,281	40,095	Spain	21,360	17,059
Greater Eurasia	4,188	n/a	Sri Lanka	291**	106**
Greece	13,500	1,700	Surinam	21	n/a
Hong Kong	899	361	Sweden	4,800	750
Hungary	5,000	330	Switzerland	4,105	2,741
India	14,916	1,610	Syria	4,878**	2,021
Indonesia	17,220	n/a	Tanzania	124	68
Ireland	1,300	450	Trinidad/Tobago	44	n/a
Israel	4,929	1,000	Ukraine	320	n/a
Italy	85,000	95,000	United Kingdom	29,000	9,000
Ivory Coast	146	12	United States	98,000	30,000
Jamaica	117	37	Vietnam	5,300	560
Japan	190,000	43,256	Yugoslavia	4,850	1,747
Kazakhstan	3,000	n/a	Zambia	45**	87
Kenya	384	342	Zimbabwe	93**	no school

* Although the survey was conducted in 1992, the date of the statistics varies from 1990 to 1994. Some statistics
are from official sources and some are from information available to the UIA's section.
** Number of architects in UIA section.